# CATHERINE THE GREAT
## AND OTHER STUDIES

CATHERINE THE GREAT

# CATHERINE THE GREAT

## AND

## OTHER STUDIES

G. P. GOOCH

ARCHON BOOKS

HAMDEN, CONNECTICUT — 1966

FIRST PUBLISHED 1954
LONGMANS, GREEN AND CO. LTD.

REPRINTED 1966 WITH PERMISSION IN AN
UNALTERED AND UNABRIDGED EDITION

LIBRARY OF CONGRESS CATALOG CARD NUMBER: 66-18227
PRINTED IN THE UNITED STATES OF AMERICA

# PREFACE

THE portrait of Catherine the Great completes the trilogy on the Enlightened Autocrats of the eighteenth century, of which the previous instalments dealt with Frederick the Great and Maria Theresa. None of them attempts a full-length picture, for we possess excellent biographies, large and small, of them all. The purpose is twofold: firstly to illustrate the type of government most widely adopted and most warmly admired in the Age of Reason which ended with the French Revolution; and secondly to bring to life leading actors on the European stage as they reveal themselves in their memoirs, correspondence and table-talk, and in the comments of friend and foe. No artist could wish for more colourful or more contrasted sitters. Their sole bond is their conviction of the superiority of efficient paternalism over all other methods of government, and their determination to fulfil their exacting duties to the limit of their strength. The two Germans—for Catherine was a German—were Intellectuals, with a genuine interest in the things of the mind, for whom the philosophy of the *Aufklärung* replaced inherited beliefs. The two Austrians, Maria Theresa and her son Joseph, on the other hand, untouched by the rationalism of the century of Voltaire, devoted their entire energies to governing their ramshackle empire. The interaction of temperament and circumstance; the clash of tradition with the requirements and temptations of the hour; the ideologies and ambitions, the austerities and dissipations, the joys and sorrows of those in high place: such are the themes of the drama unfolded in these studies. Since Karl Marx claimed attention for economic influences a century ago increasing emphasis has been laid on the impersonal factors in history, but interest in leading actors on the stage remains as keen as ever.

In the second item in this volume the scene shifts from Eastern Europe to the West, from the council chamber to the drawing-rooms of Parisian hostesses, from courts and cabinets to society and literature. Though there have been salons in France from Mme de Rambouillet to Juliette Adam, no period has witnessed such a cult of the art of conversation as during the middle decades of the eighteenth century, when Mme Geoffrin and Mme Necker, Mme du Deffand and Julie de Lespinasse, catered for the intellectual *élite* of the capital and opened their doors to any foreigner distinguished by birth or brains. The leadership of the country, which had been located at Versailles during the long reign of *le Roi Soleil*, had passed to the proud city, 'le café de l'Europe', as the Abbé Galiani called it, where literary reputations were made or marred. It was of such feasts of reason in refined surroundings that Talleyrand was thinking when in old age he looked back regretfully to the close of the *Ancien Régime* and declared that no one who had not lived in France before the Revolution had known the sweetness of life. The duller and more discreditable the Court of Louis XV, the more brightly shone the rays of the *Encyclopédistes*, who dreamed of a brave new world when reason should hold sway and tormented humanity should have its chance.

From the salons of Paris to the High Priest of the *Aufklärung* is but a step, yet only a single aspect of the most celebrated, many-sided and influential Frenchman of his age is presented in these chapters. Poet, dramatist, historian, essayist, philosopher, publicist, controversialist, correspondent of rulers and writers all over Europe, Voltaire proclaimed his gospel of rationalism and humanitarianism for sixty years through the lucid medium of the *lingua franca* of the eighteenth century. He was not only the first French historian worthy of the name, but 'one of the fathers of history', as Émile Faguet describes him, author of the first biography of a hero King, of the first panorama of the *Ancien Régime*, of the earliest comprehensive survey of the development of civilisation. For the thesis of Bossuet—that history was the implementation of a divine plan—he substituted the contention that man had had to make his own way in the world, and that the victories of reason over ignorance, superstition and intolerance constituted the essence of progress. Though not a profound scholar, he knew more about the evolution of mankind than anyone before the dawn of the nineteenth century. That there were more things in heaven and earth than were dreamed of in his philosophy is true enough, but that is equally true of Gibbon, and indeed of all the luminaries of the Age of Reason. Though our knowledge is far wider and our understanding much deeper than that of Voltaire, we are no nearer an agreed Philosophy of History than when the *Essai sur les Moeurs* was published two hundred years ago.

The volume closes with an analysis of the most impressive of political apologias and an attempt to derive lessons from the career of the Iron Chancellor. The most skilful practitioner of *raison d'état*, the doctrine which has governed the conduct of rulers and statesmen throughout the ages, owed his success not merely to his steely will and to Moltke's legions, but to his instinctive knowledge of when to strike and when to stay his hand. His maxim that politics are the art of the possible stands out as a salutary warning to megalomaniacs, dynastic or otherwise. The second principal lesson of his career is equally important: the undiluted nationalism which he preached and practised has become out of date in a rapidly shrinking world. 'Patriotism is not enough'.

*Catherine the Great* and portions of *Four French Salons* appeared in the *Contemporary Review*, *Bismarck's Legacy* in *Foreign Affairs*. The author desires to express his gratitude for permission to reprint.

G. P. G.

# CONTENTS

# PLATES

# I

## CATHERINE THE GREAT

### I. *The Years of Apprenticeship*

OF the three celebrated 'Philosophic Despots' of the eight-teenth century Catherine the Great could boast of the most astonishing career. The proud title conferred by the Prince de Ligne has been ratified by history. Frederick the Great was a Prussian, building on the granite foundations laid by the Great Elector and Frederick William I. The Emperor Joseph II was an Austrian, carefully groomed for the proudest throne on the Con-tinent. Catherine was a member of one of the most insignificant of the petty German states which peppered the plains of Central Europe between the Baltic and the Alps when Germany was merely a geographical expression. Knowing nothing of Russia nor of the Russian tongue till she was summoned across the frontier in her fifteenth year as a mere pawn on the dynastic chessboard, she turned her back for ever on the country of her birth and identified herself heart and mind with her new home.

The rising Slavonic power which had been put on the map by Peter the Great had fallen from its high estate during the puny generation which followed his death. 'I found the French crown lying in the mud,' declared Napoleon, 'and I placed it on my head.' Catherine might have made a similar claim. It was her achievement to restore the prestige of Russia and the authority of the Crown, to enlarge her dominions, to make her voice heard in the councils of Europe—in a word, to win for her empire the place among the Great Powers which since her day has never been lost. It was not in the material sphere alone that she left the im-print of her arresting personality. Till the hour of her accession

Russia had been regarded as a primitive, semi-Asiatic state on the outer fringe of civilisation, separated from the lofty traditions of Central and Western Europe by barriers of race and language, religion and culture. Peter the Great, a barbarian of genius, had been more interested in cannon and shipbuilding than in literature and the arts. It was Catherine's aim to Europeanise her adopted country by establishing direct contact with the High Priests of the *Aufklärung*, and to remove the stigma that the Colossus of the North stood for nothing except brute strength. Her purpose was in large measure accomplished, for though neither she nor her successors could eradicate the instinctive distrust of Western influences, she removed at any rate some of the obstacles to cultural cross-fertilisation. Much of her work survived till the coming of the Bolshevists, and the Communist revolutionaries themselves adopted the principles of centralised autocracy and territorial expansion which she had inherited and bequeathed. Both as a person and as a ruler her figure seems to loom ever larger in the history of eighteenth-century Europe. Two volumes of Bilbassoff's unfinished *magnum opus* are devoted to her bibliography down to 1896, and during the last half-century the broad stream has never ceased to flow.

Several years before the publications of the Imperial Historical Society of St Petersburg and the opening of the rich Woronzoff archives furnished the student with 150 volumes of correspondence and memoranda, and thereby rendered possible a documented history of the reign, the appearance of her Memoirs in 1859 enabled readers for the first time to visualise the atmosphere and sentiments of the formative years. Directly the breath was out of her body, her son and successor, the Emperor Paul, searched her papers and discovered a record in French of her early life, in her own handwriting, in an envelope directed 'For His Imperial Highness, the Czarewich, the Grand Duke Paul, my beloved son'. The manuscript breaks off in the middle of a sentence describing an interview with the Empress Elizabeth in 1759, three years before the author's accession to the throne. Paul lent it to a friend, who took a copy, and twenty years later copies were made from the first copy. On his accession to the throne in 1825 his son the Tsar Nicholas ordered the police to seize all copies. He was too late, for in 1859 Alexander Herzen, the celebrated exile and publicist, published the *Mémoires de l'Impératrice Catherine II* in London.

The volume of 350 pages provides no clue to the date of composition, but a few references to subsequent occurrences, the latest being the visit of the Emperor Joseph II in 1780, suggest that it may have been composed or revised at different periods. The nearest equivalent both in date and character is the autobiography of Wilhelmina of Prussia, for both works are a shrill indictment of the relatives and officials who made their lives a misery. If we are to seek a political purpose in the narrative it must be found in the desire to justify the *coup* of 1762. The errors and distortions of the favourite sister of Frederick the Great were exposed by Ranke and Droysen, the latter roughly dismissing her testimony as without historical value. No historian has treated the Memoirs of Catherine with such disdain, partly because they form our main authority for her early life, and partly because they provide a fascinating revelation of the personality of the only woman ruler who surpassed Elizabeth in sheer ability and equalled her in the enduring significance of her work. If the reign of the Virgin Queen forms the most glorious chapter in English history, few students will quarrel with the verdict of Waliszewski, the most popular of Catherine's biographers, that Russia today is largely what she made it. None of her ministers or favourites, not even Potemkin, enjoyed so much influence as Burleigh possessed over Elizabeth.

Sophie, familiarly known in the family circle as Figchen (a diminutive of Sophie), Princess of Anhalt-Zerbst, one of the eight branches of the Anhalt line, was born in 1729 in Stettin, where her father Christian August commanded an infantry regiment of the Prussian army. He had little to give his children except his love. His wife Johanna, as a member of the House of Holstein-Gottorp, was related to the Romanoffs, and it was to her unloving and intriguing mother that the girl owed her chance. For the Empress Elizabeth, on her accession in 1742, sent for her nephew Peter, son of the Duke of Holstein-Gottorp and of Anne, elder daughter of Peter the Great, with the intention of making him her heir. Two years later, in 1744, a second messenger set forth from St Petersburg, inviting Princess Johanna, with her daughter Sophie, to start for the Russian capital without delay on a long visit.

Though no motive was indicated it was not very difficult to guess, since the Tsarina had recently asked for a portrait of the girl. They visited Berlin *en route* at the invitation of the King of Prussia, who encouraged the match in the belief that Johanna would counterwork the designs of the Prussophobe Chancellor Bestuzhev.

It is at this moment that the reminiscences begin, and we are at once introduced to her cousin, the future Tsar Peter III, whose figure darkens the whole of the vivid narrative. 'I first saw him at a family gathering at Eutin after the death of his father. He was eleven, I was ten. I heard the family say that he was fond of drink and that it was difficult to keep him sober at table. Vivacity he possessed, but he was thin and delicate, and had a bad complexion.' He had lost his mother soon after his birth, and his father, from whom he inherited his diminutive stature and ugly features, at the age of eleven: tenderness he had never known. The young people met again in Russia, when Figchen found him less attractive than ever, for smallpox had left its scars. Among the many differences between them was the fact that his heart was anchored in Holstein, while she shed her nationality and her religion as readily as her Christian name.

Only a young woman of exceptional toughness and tenacity could have confronted the situation which greeted her without giving way to depression and despair. The sketch of the Tsarina Elizabeth in Catherine's Memoirs differs little from the portrait painted by her biographers Waliszewski and Nisbet Bain. She inherited the coarse manners and low standards of her parents, detested all serious occupations, and lived for pleasure. The few ill-written notes which survive show that she was almost illiterate, while Razumowski, the Favourite, once a Cossack shepherd boy, could not write at all. Though she spoke French well and German passably, the indolent woman cared nothing for literature and the arts. She loved dancing, riding, hunting and, above all, her Parisian clothes. A fire in 1753 is said to have destroyed 4,000 robes, and at her death 15,000 dresses and piles of silk stockings and shoes were found in her wardrobes. There were also men's clothes, for she liked masked balls, where she appeared as a French *mousquetaire*, a Cossack Hetman or a Dutch sailor. She often stayed up all night and spent hours at her toilet. Though not instinctively cruel like her savage father and disliking the spectacle of wounded soldiers, she would order torture for trifling offences. Violent and capricious, she swore like a trooper, and was known to throw her slipper in the face of an offender. Was she secretly married to Razumowski and had they children? We cannot be sure. While she frittered away her time on amusements, the business of the State was left to corrupt and dissolute adventurers—Lestocq, her French doctor, Bestuzhev, the Chancellor, who contolled foreign policy, and the Shuvaloffs. No Court in Europe was less fitted to train the wife of a future ruler in habits of virtue, industry and dignity.

Catherine, as she was renamed after exchanging the Lutheran for the Orthodox faith, found no moral support in her ambitious mother, who cared for little except money and was detested by the Tsarina and Peter. Her trials were rendered bearable only by the dream of power, and the frequent illnesses of the dissolute ruler made the prospect something more than wishful thinking. Her task was to keep on good terms with the Empress by never thwarting her will, and to gain as much influence as possible over the husband she despised. No young foreign bride ever played her hand with more consummate ability. The Tsarina was as kind to her as she could be to anyone, while the pitiful Peter quickly recognised the outstanding gifts of his girl wife and saluted her as Mme Ressource. 'I noticed he was very young,' she records. 'I held my tongue and listened, which gained his confidence. He said he was glad we were cousins, so he could talk freely. He told me he was in love with a lady of the Empress and wished to marry her, but he had resigned himself to our marriage at the wish of his aunt.' Rigorously excluded from affairs of State, he amused himself with childish frivolities, while Catherine worked hard at the Russian language, played the piano, learned to ride and read omnivorously, keeping her mouth shut and her eyes open. Her mother excited such universal dislike that one day she was told to go home. It was a passing storm, for the ruler knew that she would soon be rid of her disagreeable guest and she was well satisfied with the prospective bride. Catherine's comment forms the most revealing sentence in the Memoirs. 'I did not care about Peter, but I did about the crown.' Elizabeth congratulated her on her progress in Russian, and was delighted when she could converse freely.

B

Her stock rose steadily. 'I treated everyone as well as I could, and strove to gain the friendship, or at any rate to diminish the hostility, of those whom I even suspected of being ill-disposed towards me. I never took sides nor mixed myself up in affairs. I was always serene, considerate and polite to everyone. I was very gay by nature. I noticed with pleasure that from day to day I gained the affection of the public, which regarded me as an interesting and intelligent child. I displayed great respect for my mother, limitless obedience to the Empress, the most profound consideration for the Grand Duke, and I took special pains to win affection. I never thought myself very pretty, but I pleased people.' Though autobiographers usually flatter themselves, there is no reason to doubt the substantial accuracy of this picture. Throughout life she always knew how to charm when she had a purpose in view.

On August 21, 1745, one year after her arrival, Catherine was married. 'As the day approached I became more melancholy. My heart told me not to expect much happiness: ambition alone sustained me. Something at the bottom of my heart assured me that sooner or later I should become Empress of Russia.' Her mother had only waited for the ceremony, and the Tsarina forbade correspondence when she departed, 6,000 roubles in debt. She had never cared very much for anyone, and she quickly faded out of her daughter's life. After the death of her husband she migrated to Paris, where she contracted a *liaison* and died in debt, too soon to see her Figchen on the throne. Marriage made little difference in the life of the Grand Duchess. 'My dear husband', she acidly records, 'took no notice of me, but was always occupied with his valets, playing at soldiers, exercising them in his room, changing his uniform twenty times a day. I yawned, I was bored, having no one to speak to. He thought he could play the violin, but he could only scrape the strings. He played with toys, dressed up the staff in masks, and made them dance in my bedroom.' He insisted on her playing cards with him, and when he lost he would sulk for days. He had no manners and put out his tongue at people like a naughty child. He kept hunting-dogs in a room so close to her bedroom that she was annoyed by the barking and the smell. One day she heard screams and found him mercilessly flogging one of the animals, which was held tight by one of his

Holstein guards for the purpose. Her protests were futile, for expressions of pity he could not abide. Nothing was worse, she wrote to Frau von Bielke many years later, than to have a child as one's husband. 'I could have loved mine if it had been possible, and if he had wished for my love.' Her Grande Gouvernante, Mme Tsoglokoff, who was assigned to her by the Tsarina, was almost as much of a trial as Peter himself. She was always re-marking, 'The Empress would not like that.' 'I felt totally isolated, cried all day and spat blood.'

It was fortunate that she liked books. Her French governess in Stettin had taught her to enjoy the French classics, and she turned her long hours of solitude to good account. 'After my marriage I did nothing but read—for the first year only novels, but then I was bored by them.' A new world of delight opened up in the company of Mme de Sévigné and Voltaire, Tacitus, Montesquieu and Bayle. Her intellectual tastes, which her husband could never share, annoyed him by emphasising his own inferiority. When she went out riding, she always took a book in her pocket. 'Often when I was reading Peter entered and walked up and down, talking of things which interested him but not me. Sometimes these promenades lasted an hour or more, several times a day, and I had to walk with him till I was exhausted. When he left the room the dullest book was a delight.' Her husband was no happier than she, and he lacked her consolation of hope. 'I was not born for Russia,' he remarked to his wife in 1757. They did not suit each other, he added, and he felt sure he would die there. She urged him to try to make himself loved, and to ask the Empress to let him enter the Council and acquaint himself with affairs. It was a hopeless project, for Peter, who felt himself a German as reigning Duke of Holstein, adored Prussia and her ruler, and in consequence detested Russia's intervention in the Seven Years War on the Austrian side.

Years passed without the birth of an heir, and the impatient Tsarina, wondering whose fault it was, despatched a doctor to Peter and a *sage-femme* to Catherine. When at last a son was born in 1754, the tide of speculation on his paternity began to flow and has never ceased. Herzen's Preface declared that the Memoirs clearly indicates Serge Soltikoff as the father of her child, but he mistakes a possibility for a certainty. The best evidence of Paul's legitimacy emerged when he displayed the same mental instability as his father and for similar reasons met a similar tragic end. Yet her innocence can no more be established than her guilt. She admits her infatuation for her first Favourite. The Soltikoff family, she records, was one of the oldest in Russia, and the mother of the Tsarina Anne was a member of the clan. General Soltikoff had two sons, both of them Chamberlains of the Court, and Serge, the younger, though a married man, made love to the Grand Duchess. 'I tried to keep him back. Unhappily I listened to him. He was handsome as the day. There was no one like him at the Court of the Empress or at ours. He was a distinguished cavalier.' Elizabeth had set a bad example which it was only too easy to follow. Some of Catherine's biographers have expressed surprise, not that she fell, but that with such an odious husband she held out so long. She made no claim to chastity and thought its importance greatly overdone. 'I was attractive: that was the half-way house to temptation, and in such cases human nature does the rest. To tempt and to be tempted is much the same. Despite the inculcation of moral precepts, directly the senses begin to speak one is carried much further than one imagines, and I know not how they can be kept in check. Flight may perhaps help, but how could one flee in the midst of a court? Moreover, that too would cause tongues to wag. If, therefore, one does not flee, nothing in my opinion is more difficult than to resist what gives us pleasure. All arguments to the contrary are prudery. They do not spring from the human heart, which no one can command.' Mme Tsoglokoff encouraged her to amorous escapades. There were some situations, she remarked one day, where a major interest demanded an exception to the rule. 'You must have cast your eye on somebody. I leave you the choice of Soltikoff or Narischkin, but I think it is the latter.' 'No, no,' exclaimed Catherine. 'Then it is the other,' continued the temptress; 'you will see I shall not make trouble for you.' The meaning was clear enough. Since an heir was demanded in the interests of the State, why not choose another sire? There can be little doubt that this shameful suggestion came, not from the lady-in-waiting, but from the Empress herself.

The birth of a son after nine years of marriage, brought no increase of happiness, for the Empress promptly took charge of the child and the mother did not see him for weeks. In this time of suffering and loneliness her thoughts centred on Soltikoff. During his absence in Sweden the Chancellor Bestuzhev had sent her all the news he received, and it was a blow to learn that her handsome cavalier was to be Russian Minister at Hamburg. On his return to St Petersburg he asked permission to visit her, but failed to turn up. When she wrote to complain he came and was forgiven, but the spell was broken. Yielding to his advice to appear in public, she dressed smartly and showed her disdain for those who slighted her. 'In a word I appeared rather as head of a very large party than as a person humiliated and oppressed.' Peter now complained of her insupportable pride and public disdain for some of his friends. He was drinking more than ever, she records, always smelled of wine and tobacco, and seemed more interested in his toy soldiers—wood, metal and wax—than in his wife and son. Whether at this stage he entertained the doubts as to the legitimacy of the child which he was later to express we do not know. That he disliked his wife was as obvious as that his affections were centred on Elizabeth Woronzoff, whom he desired to marry, and whom he could trust to provide him with a child indubitably his own.

The Soltikoff *intermezzo* was soon over, and the second of the long line of Catherine's Favourites was a more interesting and important person. During his tenure of the British Embassy to Augustus III, Elector of Saxony and King of Poland, residing partly at Dresden and partly at Warsaw, Sir Charles Hanbury-Williams engaged the services of Stanislas Poniatowski, a handsome and intelligent young Pole whose mother was a Czartoryski, the most influential of the oldest Polish families. On his transfer to St Petersburg Sir Charles invited the young Count, who was believed to be Russophil, to accompany him as Secretary of Embassy. The British diplomatist, an ex-Member of Parliament and a minor poet, quickly won the confidence of the Grand Duchess, and their correspondence, published by Lord Ilchester in 1928, is our most precious source of information for the critical years following the birth of an heir. Her letters, written in French, are extraordinarily frank, while some of his seem to breathe the ardour of a lover, though no scandal was involved. Longing for a friend with whom she could discuss her hopes and anxieties without fear of betrayal, she craved his guidance and adopted his advice. Here is her first surviving letter, dated August 3, 1756. 'It is a comfort to be able to write to you. Your friendship leaves no doubt you will continue to give me your counsel, which has been so useful to me. I will write anything which seems worthy of your attention, believing that I have no friend more faithful, more sincere and more enlightened than yourself. A certain person's health is worse than ever. She coughed and was short of breath and she tried witchcraft when the doctors failed.' 'Though I am loyal and sincere,' replied the Ambassador, 'I have not your knowledge of this country. To rule one must create divisions. Continue to listen to all their proposals, but let your answers ever be polite and indefinite. I implore you to tell me everything you hear about the health of a certain person. Nothing interests me so much.' The 'certain person', needless to say, was the Empress Elizabeth.

The Grand Duchess overflowed with gratitude. 'What do I not owe to the providence which sent you here like a guardian angel, to unite us in terms of friendship? If one day I wear the crown, I shall owe it partially to your counsels. Without you I should have been the ward of the Great Chancellor, over whom I believe I possess some influence.' Next day she touched on the delicate question of the succession. 'You know the universal discontent, particularly among the soldiers, added to the fear of having three or four living pretenders to whom she would prefer her relatives. The uncertainty attaching to a child of two, added to her timorous disposition, will, I venture to hope, prove safeguards during her life. Afterwards, within two or three hours, every dirty trick will certainly be played; yet, whether they wish to exclude us or tie our hands, they will not be able to do it alone. There are but few officers who are not in the secret, and, if my arrangements for being in time do not fail, it will be my fault if they gain the upper hand. Be assured that I shall never play the King of Sweden's easy-going and feeble part, and that I shall perish or reign.'

The Grand Duchess was now planning every move. 'What a heart, what firmness!' commented the Ambassador. 'I admire you, I adore you more every day. I have no guide, no protector but you. You are born to command and to reign; old age alone will kill you. I kiss your feet. I am entirely yours. Your orders

are my law, your protection my ambition.' Her next letter brought
further details of her plans. 'After being informed of her death
and being certain there is no mistake, I shall go straight to my
son's room. Pray Heaven to give me a clear head!' The Ambassador approved her scheme and added, 'I am not afraid of anything after her death, but I greatly fear the men who might take
action before it occurs.' He was thinking of Bestuzhev, the Chancellor, who strove to keep on good terms both with the Empress
and the Grand Duchess, and whom Sir Charles described as 'a
very slippery eel'. 'I shall faithfully guard your secrets,' continued
the Ambassador, 'and give you the best advice I can. I shall tell
you nothing but the truth. Never will I flatter you.' The latter
promise was not very strictly observed. 'My heart, my life, and
my soul are all yours. I look on you in everything as a being
superior to myself. I adore you so much that I can never be
worthy of your esteem. . . . When you are settled on this throne,
if I am not here I shall come at once. I hope you will ask my
Master to send me as English Minister at your Court. I should
like the right to come and go and to profit by your leisure hours,
for I shall always love Catherine better than the Empress. I
esteem you, I honour you, I adore you. I shall die convinced that
there was never a sweetness, a soundness, a face, a heart, to equal
yours.'

Despite this almost daily exchange of confidences and counsel,
in which high politics were mingled with endearments and flattery,
the Ambassador brazenly assured Bestuzhev that he was not in
correspondence with the Grand Duchess and had no wish to be.
When the Chancellor begged him to say a good word to her on
his behalf, he refused on the ground that he did not wish to be
mixed up in any intrigues. 'It would have been to furnish him
with weapons,' he explained to Catherine, 'and perhaps he would
have thrown the blame for his bad conduct on me.' Representa-
tions would in any case have been useless, for Catherine despised
and distrusted the Chancellor. 'I am sick of his knavish tricks. I
cannot imagine why he behaves so badly towards me or what
causes his hatred for Poniatowski.' His avarice was so notorious
that on the outbreak of the Seven Years War, when England
vainly strove to keep Russia off the back of her Prussian ally, the
Ambassador was authorised to purchase his friendship with

100,000 crowns. Yet Catherine felt that it would be a mistake to break with him. 'If you ruin the Chancellor,' she wrote, 'my fate is certain. He is an enemy of Prussia, but not of England.' Throughout the Seven Years War, which involved all the Great Powers except Spain, the Empress was Francophil, Peter Prussophil, Catherine and Bestuzhev Anglophil. The Ambassador supplied the Grand Duchess with money as well as advice, and she confided that she was studying English three hours a day.

Early in 1757 Hanbury-Williams asked for his recall on the ground of ill-health, and he returned home to die and to be buried in Westminster Abbey. All that man could do to win for England the consort of the heir to the throne—by flattery, friendship and finance—he had done, and he left Russia without anxiety. 'There is no need to think of your safety. The title of the Grand Duke is as clear as daylight; none better in Europe. Everyone will prostrate themselves before you, and you will ascend the throne with the same ease as I sit down to meat. If a will is found and is not wholly favourable to you, suppress it. Lay claim to no title but the lineage of Peter the Great. Let your countenance exhibit determination and serenity. If the Grand Duke Paul is well, you should show him in your arms for a moment.' A suitable Foreign Minister might be found in Panin, at that time Minister at Stockholm. The most hopeful factor was the ebbing vitality of the Empress, who suffered from a chronic cough, breathlessness and pains in the stomach. 'Yesterday she had three attacks of giddiness or fainting,' reported Catherine cheerfully. 'She is very nervous, terrifies herself, weeps, and is afraid of losing her sight. Sometimes she forgets where she is and fails to recognise those around her. They give her innumerable drugs. My surgeon expects an apoplectic seizure.' There was longer to wait than she expected, but the end was within sight.

One of the ties between the Grand Duchess and the Ambassador had been their common affection for Stanislas Poniatowski. 'I loved him before you saw him,' wrote Sir Charles. 'For six years I brought him up. I have always looked on him as my adopted son.' He arrived at St Petersburg at Christmas 1756, but he was soon recalled by his parents to seek re-election to the Polish Diet. The services of Sir Charles were enlisted in procuring his appointment as Polish Minister, and Augustus III was ready to oblige his

Russian ally. 'Towards the close of this year,' runs the first sentence in Catherine's Memoirs for 1757, 'Count Poniatowski returned to St Petersburg as Minister of the King of Poland.' He had been absent only three months. Whether the *liaison* began soon after he had arrived in the suite of Hanbury-Williams or on his return we do not know. Everyone knew what was going on in 'the little Court', and when Catherine gave birth to a daughter in 1758 Peter had good cause to exclaim: 'God knows how my wife became pregnant. I do not know if the child is mine and whether I must assume responsibility for it.' Having no morals of his own, he took his wife's infidelity in his stride. On leaving Oranienbaum in disguise early one morning in July 1758, the lover was arrested by one of the palace guards and brought before the Grand Duke. Everything could be arranged, observed the latter, if he were told the truth. He believed that the prisoner had designs on his life, and his threats of retaliation frightened Catherine into a step which her pride had hitherto forbidden. She made herself pleasant to her husband's mistress, and Poniatowski also sought her good offices. Elizabeth Woronzoff played up, and Peter assured his wife's lover that he was not jealous. For some weeks there was a harmonious *mènage à quatre*. 'I often visited Oranienbaum,' records Poniatowski in his Memoirs. 'I arrived in the evening, and went up to the rooms of the Grand Duchess, where I found the Grand Duke and his mistress. We supped together, after which he took her away, saying to us: "Well, children, you no longer need me." And I remained as long as I wished.' This curious idyll was of brief duration, for the Tsarina asked the Saxon Court to remove him on account of a letter to Bestuzhev, who, after many years as Chancellor, lost favour and was arrested. Though Catherine consoled herself with other lovers, she retained a certain affection for the charming young Pole, and in due course rewarded him with the Polish crown. His next visit to St Petersburg was as a dethroned King thirty-five years later.

Desiring to kill two birds with one stone, the Grand Duchess begged for an audience with the Empress, firstly to remove any suspicions which the latter might cherish owing to her relations with Bestuzhev, and secondly to describe her misery as the wife of the Grand Duke. In both she was successful. Elizabeth had always detested her nephew and did not care who heard what she said. 'My nephew is an imbecile; let the devil fetch him.' Catherine, she declared, loved truth and justice and was a very intelligent woman, but her nephew was a beast. The Grand Duchess threw herself in tears at the feet of the ruler and begged to be sent back to her relatives.

ELIZABETH. How can you wish such a thing? Remember that you have children.

CATHERINE. My children are in your hands and could not be in better keeping. I hope you will not abandon them.

ELIZABETH. How shall I explain your departure?

CATHERINE. Your Majesty can state why I have incurred your disgrace and the hatred of the Grand Duke.

ELIZABETH. How would you be able to live with your relatives?

CATHERINE. As I lived before you summoned me here.

After answering the charge of mixing herself up in things which did not concern her the clouds rolled away, despite the efforts of the Grand Duke, who was present at the interview, to envenom the sovereign. Tears came into her eyes, and the long interview ended at three in the morning. Before Catherine was in bed she received a message from the Empress that she was not to worry and that they would have a further conversation alone. Of that later talk we merely learn that Elizabeth demanded and Catherine promised the exact truth in reply to questions, for at this point her Memoirs break off with an unfinished sentence. 'Puis elle me demanda des détails sur la vie du grand-duc . . .' Her apologia reveals a good deal of her character but by no means the whole, for even at this stage she was a more formidable personality than it suggests. 'The Grand Duchess,' reported the experienced Chevalier d'Éon, the mystery-man among the secret diplomatic agents of Louis XV, 'is romantic, ardent, passionate. Her eyes are brilliant, their look fascinating and glassy—the look of a wild beast. Her forehead is lofty and, if I am not mistaken, a long and terrifying future is written on it. She is prepossessing and affable, but when she comes close to me I instinctively recoil. She frightens me.' The Grand Duke may well have felt something of the same shrinking and have dreaded the conflict of wills when his turn came to ascend the throne. The Empress vetoed his request to be allowed to return to Holstein, and the unhappy man had to obey. The whole Court, and indeed the Chancelleries of Europe, waited breathlessly for her death, and speculated on the inevitable struggle for power between the semi-imbecile Peter and his dynamic wife.

When Soltikoff, Poniatowski and Hanbury-Williams left the stage, Catherine found comfort and companionship in Princess Dashkoff, the only woman who ever became—and for a short time remained—an intimate friend. Catherine Woronzoff was the niece of Michael Woronzoff (Vice-Chancellor and, after the fall of Bestuzhev, Chancellor) and sister of the ugly mistress of the Grand Duke. Though she was still in her teens, they were attracted to each other by their intellectual tastes. 'The only two women who occupied themselves with serious reading were the Grand Duchess and myself,' she writes in her Memoirs. She translated an essay of Voltaire on epic poetry into Russian, and the Grand Duchess showed her friend her own dissertation on legislation. They often saw each other when the Dashkoffs were in the capital, and if they could not meet they exchanged affectionate little notes. When the Empress Elizabeth was on her death-bed the anxious Princess visited her friend at midnight to warn her of approaching danger. 'In heaven's name place your confidence in me. Issue your orders: I will not endanger your safety.' She had no plans, replied Catherine, concealing the fact that all arrangements for the approaching crisis had long been made. The most important preliminary had been the selection of Gregory Orloff as her new lover, a tall and handsome young officer who had fought bravely in the Seven Years War, a *bon vivant*, loving women, liquor and the gaming-table and ready for any dare-devil escapade. With his four brothers, all of them officers, he could count on considerable support among the troops in the capital, on whose mood, at a given moment, everything would depend. The paternity of Catherine's daughter, who died in infancy, had been a mystery, but that of 'Bobrinsky', born in April 1762, presented no such problem, and his mother never pretended that he was her husband's son.

Peter's first act on ascending the throne was to make peace and an alliance with his hero Frederick the Great, thereby saving Prussia from annihilation at the crisis of her fate. His decision was neither unexpected nor resented, for the emotions of the Russian people are rarely stirred unless their country is invaded.

Yet a bolder and more perilous resolve had long been ripening in his disordered brain. In the first conversation with Princess Dashkoff after his accession he hinted his intention to substitute his mistress for his wife upon the throne. The plan was known to Catherine, for Peter could never keep his mouth shut. It was now a contest of wits and wills, both parties realising that there was not much time to lose. Which of the ill-assorted partners would strike first? Would the new Empress be divorced and her son declared a bastard, or would the Tsar be dethroned? 'The Empress finds herself in a cruel situation,' reported the French Ambassador, 'and she is treated with studied contempt. She bears the behaviour of the Emperor towards her and the arrogance of Mlle Woronzoff with the utmost impatience. I cannot conceive that the Empress, whose courage and impetuosity are known to me, will not sooner or later proceed to extremes. She has friends who, if she gives the signal, would risk everything on her behalf. Only some occasion is required for an explosion.'

Catherine was as popular as Peter was disliked and despised. The support of troops in the capital was secured by the Orloffs, and Princess Dashkoff influenced officers in her husband's regiment. She also claimed to have won over Count Panin, recently appointed Governor of the little Grand Duke Paul, now a lad of eight. When she fell ill the Empress wrote: 'I cannot afford to lose a friend like you.' The Princess rode into St Petersburg at the side of Catherine on June 28, when the latter was proclaimed Empress of Russia by the Archbishop of Novgorod in the church of Our Lady of Kazan. The Tsar had ignored various warnings, among them those of Frederick the Great, to whom his survival meant so much. Not a drop of blood was shed. He had never made friends among his subjects, for his heart was in Germany and he had welcomed Prussian victories over Russia in the Seven Years War. His Holstein guards would have fought for him at the word of command, but his will, like that of the unhappy Alexis before him, was weak, and he had never been anxious to reign. Meekly accepting his fate, he signed his abdication. A few days later he was dead.

In considering Catherine's relation to her husband two problems arise. Was he the repulsive degenerate portrayed in her Memoirs? And what was her share of responsibility for the final catastrophe?

The answer to the first question is provided in Nisbet Bain's biography of the unhappy ruler, which utilises unpublished despatches of the *Corps Diplomatique*. Peter, we are told, was not a mere idiot and he possessed many amiable qualities. He was neither a profligate nor a drunkard, and he never shed blood. He was a kind master, a grateful nephew, an indulgent husband and a most generous friend. He enjoyed books on travel and war, liked music and played the violin. The marriage was not more miserable than most princely partnerships. Finding it impossible to love each other, they tacitly agreed to seek happiness elsewhere, and there were no complaints of infidelity on either side. Peter chose an ugly mistress, Catherine handsome cavaliers. Though notoriously unfitted to rule an empire, he would have made a good average country squire. His heart was good, if his head was weak. Yet, while his character is vindicated against the graver charges of his wife, her picture of his tragic insufficiency is fully confirmed by his English biographer. Mentally he was little more than a child. He indulged in schoolboy pranks with his Holsteiners, played for hours with toy soldiers, preferred low company, and lacked all sense of dignity. The poor half-crazy creature with his nerves perpetually on edge could never keep still, making faces and thrusting out his tongue. Completely destitute of horse sense and *savoir faire*, he alienated the army by his preference for his Holsteiners and his infatuation for Prussian models. Such a half-wit could have no friends, and in eighteenth-century Russia such an experiment in irresponsible autocracy could have only one end.

When the Tsar was dethroned and imprisoned at Ropsha, a small château near the capital, the question arose whether he should live or die. That his liquidation would be in the interest of the Empress was obvious, but her German upbringing prevented her from rating human life quite so cheaply as was traditional in Eastern Europe. There is no evidence that she ever contemplated violence: having obtained the power she coveted, she had no desire to shed blood. So well was her squeamishness understood that the Orloff brothers decided to act on their own responsibility. That Gregory, the reigning lover, may already have dreamed of marrying her was an additional reason for removing the legal obstacle. Once the plot was hatched it was easy enough to carry it out, for Alexis, the ablest of the brothers, was the chief jailer, played cards with the captive every day, and could make preparations at his leisure.

Several imaginary accounts of the final scene found their way into print, but the only first-hand evidence is contained in a distracted letter from Alexis himself written immediately after the catastrophe and despatched by courier to the Empress. 'Little mother, most merciful sovereign lady, how can I explain and describe what has happened? Thou wilt not believe thy faithful servant; but, so help me God, I speak the truth. I am ready to die, but I do not know how this mischief occurred. We are ruined if thou dost not have mercy. Little mother, he is no more. What were we thinking of to raise our hands against our Gosudar? But the mischief is done. He struggled behind the table with Prince Theodor (Baryatinsky), but we separated them and he is no more. I do not remember what we did, but we are all guilty and worthy of punishment. Have mercy on me, if only for the sake of my brother. I make my confession to thee and there is no need to investigate. Forgive us or order our speedy death. The world is unmerciful. We have angered thee and lost our souls for ever.' The letter, first printed in 1881 from a copy by Rostopchin found in the Woronzoff archives, was discovered in the cabinet of the Empress immediately after her death. Her successor had instructed the Grand Duke Alexander, the Chancellor Bezborodko and Rostopchin to examine her papers, and the unsigned letter was identified as in the handwriting of Alexis Orloff. Though Paul was relieved to discover that his mother's hands were not stained with his father's blood, he threw it into the fire to conceal the fact that the self-confessed assassins remained in favour at Court.

Most onlookers throughout Europe, among them Frederick the Great and Horace Walpole, held Catherine responsible for the crime on the ground that in such a semi-savage community as Russia the deposition of a ruler virtually involved assassination. Qui veut la fin veut les moyens. If her hands were not red there were stains on her clothes. When Princess Dashkoff visited her friend on the following day she was greeted with the words: 'My horror is inexpressible; this blow strikes me to the earth.' The proof of her innocence, adds the Princess in her Memoirs, was to be found in Alexis' letter. That Catherine quickly recovered is not surprising, for the removal of the sword of Damocles over her head was an immeasurable relief. At last, after a long agony of frustration and insecurity, she was not only out of danger but on the open road. She had suffered her brainless husband for seventeen years: now she reaped her reward. Nothing more was heard of Panin's plan that she should become Regent for her son. The child meant nothing to her except as a potential rival who had to be watched. The hour of destiny of which she had dreamed in hours of depression had struck, and at the age of thirty-three she strode confidently forward towards the shining goal of power and fame. Like Frederick the Great, she was born to rule.

Catherine's version of the revolution was conveyed in a long letter to her old lover Stanislas Poniatowski, written two weeks after the final catastrophe, in which there is not the slightest sign of emotion or regret. Peter, she declared, had lost the little wits he had. He wanted to change his religion, marry his mistress and imprison his wife. On the day of the conclusion of peace with Prussia he publicly insulted her at table and ordered her arrest. The order was withdrawn, but henceforth she had listened to proposals to seize him and shut him up. 'We could count on many captains of the Guards. The secret was in the hands of the three Orloff brothers. They are extremely determined people and much loved by the common soldiers. I am under great obligations to them.' After a detailed account of the deposition of the ruler the letter hurries over the final scene. 'I sent the deposed Emperor to a remote and very agreeable place called Ropsha, twenty-five versts from Peterhof, under the command of Alexis Orloff, with four officers and a detachment of picked good-natured men, while suitable rooms were being prepared for him at Schlusselburg. But God disposed otherwise. Fear had caused a diarrhoea which lasted three days and he passed away on the fourth, when he drank excessively. He had all he wanted except his liberty. The only things he asked me for were his mistress, his dog, his negro and his violin; but for fear of the scandal and increasing the agitation of his guards I only sent him the last three. The haemorrhoidal colic affected his brain. For two days he was delirious, and the delirium was followed by extreme exhaustion. Despite all the help of the doctors he expired while demanding a Lutheran priest. I feared the officers might have poisoned him, so I had him opened, but not the slightest trace of poison was found. The stomach was quite sound, but inflammation of the bowels and a stroke of apoplexy had carried him off. His heart was extraordinarily small and quite decayed. So at last God has brought everything to pass according to His designs. The whole thing is rather a miracle than a pre-arranged plan, for so many lucky circumstances could not have coincided unless God's hand had been over it all. Hatred of foreigners was the chief factor, and Peter III passed for a foreigner.'

Catherine's narrative might have sounded a little more plausible did we not know that the confession of the chief executioner was locked up in her cabinet. 'It is announced that it is the natural result of the despair caused by his deposition,' reported the French *Chargé d'Affaires*, 'but in secret people say that he was poisoned.' On Panin's advice the body was exhibited in order to avert a repetition of the experience of 'the false Demetrius', but the public was not permitted to see much of its late ruler. Since a big hat was drawn over part of his face and a large tie was wound round his neck, it was not very difficult for the spectators to draw their own conclusion as they filed past the mangled corpse.

## II. *Mother and Son*

CATHERINE'S relations with her son constituted the most embarrassing problem of her reign. If the excesses of her private life may be charitably explained as partly pathological, the harsh treatment of her heir was a calculated policy which casts a dark shadow on her fame. In the sphere of *haute politique* her head ruled her heart, but the head can also make grave mistakes. Such conflicts are a very old tale, and rarely has the instinctive antagonism of youth and age been so painful and so prolonged. There was more melodrama and ideological colouring in the fate of Don Carlos and Alexis, but the experience of Paul was complicated by an unusual if not indeed unique consideration. Was he the legitimate son of Peter III, or the offspring of the earliest of his mother's many lovers? Most of the courtiers and the *Corps Diplomatique* inclined to the latter hypothesis. Perhaps the Grand Duchess her-

*PAUL I*

self was not quite sure, and the question remains open two centuries after his birth. His putative father had his doubts, and sometimes spoke of declaring him a bastard when he came to the throne. It would be surprising if Paul himself, who detested his mother, did not speculate whether he was a Romanoff or a Soltikoff. The most convincing argument for his legitimacy was his ill-favoured countenance, which he was unlikely to have inherited from one of the handsomest men of the age. Corroborative evidence may be found on the psychological plane. When Prince Adam Czartoryski, the bosom friend of the Tsar Alexander I, arrived in St Petersburg shortly before Catherine's death, he heard speculations about the paternity of the Grand Duke Paul, and dismissed them as idle gossip. In observing the extreme resemblance between this Prince and Peter III, he records in his Memoirs, he could not doubt that he was his son.

A second significant factor in the lifelong estrangement was the decision of the Empress Elizabeth to remove the child from his mother's care from the moment of his birth, permitting her to see him only at infrequent intervals. Tenderness he never knew. Whether in happier circumstances they would have taken to each other we can only guess. Catherine's delight in children was revealed towards the close of her life when her two eldest grandsons provided her with the purest—perhaps the only pure—joys she had ever known. When she succeeded to the throne at the age of thirty-three, and could do what she liked with the boy, it was too late to find the way to his heart, and she hardly appears to have tried. Terms of conventional endearment were occasionally exchanged, but the relationship inevitably worsened with advancing years. Paul was haunted not merely by the nightmare of his father's assassination, and the gnawing uncertainty of his own prospects, but also by the gravest doubts whether his mother's hands were stained with blood.

Beginning as strangers, they soon became rivals. Primogeniture formed no part of the law or practice of the Romanoffs, for since Peter the Great the succession had been decided by the whim of the ruler or a palace revolution. Yet Paul's claim to the throne when he grew to manhood was extremely strong, though Peter III left no will. At the time of the murder he was in his eighth year, and it was expected in some quarters that the Empress might

c

act as Regent till he came of age. That she had no intention either of surrendering power, or, like Maria Theresa, sharing responsibility, was quickly apparent, and her decision was rendered a little more plausible by the contrasts of temperament and abilities. Catherine, possessing a first-class brain and a will of tempered steel, was born to rule, and her territorial acquisitions at the expense of Poland and Turkey enhanced her prestige at home and abroad. Paul, on the other hand, though not without estimable qualities, was ill-balanced, irritable and irresolute. Though not utterly contemptible like his father, he inherited the inability to inspire confidence and to win friends. With a more winning personality he might have formed a party, and with a stronger will he would surely have reached for the crown. Resenting his fate, yet sullenly accepting his fetters, his whole career till his accession at the age of forty-two was a tragedy of frustration.

In eighteenth-century Russia everything depended on the ruler, and the Empress Elizabeth was as variable as a weathercock. That she hated and despised her nephew, whom she had summoned from Holstein, was no secret, but would she dare to send him back? Several alternatives flitted through her disordered brain as her end approached, among them that of proclaiming the infant Paul as her heir. Drunken and dissolute though she was, she dreaded to entrust her country to a half-witted degenerate whose hero was her enemy Frederick the Great. Though she was too self-indulgent to concern herself overmuch with the lonely child, she chose as his Governor one of the few relatively respectable members of her entourage, Count Nikita Panin, who had represented his country at Stockholm for many years. The boy warmed to the first human being who had shown him kindness, for his father cared as little for him as his mother. Had the Empress carried out the project for the succession with which she coquetted, the destiny of Paul and his parents would have been unimaginably different. But her will was never very strong, and she passed away without taking the plunge.

The new Tsar surpassed the most sinister anticipations of his subjects. Within a few weeks he had humiliated the army by concluding an inglorious peace with Prussia, and alienated the clergy by his mockery of the ceremonies of the Orthodox Church. His wife was treated to the usual insults and threats. It was widely

believed that if the Woronzoff were to present him with a son he
would divorce Catherine, marry his mistress, declare Paul a
bastard and recognise the baby as his heir. Since the Ambassadors
reported to their respective governments that a revolution was at
hand, there was little surprise throughout Europe when he was
dethroned, imprisoned and slain. During his brief reign the interests of mother and son were identical in the sense that an attack
on either involved the downfall of both. When Peter was gone,
their interests diverged, and a short battle for power occurred.
Panin, who had taken part in the coup, desired the recognition of
his little charge as the heir, and dreamed of standing at his right
hand during the long minority; but the indolent Governor was
never a fighter, and the boy was too young to fight for himself.
Fearing to commit himself to a losing cause, Panin bowed to the
stronger will. He had little choice, for the ruthless Orloffs were
determined to trample all opposition underfoot.

In the early morning of June 28, 1762, when Catherine rode
from Oranienbaum to the capital, Paul was sleeping peacefully in
the Summer Palace. On entering the church where she was to be
proclaimed, his mother sent for him to witness the coronation
ceremony. Awakened by an officer with a military escort, the
frightened lad was carried out in the arms of Panin, who endeavoured to reassure him. After taking the oath he appeared
with the Empress on the balcony. The tragedy of his father's
deposition and death was never far from his thoughts. Hitherto
his mother had been an object of indifference to him: henceforth
he thought of her with aversion and dread.

Though Catherine had won the first round in the long duel
with her unhappy son, she felt the ground quaking under her feet.
She was a foreigner, and her complicity in the murder of her
husband was generally assumed. One of her first acts was to
declare Paul her heir, a step of doubtful utility if intended to
buttress her own position as the rightful occupant of the throne
for life. Fearing to leave him in the capital, she took him to
Moscow for her coronation, but on their arrival he was too ill to
appear. From time to time the cry was heard among the soldiers:
'Long live the Emperor, Paul Petrovich!' The *Corps Diplomatique*
reported to their governments the probability of another *coup*, and
Louis XV instructed his Ambassador to establish contact with the

Opposition. On the rare occasions when he was allowed to appear in public, Paul was greeted with applause. Panin had not lost interest in his charge, and when Catherine proposed to marry Gregory Orloff, he courageously voiced the widespread objection to the plan. During the brief reign of Peter III she had given her third lover a son, and it was feared that a new marriage might lead to the substitution of 'Alexis Bobrinsky' as heir to the throne. The little Grand Duke was beginning to ask why his father had been murdered, and why his mother, not he, was on the throne. So great was her alarm that she desired to take him on her visit to Livonia in 1764. When Panin pleaded the boy's ill-health, she ordered that during her absence he should reside at Tsarkoe-Selo, and that he should join her at the first sign of trouble in the capital.

The general *malaise* was intensified by the murder in the prison of Schlusselburg of the young Ivan VI, great-grandson of the elder brother of Peter the Great, who had sat on the throne for a few months till Elizabeth seized power in 1741. Whether Catherine had a hand in the crime no one could be sure, but it was obvious that the disappearance of a rival claimant was a relief to her anxious mind. The French Ambassador reported rumours that the next victim might well be Paul himself. The death of Ivan increased his peril, for henceforth he was the only rallying point for the Opposition. In 1765 a leading ecclesiastic omitted the name of the Empress from the public prayers, and exhorted the congregation to pray for the Grand Duke as the only legitimate ruler. In 1766, at the age of twelve, Paul declined to appear at a Court supper to celebrate the anniversary of his mother's accession. Alarmed by the hostility around her, she was credited with the idea of marrying her discarded lover Stanislas, whose election to the Polish throne she had engineered, so that in the event of being forced to abdicate she might find a dignified retreat in Warsaw.

In the hope of strengthening her popularity, Catherine decided on a visit to Moscow in 1767, taking her son with her. A year's residence failed to rouse enthusiasm, whereas every opportunity was seized by the citizens to acclaim the delicate lad who was left behind under the care of the Orloffs when his mother returned home. When some Moscow nobles expressed their desire for her abdication, Panin explained the the Grand Duke was too young to reign and still required the guidance of his mother. Knowing Panin's easy-going nature and respecting his character, Catherine had no fear that he would make trouble. Moreover, his dismissal might have been interpreted as a threat to the interests, and even to the life, of his charge. Though the lad was too young to organise opposition, she resented his popularity and treated him with a studied coolness. She loved good looks, and his ugly, morose, distrustful countenance seemed to repel familiarity. Whether the warm-hearted d'Alembert might have brought some serenity and warmth into his life had he accepted the invitation— with a princely salary, a house and the privileges of an ambassador —to teach him mathematics we can only guess. Panin instructed him in the recent history of Europe, and from other teachers he learned to dance, to ride and to speak French. The diary of his tutor Poroshin depicts an intelligent, impressionable, highly-strung youth. 'His Highness has that most detestable of habits of doing everything in haste. He is in a hurry to get up, to eat, to go to bed. Responsive and affectionate, he forms an attachment very quickly, but the object of his sudden affection has to exert himself to retain it at the same level, otherwise the whole thing is very soon forgotten.' Paul, never at peace with himself, lived in a twilight of sinister memories and haunting fears. His health was poor, and every illness started rumours of foul play. In 1771 a few officers of the Preobrajenski regiment, a name only too celebrated in the classic land of palace revolutions, plotted to arrest the Empress and proclaim her son. The scheme was betrayed, the conspirators tortured and banished to Siberia, but the *malaise* remained.

In September, 1772, Paul reached his legal majority at the age of eighteen: now, if ever, was the time for a change. The Synod, except for a single Archbishop, declared in his favour, and the air was thick with rumours. Panin, however, had no desire to burn his fingers, and Paul maintained an attitude of sullen reserve. Though his mother kept watch on his movements, she could find no cause for complaint. At this moment, without consulting him, she ceded to Denmark the Duchy of Holstein-Gottorp, which had been so dear to his father's heart—a decision interpreted by the French Ambassador as a move to sever the only link between her heir and the Western world.

A momentary *détente* occurred in the same year when the Empress tired of Gregory Orloff, whom Paul had always detested as a ringleader in the murder of his father. For the first time he received marks of affection to which he appeared to respond. 'We have never had a jollier time at Tsarkoe-Selo than these nine weeks I have spent there with my son, who is becoming a nice lad,' she wrote to her Hamburg friend, Frau Bielke, in August, 1772. There had been plenty of laughter and high spirits. 'I return to town on Tuesday with my son, who does not want to leave my side, and whom I have the honour to please so well that he sometimes changes his place at table to sit next me.' How much of this display was genuine? The Prussian Envoy reported that the Grand Duke saw through his mother's game and resented her unaccustomed smiles. The French Envoy attributed them to her feeling of insecurity after her breach with the Orloffs. So alarmed was she that her old lover was consoled with estates and a pension, pictures and silver. He was soon back at Court, though his office of *amant en titre* was now filled by Wassiltchikoff. After welcoming what he expected to be the final eviction of his hated enemy, Paul was disgusted by his partial restoration to favour. Taking advantage of his mother's recent pose of affection, he had threatened to leave the country if the fallen idol returned. He had wept with anger when he saw him once more at Court, reported the French Envoy, and refused to speak to him. When at last he consented to do so he was rewarded with a present of 50,000 roubles, but the ex-favourite wondered what would happen when he came to the throne. Once relieved of the fear of retaliation by the Orloff faction, the Empress dropped her displays of tenderness as an actor removes his mask. Members of the *Corps Diplomatique* deplored their inability to be on good terms both with the ruler and the heir: to accept an invitation to his suppers was to incur her sour looks. When the Swedish Ambassador planned to congratulate him on his coming of age, he was dissuaded by a more experienced colleague. At the age of nineteen the Austrian Ambassador described him as the idol of the nation, but his popularity increased the dislike and the apprehensions of his mother.

On attaining his majority, the time had come for Paul to marry, and his mother's choice fell on Wilhelmina, a daughter of Caroline, 'the Great Landgravine' of Hesse-Darmstadt, the friend of

Goethe, Wieland and Herder. The plan was welcomed for political reasons by Frederick the Great, whose nephew and heir had married an elder sister of the prospective bride. A faint ray of sunshine flickered in the soul of the melancholy lad at the thought of a little more liberty and a home of his own. He had displayed a boyish attraction for one of his mother's ladies, but his affections had never been seriously engaged. Unlike Peter III, he had a heart and a brain. 'The Grand Duke cannot conceal his joy,' reported the Prussian Ambassador; 'he regards it as his greatest happiness to be united to a princess he adores.' It was not all plain sailing, for the family feud was too bitter to be healed by wedding bells. Would her son become more independent, and might not a wife encourage him to assert his rights? The Great Landgravine, who had accompanied her daughter, returned to Darmstadt directly after the wedding, and the Empress reported that her son appeared very much in love. The Grand Duchess, she declared, was pure gold. On closer acquaintance, Catherine's eulogies rapidly diminished, for, as she confided to Grimm, she only wanted to amuse herself. Paul, on the other hand, began to take more interest in the things of the mind. He engaged La Harpe, the Swiss journalist, to send him gossipy bulletins which were ultimately published as *Correspondance littéraire adressée à Son Altesse Impériale le Grand-Duc de Russie*—a pale imitation of the more high-brow enterprise of Grimm and Diderot.

Paul's spell of happiness was brief, for his mother's suspicious hostility was undiminished. Panin, to whom he was genuinely attached, had never possessed her full confidence since his championship of the Regency. He was now informed that the education of the Grand Duke was finished, and that his mission was fulfilled. The parting was regretted by Paul, and his resentment was increased by the appointment to his little Court of General Nicholas Soltikoff—later to be entrusted with the education of his sons—whom he regarded as little better than a spy. A further blow to his pride was inflicted when his request to become a member of the Council was roughly declined. After a distressing scene, the Empress reiterated her decision in a letter of the same day. 'I told you that your request needs mature consideration. I do not think your entrance into the Council would be desirable. You must be patient till I change my mind.' Paul now began to suffer from a persecution mania which grew from year to year. One day, finding fragments of glass in his food, he carried the plate to his mother and accused her of planning his murder. Tension increased when Pougatcheff, the Cossack adventurer, announced that he was Peter III and that his aim was to depose the Empress and place their son upon the throne. When the rebellion was suppressed and its leader executed, a new cause of friction emerged, for Potemkin, the ablest of Catherine's lovers, gained a commanding influence. While the Court was at his feet and there was talk of his marrying the Empress, Paul looked on in impotent despair from the wings, compelled to borrow money for his daily needs. In the new capital he was nobody, but on a visit of the Court to Moscow in 1775 he was once again acclaimed. 'You see how popular you are, Prince,' observed Count Razumowski, 'if you wished.' Paul made no reply, for he lacked the spirit to rebel.

His marriage, like almost everything else in his life, proved a disappointment. The frivolous Hessian princess had never encouraged his affection, and it was rumoured that Razumowski, a celebrated lady-killer, was her lover. The Empress believed—or affected to believe—in her transgression, and warned Paul to keep a sharp look-out. She also lectured him on his wife's extravagance. No one in Europe, she declared, had such a civil list. It was a trial, she wrote to Potemkin, always to be paying her debts and never to receive a word of thanks. The intermezzo which had begun so auspiciously was soon over, for she died in childbirth in 1776. She had never courted popularity, and few tears were shed at her passing. For her husband it was a blessing, for she could never have made him happy, and such a self-willed consort would have introduced yet another element of disruption into a deeply-divided family.

Not a moment was lost in looking round for another bride for the Grand Duke. Prince Henry of Prussia, who happened to be in St Petersburg, offered his services and proposed Sophia Dorothea, eldest daughter of Prince Eugene of Montbéliard, a junior branch of the Württemberg dynasty, a great-niece of Frederick the Great, who was presumably Prussophil. Her engagement to a brother of the late Grand Duchess, the heir to the Landgrave of Hesse-Darmstadt, was broken off, and the prospective bridegroom was consoled by a Russian pension. The almost penniless girl of seventeen was summoned to Berlin, whither Paul, in the company of Prince Henry, had travelled to meet her. 'The Grand Duke is exceedingly amiable,' she wrote home; 'he has every charm.' For the first time in his life he received the consideration due to his rank, and revelled in the experience. 'Nothing can exceed the attention and even court His Prussian Majesty pays to the Grand Duke, nor the pains he takes to captivate and please him,' reported the British Ambassador from Berlin. Inheriting his father's liking for Germany, Paul wrote to his mother that in the scale of civilisation Prussia was two centuries ahead of the land of his birth. The new bride, like her predecessor, was warmly welcomed by the Empress. 'My son has returned in good health and very much taken with his princess,' she reported to Frau Bielke. 'I am literally enchanted.'

Paul's second wife, the Württemberg princess henceforth known as Marie Feodorovna, was handsome, affectionate and intelligent. 'Wherever she goes,' he reported to Prince Henry, 'she has the gift of diffusing gaiety and ease. And she possesses the art not only of banishing my fancies, but even of restoring the character I had entirely lost during these three unhappy years.' To another friend he wrote that he was not made of marble, and that his heart was not so hard as people believed. The Grand Duchess seemed equally pleased. 'He is an angel, the pearl of husbands,' she confided to her bosom friend, Baroness d'Oberkirch, whose Memoirs are filled with her praises; 'I am perfectly happy.' To the kindly Panin she wrote that the adorable Grand Duke overwhelmed her with affection and caresses. The British Ambassador, Sir James Harris, saw further ahead. 'They are at present perfectly happy together, but I fear their happiness cannot be durable in a court so unprincipled and so singularly composed. He betrays a levity that sometimes flatters the lady he addresses himself to; and she must be possessed of a very uncommon share of resolution and rectitude if she avoids the many snares which will be laid in her way, and from which none of the Empresses of these dominions, without exception, have escaped. He is very temperate in his food and still more in his drinking, and has, by these regularities, strengthened a constitution naturally infirm. In a word, without superior capacity, he has a sufficient portion of understanding, if

he gets the better of a certain fickleness in his affections and
timidity in his actions which may be only the effect of youth, and
of his situation, to govern this country.'

Though the Grand Duchess was shocked by the profligacy of
the Empress, she possessed sufficient tact to avoid a breach. The
opening phase of Paul's second marriage was the brightest chapter
of an unhappy life. 'She deserves his affection,' reported the
British Ambassador, 'and he is very fond of her.' Yet the funda-
mental cause of his spiritual sickness remained: excluded from all
official responsibility, he had little to do except to brood over his
fate. His mother's successive lovers became automatically his
enemies, as he was theirs. If Orloff had been the most detested,
Potemkin was the most formidable and the most to be feared.
'Prince Potemkin rules her with an absolute sway,' reported
Harris in 1779; 'thoroughly acquainted with her weaknesses,
her desires and her passions, he operates on them and makes them
operate as he pleases. Besides this strong hold on her, he keeps
her in constant dread of the Grand Duke, and has convinced her,
from the numerous friends and adherents he has made, that he is
the only person who can discover in time and protect her against
any undertaking from that quarter.' The birth of his sons brought
little satisfaction, for the Empress promptly took charge and
lavished on them the affection which she denied to her son.

When the Emperor Joseph II paid his first visit to Russia in
1780 he reported his impressions of the two Courts to his mother,
Maria Theresa. Like everyone else, he admired the Crown
Princess, and his verdict on Paul was extremely favourable. 'The
Grand Duke is greatly undervalued abroad. His wife is very
beautiful and seems created for her position. They understand
each other perfectly. They are clever and vivacious and very well
educated, as well as high-principled, open and just. The happiness of others is more to them than wealth. With the Empress
they are ill at ease, especially the Grand Duke. There is a lack of
intimacy without which I could not live. The Grand Duchess is
more natural. She has great influence over her husband, loves
him and rules him. She will certainly play an important part some
day. She is very affectionate towards me, but one has to be careful
since too close a relationship might create difficulties. That the
Grand Duke mentioned his false position proves his confidence

in me, but it is not easy to please both parties at the same time. He has many qualities deserving respect, but it is extremely difficult to play second fiddle here when Catherine II plays the first. The more I learn of the Grand Duchess the greater is my admiration. She is exceptional in mind and heart, attractive in appearance and blameless in conduct. If I could have met a Princess like her ten years ago I should have been most happy to marry her.'

The chief episode in the middle years of the Grand Duke was his tour of the European capitals in 1781-2, travelling as the Comte du Nord. The pleasure of the journey, which occupied over a year, was diminished by his mother's veto on a visit to Berlin, where the Prussophil Prince was eager to renew acquaintance with his hero; for the Empress had transferred her political favours to Austria with a view to joint adventures at the expense of the Turks. Despite this harsh decree, which had led to angry scenes, he delighted in his freedom from unfriendly surveillance and in the consideration he received from his hosts—King Stanislas in Poland, the Emperor Joseph in Vienna, Pope Pius VI in Rome, the Grand Duke Leopold in Florence, and, above all, the French King and Queen at Versailles. The Grand Duchess and Marie Antoinette made friends, and a happy time was spent at her old home at Württemberg. We can follow the travellers in the diary of Baroness d'Oberkirch, who accompanied them through France, rejoicing in their social triumphs. She liked and respected the Grand Duke, and the Grand Duchess she adored. The frequent letters from the Empress, filled with details about the children and inquiries about the journey, made a pleasant impression. In her correspondence, no less than in society, Catherine could be charming, and here she was seen at her best. No uninstructed reader of these chatty bulletins would guess what troubles there had been and were again to be. She welcomed the temporary relief from the chronic apprehensions arising from the presence of her frowning heir.

Joseph's prediction that Paul's situation on his return might well be even more disagreeable than before was fulfilled, for reports of his verbal indiscretions had reached St Petersburg from various capitals. At Vienna he had angrily exclaimed that he would dismiss his mother's counsellors with a whipping when he gained control. In Naples he complained that the Empress could keep her throne only by trampling on the laws. In Paris he bitterly observed that if he possessed a faithful dog his mother would have it drowned. Every year made his frustration harder to bear. He and his wife had to appear at official balls, but mother and son saw little of each other. Princess Dashkoff relates that she reluctantly avoided 'the young Court' so that she should not be questioned or suspected by the Empress. On the death of Gregory Orloff Catherine presented her son with the palace of Gatschina, which she had built for the Favourite. Paul's family grew apace, six daughters following one another, with two more sons at the end of the list. He took some pleasure in his younger children, who were left to their parents' care, but his capacity for care-free happiness had been frozen in his youth. The Empress displayed as little affection for him as for her worthless bastard, Alexis Bobrinsky, the child of Orloff, now growing to manhood and sowing his wild oats in the capitals of the West. Most of the sentiment of which her heart was capable was concentrated on her lovers, and when Lanskoi, perhaps the most passionately worshipped of them all, died in 1784, she shut herself up with her grief for a couple of months till a new paramour restored her resilience. Paul watched these performances with contemptuous disgust, for his morals were above the average. The Grand Duchess, who was described as an angel by the Prince de Ligne, gave the Empress no ground for criticism, though her wholesome bourgeois *ménage* constituted an unspoken and unceasing rebuke.

On his arrival at St Petersburg in 1784 the French Ambassador, Comte de Ségur, son of the Minister of War, strove in accordance with his instructions to establish friendly but not too intimate relations with 'the little Court'. First impressions were extremely favourable. 'The homage they had received in Paris had predisposed them in favour of all Frenchmen, and when they admitted me into their society I learned to know all the rare qualities which at this period won general affection. I say their society, because, except for official occasions, their circle, though fairly large, seemed—especially in the country—more like a friendly gathering than a stiff Court. No private family did the honours of the house with more ease and grace. Dinners and balls, performances and fêtes—everything bore the imprint of the best tone and the most delicate taste. The Grand Duchess, majestic, affable and natural,

pretty without coquetry, amiable without affectation, created an
impression of virtue without pose. Paul sought to please and was
well informed. One was struck by his great vivacity and nobility
of character. These, however, were only first impressions. Soon
one noticed, above all when he spoke of his personal position and
future, a disquiet, a mistrust, an extreme susceptibility, in fact,
oddities which were to cause his faults, his injustices and his misfortunes. In any other rank of life he might have made himself
and others happy; but for such a man the throne, above all the
Russian throne, could not fail to be a dangerous shoal on which
he could not climb without expecting to be speedily hurled down.
The history of all the dethroned and butchered Tsars was his *idée
fixe*, darkening his mind and unhinging his reason.'
   A later portrait by the same accomplished hand many years after
his return to France in 1789 registers the decline and fall of
what might, in happier circumstances, have been a noble nature.
'He combined plenty of intelligence and information with the
most unquiet and mistrustful humour and the most unsteady
character. Though often affable to the point of familiarity, he was
more frequently haughty, despotic and harsh. Never had one seen
a man more thoughtless, more frightened, more capricious, in a
word, less capable of rendering himself or others happy. His reign
proved it. It was not malignity which inspired so many injustices,
or led him to disgrace or exile so many people; it was a sickness
of the mind. He tormented all who approached him because he
unceasingly tormented himself. The throne always seemed to
him surrounded by precipices. Fear upset his judgment. Imagined perils gave rise to real ones, for a monarch inspires the
mistrust which he exhibits and the terror he feels.'
   Paul complained of his fate to any foreigner who was willing to
listen, beating his clenched fists against the bars of his cage without attempting to break out. He was allowed no say in the
marriage of his sons. His mother's alignment with Austria was a
fresh trial for the Prussophil Prince, and he confided in cipher to
Frederick William II, whom the Empress disliked and despised,
that his sentiments were unchanged. Still more bitterly resented
was her veto on military service in the second Turkish war, for
the army was his chief interest, and her permission to share in the
simultaneous campaign against Sweden in Finland was a slender

consolation. Life was rendered endurable only by the thought that some day the nightmare would end and he would find himself on the throne. Even here, however, there was an element of doubt, for as the precocious and attractive Alexander grew to manhood, a new danger loomed up. Since Peter the Great had proclaimed the right of the reigning sovereign to nominate his successor, who could tell whether Catherine might not change her mind and exclude him from the throne? He sought comfort in the mysticism which swept across Europe like a wave in the closing decades of the century, which had invaded the dissolute Court of Frederick William II, and which was proclaimed by Saint-Martin in France and Novikoff, the chief of the Freemasons, in Russia. Rebelling against the fashionable scepticism of his mother's Court, he spent much time on his knees in prayer, his face bathed in tears, sometimes uttering groans which were heard in the neighbouring guardroom. What little self-control he had exerted had given way, and his outbursts became the terror of his entourage. Though the Empress inspired little respect, it was not her Favourites alone who dreaded a change for the worse. Paul's loss of popularity was noted and welcomed by his mother as diminishing the probability of a military *coup*.

The Grand Duchess, ever loyal and serene, was respected by her partner, but she gave more affection than she received. 'I shall be separated from my beloved husband,' she wrote to the Baroness d'Oberkirch when he left for the Swedish campaign in 1788. 'Thousands of versts will be between us, and he will be exposed to all the horrors of war. My heart is almost broken by anxiety for the life of him for whom I would willingly sacrifice my own.' Paul's craving for affection, on the other hand, found deeper satisfaction elsewhere. Catherine Nelidoff, one of his wife's ladies-in-waiting, had accompanied them on their European tour, and his delight in her company was unconcealed. Though extremely plain, she had plenty of personality. It was the only idyll, the only completely satisfying experience, in his tragic career. Though tongues began to wag, the relationship seems to have been platonic. The best testimony to its innocence was supplied by the friendship ultimately accorded to her by the Grand Duchess when, after a long phase of acute jealousy, she became convinced of her unselfish devotion to the Grand Duke. When he transferred his attentions to Mlle Lapoukhin, she withdrew after ten years of favour to the Smolny Convent, where she had been educated. She was wise to depart, for Paul became more moody and unpredictable from year to year.

A vivid picture of the atmosphere in Russia during the closing phase of the reign is painted in the Memoirs of Prince Adam Czartoryski, who, having lost his country, settled in Russia in 1795. 'The Empress Catherine, principal author of the ruin of Poland, whose very name strikes horror and is cursed by every Polish heart: Catherine, who, judged from a distance, possessed neither virtue nor even decency, had won the veneration and even the love of her entourage and her subjects, above all in the capital. From the date of her accession, the Muscovite Empire had gained in consideration abroad and in order at home far beyond that which prevailed under Anne and Elizabeth. Minds were still full of old fanaticism and low adoration of their autocrats. The prosperous reign of Catherine had confirmed the Russians in their servility, though a few rays of European civilisation had begun to penetrate. Thus the whole nation was in no way scandalised at the depravity, the crimes and murders committed by their sovereign. Everything was permitted. No one dreamed of criticising her debauchery. It was thus that the pagans respected the crimes and obscenities of the gods of Olympus and of the Caesars of Rome. The Grand Duke Paul figured as the shadow in the picture, and enhanced the effect. The terror he inspired fortified the general attachment to the rule of Catherine. Everyone desired the reins of government to remain as long as possible in her strong hands. The universal fear of Paul increased the admiration for the power and the lofty abilities of his mother who kept him on the lead, far from his rightful throne.' In a word, her best insurance against a palace revolution was the unpopularity of her pathological son. In the words of Countess Golovin, his soul was noble but his head was confused.

That the Empress desired her gifted and handsome grandson Alexander to succeed her was neither a secret nor a surprise, and there was no constitutional obstacle to her freedom of choice. When she felt her powers declining, she worried increasingly about the future of her realm. 'I see into what hands the Empire will fall when I am gone,' she exclaimed. The most revealing clue to her intentions occurs in a letter to Grimm in 1791 in which, with reference to the French Revolution, she foretold the coming of a Genghis Khan or a Tamerlane, and added the words: 'This will not occur in my time, and I hope not in the time of M. Alexander.' Throughout the last months of her life she made half-hearted attempts to implement her plan. Thirty years later Paul's widow confided to their daughter Anne, wife of Prince William of Orange, that a few weeks before her death the Empress invited her to sign a paper demanding that Paul should renounce his right to the throne. Though only too well aware of his unfitness to rule, she indignantly refused, and an appeal to Alexander to save his country from the rule of a madman was equally fruitless. Whether Catherine was about to proclaim her grandson her successor, as was rumoured in the capital, or whether she left a will to that effect which was destroyed by her son, we cannot be sure, for while she was considering the next step she was suddenly struck down at the close of 1796. Paul, at any rate, was prepared for the worst. When Nicholas Zuboff, brother of the latest Favourite, hurried to Gatschina with the news of the fatal event, the terrified Grand Duke, believing that the moment of his arrest had come, exclaimed to his wife: 'We are lost!' The sudden change from moody impotence gave another turn of the screw to his disordered brain.

The feud between mother and son lasted beyond the grave. Paul's first act as sovereign was to proclaim the principle of primogeniture in regard to the Crown, the second to pay off old scores. Surviving associates of his father were restored to favour, regardless of personal merit, while those who had served his mother's purposes felt his heavy hand. He was his own master at last, yet he was no happier on the throne. Happiness was beyond his grasp. Though he had escaped from his most formidable enemy, he could never escape from himself. Haunted by the grim memories of the past, yet deaf to their strident warnings, he staggered blindly forward to his doom. Like his degenerate father, he dug his own grave. The worst of Catherine's offences was not her immorality but the cold-blooded maltreatment of her son, for the sins of the spirit are worse than the sins of the flesh. Had she revisited the scenes of her glory during his brief reign she would have pointed to his dangerous antics in justification of

*POTEMKIN*

her parental severity. But then the Recording Angel might have replied: 'You, more than anyone, made him what he was. You bruised his soul beyond the power of the healer's art.'


## III. *The Favourites*

A PICTURE of Catherine the Great without her lovers would be as untrue to life as that of Louis XIV and Louis XV without their mistresses. The third female ruler of Russia merely followed the evil ways of the Empresses Anne and Elizabeth, the former dominated by Biron, a boorish Courlander, the latter in bondage successively to the Ukranian shepherd-boy Razumowsky and Ivan Schuvaloff. But her reign was longer, and the number of her Favourites far greater than any of her predecessors or successors on the throne of the Romanoffs. George Soloveytchik, the latest of Potemkin's biographers, lists twenty-one. More than half of them were little more than shadows, playing a very minor part in the drama, pretty toys of the masterful woman who drew them from obscurity and threw them aside when she had had enough. Three, on the other hand, helped to make history, and one of them filled Europe with his fame. Some were chosen by herself, others pushed forward for her inspection. As soon as one was selected, speculation as to his successor began. There was keen competition, for the winner was greeted with a *beau geste* of 100,000 roubles, received jewels and emoluments during his term of office, and was presented with landed property when he finished the course. In almost every case the parting occurred without scenes or tears, and occasionally a discarded lover reappeared at Court.

Though eager for a good Press throughout Europe both for herself and her adopted country, Catherine was never known to blush for her private life. The moral standard of her contemporaries was so low that few could throw stones, and Maria Theresa was the only ruler who frowned on the sins of the flesh. In the early years there was an interval between the removal of one Favourite and the rise of another, but before long the transition was arranged in advance. That the apartments immediately under those of the Empress and connected by a private staircase

D

would remain untenanted was as unimaginable as that there should be an interregnum at the Foreign Office, the Treasury or the Ministry of War. A technique of initiation was worked out, the prospective Favourite being duly examined by her Scottish doctor, Rogerson, and then tested by her principal lady-in-waiting, Countess Bruce. Throughout the reign the reports of the British, French, Prussian and Austrian ambassadors are filled with the fortunes of the paramours, most of them young officers selected for their good looks; for all of them, whether puppets or personalities, occupied a conspicuous position on the stage.

That Catherine was over-sexed was known to all the world, but it would be doing her injustice to attribute her conduct to sensuality alone. Like other women, she longed to love and be loved. That she was mated to a repulsive buffoon was not her fault, and the emotional vacuum cried aloud to be filled. Had a loving husband been provided for her, she explains in her Memoirs, she would have been a faithful wife, for she had no natural bent for debauchery. She vetoed unrefined conversation, and when Ségur, the French Ambassador, embarked on a risky story, he was put in his place. To read her letters to Potemkin is to realise that this brilliant woman craved, not for physical satisfaction alone, but for loving comradeship in her lofty station. Part of the fascination of the study of her complex character lies in the combination of a brain as coolly calculating as that of Frederick the Great, with a tender heart. Several lovers were also friends, and one of them remained a friend for life.

The first four date from the bleak years of apprenticeship, and the first two left no deep furrows in her heart. Soltikoff, described by the French Ambassador as an ignoramus without taste or merit, quickly tired of his easy conquest and left the country. Stanislas Poniatowski, who possessed elegance, charm and intelligence, with the polish of Parisian salons upon him, was recalled to Poland and in due course rewarded by his patron with a crown. When they met again thirty years later during Catherine's celebrated journey to the South, they had little to say to each other, for she had partitioned his beloved country and was about to hack off another slice. The third lover, Elughine, is a mere shadow. The fourth, Gregory Orloff, ranks as the first Favourite *en titre*. Their son, Bobrinsky, was born on the eve of the palace

revolution of 1762, which was organised by him and his four
gigantic brothers, one of them, Alexis, taking an active part in the
butchery. Catherine's responsibility for the murder of her husband
was of the same degree as that of her grandson Alexander for the
death of his father Paul. Neither gave the order, but there was no
need. Both were aware that the mere deposition and imprisonment of a ruler was a dangerous game. Since her life was notoriously in peril so long as Peter was alive, the murderers rightly
counted on her approval.

For the next ten years the Orloffs stood in the centre of the
brilliant throng surrounding the Semiramis of the North. Her
affection for Gregory was not in doubt, and she described him to
Frau Bielke as without exaggeration the handsomest man of his
time. Yet there was very little in him, as Catherine, an Intellectual
to her finger-tips, became increasingly aware. Moreover, was not
there also a certain element of fear? What these lawless brothers
had done to Peter II might they not do again? A year after the
murder there was talk of a marriage, but the project was scotched
by the courageous intervention of Panin, the only member of her
entourage who never flattered her. Mme Orloff, bluntly declared
the Foreign Minister, could never be Empress of Russia. Moreover, the promotion of the Favourite might conceivably be
followed by the substitution of Bobrinsky for the Grand Duke
Paul. Orloff accepted the rebuff, and Catherine, who was never
vindictive, may have been secretly relieved. The favour of the
Orloffs remained undiminished. When Gregory offered to fight
the plague in Moscow and was selected to negotiate peace with
the Turks, he received new rewards, but his triumphs had gone
to his head. 'He lacks nothing but the title of Emperor,' reported
the French *Chargé*. 'His want of consideration with the Empress
strikes everyone, and the Russians recall nothing like it since the
foundation of the monarchy. Scorning etiquette, he takes liberties
with his sovereign in public which in polished society no self-
respecting mistress permits to her lover.' While she always confined herself to her *amant en titre*, he had other mistresses to
entertain. The long spell was broken, and with the encouragement of Panin, the leader of the anti-Orloff party, she decided to
act.

No sooner had the Favourite left for the South in 1772 than

Wassiltchikoff, a harmless young *protégé* of Panin, was installed in the coveted suite. Amazed and angered by the news, Gregory hurried home, but he was met on the outskirts of the capital by an order to proceed to Gatschina, the palace she had built for him, there to await instructions, on the pretext that travellers from the South required a period of quarantine. Since the reaction of the formidable brothers was unpredictable, the locks on the palace doors were changed, and trustworthy troops were held in readiness to deal with any attempted *coup*. The fallen demigod was dismissed from all his posts and a request for an interview was ignored. A rumour spread that he was among the guests at a Court ball, and the hostess fled for safety to Panin's apartments. When he was commanded to return the diamond medallion with the portrait she had given him to wear on his heart, he restored the diamonds, but kept the portrait. To the order to travel abroad for his health he replied that he had never felt better. She tried to placate him by announcing that at her request the Emperor had made him a Prince of the Holy Roman Empire. Her anxiety was exaggerated, for Gregory had no intention of risking his life for the second time. After a brief interval he reappeared at Court as if nothing had happened, and he treated his colourless successor with civility. Though some observers wondered whether he might not regain his position, there was as little question of reinstatement as of disgrace. Catherine never recalled a fallen favourite. On the other hand, when Potemkin at a later date tried to make trouble, he was gently but firmly reproved. 'There is only one thing I beg you not to do, namely, not to try to injure Prince Orloff with me. I should regard it as great ingratitude on your part, for there is no one who praises or likes you more than he. If he has failings it is not for you or me to criticise. He and his brother are great friends of mine, and I will never abandon them.' Gregory died many years before his Sovereign, and Alexis, the more ambitious and gifted of the brothers, retained his post as Grand Admiral and remained in favour to the end of her life. She had played her cards with consummate dexterity, breaking the Orloff yoke without bloodshed and without creating unappeasable resentments.

Wassiltchikoff was the first of the lovers who held no place in the ruler's heart, and no one knew better that he was only a stop-gap while she was looking round. 'Je ne suis qu'une fille entre-tenue,' he confessed, and he was as ready to go as he had been to come. From the start he bored his patron, who described him as *cet imbécile*. When she could bear him no longer she paid him off and never desired to see his face again. 'An excellent but very boring citizen,' was her concise verdict. 'Tell Panin', she wrote to Potemkin, 'that he must send him away somewhere for a cure. He is a nuisance, and besides, he complains of pains in the chest. After the cure we will send him to some place as Ambassador. He is a bore. I burned my fingers and I shall never do it again.' In the long line of lovers none meant less to her than this spectral figure sandwiched in between two full-blooded personalities.

The Prince de Ligne, who knew everyone of note in Continental Europe, pronounced Potemkin the most extraordinary man he had ever met. His father, a poor colonel, died when the boy was seven, and his mother played little part in his career. A good linguist and a classical scholar, he loved history, literature, music and, above all, theology. He distinguished himself at the newly-founded University of Moscow, and his choice seemed to lie be-tween the Church and the Army. He chose the latter and was soon a member of the Orloff circle, sharing their evil ways with women, gambling and drink. The first contact with the Empress was made on the hectic day when Peter was dethroned, and the name of 'Quartermaster Potemkin' was on the list for rewards for services on that occasion. He received military promotion and 10,000 roubles, followed at the Coronation by a silver table-set and a grant of land with 400 'souls' in the neighbourhood of Moscow. After a mission to Stockholm to announce the accession of Catherine, he became Groom-in-Waiting at the age of twenty-three. Learning that he was a clever mimic, the Empress asked how it was done, and he proceeded to imitate her German accent with a realism which made her laugh. Henceforth he was a wel-come guest in the intimate circle where formality was banned, and music, recitations and games were the order of the day. He was fascinated by the gay and witty hostess, and his intellectual in-terests attracted a woman who hated to be bored. His rapid rise to favour annoyed the Orloffs. Angry words were exchanged, and it was rumoured that the loss of an eye at this period was the result of a scuffle. Court life, they told him, was spoiling him, and

he should return to the Army. They had miscalculated their
tactics, for when he tactfully withdrew to something of a hermit's
life and the study of theology, the Empress made public and frequent inquiries about his health. Only when he was gone did she
realise how much he was missed.

Though no longer appearing at Court, Potemkin was not forgotten. In 1763 he was appointed Assistant to the Chief Procurator of the Holy Synod, and the Empress drew up his instructions. He also received military promotion, and in 1767 he was
transferred to Moscow as commander of a regiment. He took
part in the Commission for Legislative Reform as Trustee or
Protector of the Racial Minorities and member of the Civil and
Religious Committee. He loved to dicuss theological dogmas,
and, like Akbar, invited spokesmen of various creeds and sects
to argue their case in his presence. Entering every church he
passed, he lit a candle to his patron St Gregory, or St Catherine.
Volunteering in 1769 for the Turkish war, he served as aide
to Rumiantsoff, and fought bravely in the cavalry. He was
promoted major-general and Commander-in-Chief. Rumiantsoff
praised him in his reports to the Empress, who allowed him to
write personal letters. Soon she replied, and a regular correspondence ensued. The turning-point in his fortunes occurred
when a letter of December 4, 1773, reached him in the South.
'Mr. Lieutenant-General and Chevalier. You are probably so busy
watching Silistria that you have no time to read letters. Though
I do not know if your bombardment was successful, I am sure
that all you are doing is due to your devotion to myself and the
beloved fatherland. But since I am most anxious to preserve
zealous, courageous, intelligent and skilful people, I beg you not
to expose yourself to danger. After reading this letter you will
perhaps ask why it was written. I reply, in order that you should
have the confirmation of my ideas about you, for I am always your
most well-wishing Catherine.' Realising that his hour was at hand,
he hurried home to enjoy his luck.

On reaching the capital at the age of thirty-three, Potemkin
found the ball at his feet. Meeting Gregory Orloff on the staircase
of the palace, he inquired: 'Any news?' 'Only that you are going
up and I am coming down,' was the reply. The Empress had made
up her mind, but she had to feel her way, and for the moment

Wassiltchikoff remained in his official suite. When the impatient lover, resenting the delay, avoided the Court, she inquired as to the reason. Love-sickness, was the adroit reply, and he thought of entering a monastery. Though she explained that Wassiltchikoff would soon disappear, he entered a monastery, where visitors found him in alternate moods of melancholy and exaltation. Were the lovers playing a pre-arranged game, or was he not entirely convinced that his hour had struck? We cannot be sure. Once again Panin intervened. The impending appointment, he warned the sovereign, would not be approved at home or abroad, and she would soon experience his pride and eccentricities. The protest was unavailing. Potemkin, she replied, was too able to be buried alive in a monastery, and she despatched Countess Bruce to convey the promise of 'the greatest favours' if he returned to Court. The envoy found him in a monk's garb, prostrate before an ikon of St Catherine. The moment had arrived to throw off the mask, and he joyfully accepted the appointment of Adjutant-General, the customary euphemism for a newly-appointed Favourite.

Gregory Potemkin was the only performer on the Russian stage of the same calibre as the Empress, and he would have made his mark whenever and wherever he had been born. They had much in common. Both were Intellectuals, both combined wide vision with executive ability, both were hard workers. The latest Favourite occupied a political position radically different from the rest. Zuboff she was to love with no less fervour, but Potemkin alone helped her to carry the burdens of State. Though he was the *amant en titre* for only two years, they remained devoted friends till his death. For the first and last time she found the partner of her dreams. What he meant to her we can read in the love-letters which have survived. Two such temperamental egoists could hardly have expected unbroken harmony to prevail, but despite frequent quarrels it was the most memorable experience of her life.

The Empress was as happy as a child with a new toy. 'What a marvellous head he has got,' she reported to Grimm. 'He has done more than anyone to end the Turkish war, and is as amusing as the Devil.' Though herself unmusical, she admired his singing, and liked to hear him recite his own verses. For the first and last time she thought of a Favourite as an equal, and never for a

moment did he consider himself an inferior. Though himself
indiscriminate in his amours, he rebuked her for having had any
lover but himself. His estimate of fifteen, she replied, was incorrect: there had been only five. 'If in my youth I had been
allotted a husband I could love I would have remained eternally
faithful to him. The trouble is simply that my heart cannot be content even for an hour without love.' For the next two years
ecstatic happiness alternated with stormy scenes and sulks. She
was gay by nature, he moody, suspicious and often depressed.
She was a systematic worker; he had bouts of volcanic energy
followed by phases of apathy. He loved and admired her, but
she was less to him than he to her. The greatness of Russia, to be
achieved through their joint efforts, was their inspiration. There
seemed no limit to his favour, for he was consulted about everything. Such power naturally provoked jealousy, but he had no
need to worry, for he was anchored in her heart. The Orloffs,
especially Alexis, naturally resented their fall from power. Panin
disapproved the whole system of Favouritism, but Potemkin
partially disarmed his hostility by non-interference in foreign
policy except in regard to the Turks. His most pressing task was
to strengthen the Army, for, though the first Turkish war was
over, peace was recognised on both sides merely as a truce.
Offices, titles, priceless jewels, grants of land and money were
showered upon him. He was congenitally incapable of living
within his means, however ample they might be, but his debts
were always paid. Not content with lavishing every distinction
on her adored partner, the Empress sought foreign decorations
to add to his glory. She secured for him the coveted title of Prince
of the Holy Roman Empire from Joseph II, who needed her co-
operation in his Turkish schemes, the Black Eagle from Frederick
the Great and the Order of the White Eagle from King Stanislas;
but her request for the Order of the Garter was refused by
George III. He was both the *enfant gâté* and the *enfant terrible* of
the Russian Empire.

Since the failure of the project of a union with Orloff, the
Sovereign had abandoned all thought of a public ceremony, but a
secret marriage was another matter. She was not quite so volatile
as the list of her lovers suggests. Soltikoff and Poniatowski had
left Russia. Orloff, she explained, would have retained her

affection for life had he not tired of her, and she had been willing to marry him. Now she wished for nothing better than to enjoy the happy partnership with Potemkin for the rest of her life. That he, like Orloff, desired to fortify his position by a legal tie was natural, and her devoted love could refuse him nothing in her gift. According to Professor Barskoff they were married at the close of 1774 in the church of St Samson on the outskirts of the capital, she being accompanied by a single lady-in-waiting, he by a nephew and a chamberlain. As in the case of Louis XIV and Mme de Maintenon, no written record has survived.

The strongest evidence for a marriage is to be found in no less than twenty-three of the love-letters written during the two years of their closest intimacy, in which she addresses him as 'dear husband', 'my beloved husband', and describes herself as 'your wife'. 'Was she attached to you two years ago by holy ties?' she asked in the course of one of their periodical wrangles. 'Mon bijou', 'mon ange', 'mon âme précieuse', 'mon pigeon', 'mon faisan d'or', 'ma soeur âme', 'mon petit père', which constantly occur in her *billets-doux*, may have been lavished on one or two of her other lovers. None of them, so far as our evidence goes, was addressed as 'mon cher époux et ami', 'mon mari chéri', and to no one else did she announce herself as 'your wife'.

Catherine's 357 surviving love-letters to Potemkin during the years 1774–6 are partly in Russian, partly in French. Since they are undated, they have been printed in the order in which they were found, and she believed that he carried them in his pocket. Though living under the same roof, she often felt the need of expressing her emotions in a little note before she got up, and sometimes two or three times a day. Her pet names reveal an unexpected tenderness, and here alone can we peer into the depths of her heart.

There is surely something more than mere passion in the correspondence between the Empress and Potemkin. Of his share only fragments survive, but we know that he called her 'ma petite mère chérie', or 'Madam', or 'femme de feu' according to his ever-changing mood. Sometimes he signed himself 'your slave'. The first letter of the series might have been written by a happy girl revelling in the warm sunshine of her first love. 'Chéri, I suppose you thought I should not write to you today. You were wrong.

I woke at five; now it is seven and I am going to write. To tell the truth—please listen—I don't love you a bit and I don't want to see you again. You won't believe me, joy of my heart, but I can't abide you. I have given formal instructions to the whole of my body, down to the smallest of my hairs, not to show you the slightest sign of love. I have shut it in my heart behind ten locks; it is suffocating and I fear an explosion. Think of it, you, a reasonable being; can one express so much folly in such a few lines? A flood of ridiculous words gushes from my head. I can't understand how you can bear a woman with such incoherent ideas. Oh! Monsieur Potemkin, what a sorry miracle you have wrought in deranging a head commonly regarded as one of the best in Europe! It is high time for reason to assert its sway. What disgrace! What sin! Catherine II a prey to this crazy passion! You will disgust him with your folly, I say to myself. I often repeat these words. They alone can lead me back, and that is one more proof of your immense power over me. So, silly letter, off you go to the happy place where my hero lives. My little Grisha will never read these lines so full of folly but also with so much love in them. He should throw them aside. Adieu, Ghiaour, Muscovite, Cossack, I do not love you.'

The second letter is no less characteristic of a correspondence in which one party was as patient and understanding as was the other full of unmerited complaints. Potemkin now possessed everything—power, riches, the highest position in the land, a limitless field for his abilities, above all the utter devotion of his sovereign—but it was not in his nature to be satisfied. That she bore the sulks and scoldings of this *mauvais coucheur* is sufficient evidence of her craving for love. She gratefully accepted him with all his faults, and forgave him what she would have tolerated from no lesser man. Here is her reaction after one of the scenes which recurred with distressing frequency. 'There was some writing on this sheet of paper,' she replied to a scolding letter which she pretended not to have read. 'Reproaches, of course, for Your Excellency had the sulks with me all the evening, and I, with a broken heart, sought in vain for a caress. What happened? The quarrel occurred the day before yesterday when I honestly tried to explain my plans which could not injure you and would have been much to your advantage. Yesterday evening, I confess,

I did not send anyone to you as I expected you here. But when you had not turned up by nine o'clock I sent to ask for news. Then you came, with a frown on your face. I pretended not to notice your ill-humour, and that threw you out of your stride. You reproach me for that now; in place of the tender letter you asked for here is a repetition of our quarrel. Patience, ché i, let my wounded heart calm down. Tenderness will come directly it is allowed. I have only too much of it for you; it obsesses me and urges me always to your side. And when it sees its frank expression is impossible it uses guile. You must understand how strong it is. It can assume any disguise in order to reach you. After a blow of the fist it jumps back and then promptly returns as near as possible to my heart's friend. Who is he, this cherished friend? He is called little Grisha. My tenderness bears with his outbursts of anger, pardons his misinterpretation of my words, turns a deaf ear to his rough words, forgets injustices. In short, my tenderness is our love—frank and quite out of the common. Arrange to end my love if you can, but I assure you that sincerity is well worth while.' When the storm passed the Empress was once again like a merry child. 'Chéri, what funny things you told me! I am still laughing over them. What happy moments I pass with you! We spend four hours together without a moment of ennui and it is a wrench to leave you. My beloved little pigeon, I love you greatly; you are handsome, intelligent, amusing. In your company I forget the whole world. Never have I been so happy. I often try to hide my feelings, but my heart betrays my passion. Evidently it is too full and overflows. Adieu, my friend. Behave in public in such a way that no one can guess what is going on. It is great fun to put people off the scent.'

The notes sounded in these three first letters, with their rhythm of sunshine and storm, recur throughout the series. To Catherine the writing of letters was a relaxation, and she was never too busy to dash off a few lines—sometimes a single line—to her friend. 'My beauty, my chéri, unlike any king, I am full of goodwill and tenderness towards you, and you shall have my protection as long as I live. Adieu, mon bijou. Mon amour, bonjour.' When he incurs reproaches she chastises with a gentle hand. 'If your stupid ill-humour is over, please tell me, for it seems to be dragging on. Since I have given you no excuse for such lasting anger, the time strikes me as unduly long. Unhappily I am the only one to think so, for you are a wicked Tartar.' Over and over again she sent a message before the day's work began. 'Bonjour, mon coeur. Comment vous portez-vous?' 'Ours is an extraordinary relationship which cannot be expressed in words; there are too few letters in the alphabet.' 'Good morning, my pigeon. I want to know if you slept well and if you love me as much as I love you.' 'My love, your colic distresses me, for I love you beyond all measure.' 'No wonder there is talk of your conquests of women. How odd it is! Everything I used to laugh at has now happened to me, for my love for you has made me blind. Sentiments I thought idiotic, exaggerated and scarcely natural I am now experiencing myself. I can't keep my silly eyes off you. I forgot all that my reason tells me and I feel quite stupid when I am with you. We can only meet during the next three days, for then comes the first week of Lent, which is reserved for prayers and fasting, and besides my own devotions it would be a great sin to meet. The mere thought of this separation makes me cry.'

While Catherine was basking in her bliss, Potemkin's doubts as to how long it would last incurred a gentle rebuke. 'You should be ashamed of having said: My successor will not survive me! Why do you try to enslave a heart by fear? It is unworthy of you. In that case you would be motived by ambition alone, not by love. Cancel these lines and banish such thoughts. Don't worry. Perhaps I shall bore you much more than you will ever bore me. My heart is always open and I do not like change: friendship and habit only fortify my love. You do yourself injustice. You are made to be loved. I admit that your apprehension is itself a sign of tenderness, but I assure you that there is not the slightest ground for fear. No living man is your equal. You can read in my soul and my heart: they are like an open book. If you do not feel it or see it, you are really unworthy of the *grande passion* you have inspired. I love you without limits. Get that into your head. But I entreat you to pay me in the same currency, otherwise it will be difficult to avoid rivers of tears and torrents of sorrow. When I love I become cruelly tender. You have only to satisfy my tenderness by your own. All my actions have no other purpose than to bring harmony into your life. Who strives harder than I to restore tranquillity and calm? I never judge people by words spoken in anger. I make no reproaches. You have greatly hurt and angered me, but I cannot hate you. I try to believe that the old footing will be restored. My heart, my mind and my vanity are equally contented with you: what more could I desire? I am perfectly satisfied. I love you more than myself.' 'My pigeon, my friend, be joyful: away with your spleen!'

The gem of the collection is a sheet containing a declaration of their feelings in parallel columns.

| *In Catherine's hand.* | *In Potemkin's hand.* |
|---|---|
| Je suis. | Mon âme chérie. |
| Je ne l'ignore pas. | Tu sais que je suis à toi. |
| C'est vrai. | Je n'ai que toi dans ce monde. |
| Sans doute. | Je te suis fidèle jusqu'à la mort. |
| Je te crois. | Par conséquent tes intérêts me sont très chers. |
| Prouvé depuis longtemps. | La chose qui m'est le plus agréable, c'est de te servir et d'être utilisé par toi. |

After two years of such rapture as she had never known, Catherine realised that her moody partner was gradually slipping away. Ever ready to forgive and forget, she strove to hold him tight. 'Which of us two creates discord,' she pleaded, 'and which tries to restore harmony? You know who is the most indulgent, the most ready to pardon offences and injustices. I know my words have no effect, but remember that I prove them in the least of my actions. In God's name let your reason work and compare your record with mine. Is it beyond your capacity to pluck out the weeds?' Potemkin was incorrigible and she knew it. The last straw was his demand that she should dismiss her secretary Zavadowsky, which she refused on the ground that it would be unjust to an innocent man. We can only speculate on the workings of Potemkin's mind, but he may have felt that the ice was wearing thin. He loved the Empress, but did he not love power even more? If he carried his ill-humour too far, might he not one day, like Orloff, find himself suddenly dismissed? Perhaps it might be better to terminate their intimacy before a crisis arose, parting in peace and retaining his influence. That the initiative came from him is clear, but she seems to have accepted his decision without a struggle. The general impression that he had lost not only favour but power quickly proved to be incorrect. As with Louis XV and the Pompadour, the friendship continued after passion had burned itself out. He retained his offices and found an outlet for his abounding energies in the conquest and colonisation of the South. Affectionate letters continued to be exchanged, and he consoled himself for the loss of his Sovereign by *liaisons* with his five pretty nieces, above all Varvara, assuring her that he loved her as he had loved no one else.

Potemkin's successor, the colourless Zavadowski, sponsored jointly by Panin and Orloff, had been promoted from private secretary to Favourite without consulting the superman, who promptly looked round for a candidate whom he could trust. He chose Zoritch, the only foreigner except Stanislas in the list of Favourites, son of a Jugoslav officer in the Russian army. For the first and last time the Empress accepted a middle-aged lover. He spoke of himself as a barbarian, and described how 'my lady' had polished him; but his empty head was quickly turned. The title of Count failed to satisfy him, for why should he not be made a Prince, like Orloff and Potemkin? Determined to fight for his place he threatened to cut off the ears of any rival hussar and challenged to a duel his patron, who realised that he had misjudged the man. Pensioned off within a year he lived in oriental splendour in the South, where Countess Golovin visited him, 'perfumed like a Sultan'. He was succeeded by Korsakov, whose only attraction was a fine tenor voice. The experiment of fifteen months ended abruptly with the discovery of his *liaison* with Countess Bruce and the banishment of the guilty pair from Court. The Empress did not care what her Favourites did in their leisure hours, but she expected them to behave themselves at Court.

After three disappointments Potemkin scored a success in 1780 with Lanskoi, a young officer of twenty-two, described by Kotzebue as the most ignorant person at Court. The usual shower of titles and emoluments descended on him—General, Chamberlain, lands, palaces, cash—and his greedy brothers bathed in the golden stream. Though despised for his avarice, indolence and intemperance, he was adored by the Empress, who nearly broke her heart when he died after four years of comradeship. For the first time a Favourite was struck down at the height of his favour, and for the only time in her life she gave way to prolonged and uncontrollable grief. She shut herself up with his sister, and three months later she reported to Grimm that she was still bathed in tears. When the first paroxysms were over she found partial consolation in Jermoloff, another shadowy figure whom she never pretended to love. Once again Potemkin had made an unsuitable choice. When the new Favourite was persuaded by the latter's enemies that Potemkin neglected his duties and embezzled public funds, the wrathful pro-consul presented an ultimatum. 'He or I must go.' It cost the sovereign nothing to yield and she never saw the offender again.

Jermoloff's successor Mamonoff, another young *protégé* of Potemkin, possessed a better education, greater refinement and more intelligence, and he kept his place for several years. 'Sasha', reported Catherine enthusiastically to Potemkin, 'is beyond price.' *L'habit rouge*, as she called him, accompanied her on the long journey in the South in 1787 and might have retained his post till her death had he not fallen in love. She spoke indignantly of his treason. 'I cannot express how I have suffered.' She soon recovered herself and wrote to Potemkin that she had never tyrannised over anyone. 'God grant them happiness,' she exclaimed. He received the customary grants, and she only stipulated that the happy pair should leave the capital, where their presence would evoke painful memories. When Mamonov, tiring of his wife, pleaded for the renewal of their *liaison*, he found the door barred.

Potemkin's finest hour was still to come. A visit to the South had been planned in 1784, but elaborate preparations had to be made. Leaving home in January 1787, accompanied by the British, French and Austrian Ambassadors, by Mamonoff, and by the Prince de Ligne, in whose company no one could be dull, the Empress drove 100 miles a day to Kiev, where the party spent several months. The most spectacular part of the journey began when eighty ships sailed down the broad Dnieper with Potemkin as Master of the Ceremonies. That he constructed sham villages along the banks and marshalled the peasantry in crowds to create the illusion of progress was the fantastic invention of a Saxon diplomatist. The highlight of the tour was the inauguration of the port of Sebastopol, with a fleet at anchor in the harbour. Catherine expressed her gratitude to the most distinguished of her subjects by conferring on him the title of Prince of Taurida, and her letters during her journey home breathe affectionate admiration. His capture of the fortress of Oczakoff in the Second Turkish War raised his prestige still further, but his crowning triumph was the magnificent ball given by him in April 1791 in the Taurida Palace built for him by his adoring friend. When 3,000 guests were assembled in a setting worthy of the Arabian Nights, the Sovereign appeared in all her splendour and remained till two o'clock in the morning. Old memories crowded upon them, and when they parted there were tears in their eyes. 'He has come back to us,' she reported to the Prince de Ligne, 'as beautiful as the day, gay as a lark, shining like a star, wittier than ever.' He returned to his post in the South, and within six months died by the wayside, worn out by loose living and gluttony, at the age of fifty-five.

When the news arrived, Catherine fainted and wept. 'Now I have no one left on whom I can rely,' she exclaimed. Her faithful secretary Krapovitsky made brief entries in his diary. 'Tears and despair.' 'Wept.' 'Tears.' She found her chief comfort in singing Potemkin's praises to her friends. 'I have had a terrible blow,' she wrote to Grimm. 'My pupil, my friend, almost my idol, died in Moldavia. He had an excellent heart, a rare understanding and exceptional breadth of mind. His views were always spacious. He was very human, well-informed and lovable, and his ideas were his own. He was the wittiest of men. In war he never missed a chance. No one was less influenced and he knew how to employ others. He was a statesman both in the planning and the execution. He was passionately attached to me, grumbling when he thought I could do better. With age and experience he cured himself of his faults. Three months ago when he was here I told Zuboff that this change alarmed me, and unhappily my apprehensions are fulfilled. His rarest quality was a courage of heart, spirit and soul which distinguished him from other men. So we understood each other perfectly. I regard him as a very great man, capable of even bigger things.' Her last tribute of gratitude was the liquidation of his mountainous debts. A briefer but more judicial verdict was delivered by the Prince de Ligne. 'Potemkin is the emblem of the immense Russian Empire. He, too, is composed of deserts, gold mines and diamonds.'

We come nearest to the soul of this extraordinary man in occasional snapshots. When the Prince de Ligne suggested that he might become Hospodar of Moldavia he proudly replied that it did not attract him. 'I could be King of Poland if I liked. I refused to be Grand Duke of Courland. I am much more than all that.' A similar impression of measureless ambition, dazzling successes and pathological discontent is left by a little scene at dinner with his nephew Engelhardt. Suddenly turning from gaiety to gloomy silence the host began to think aloud. 'Can anyone have had better luck? All my hopes and desires have been fulfilled as if by enchantment. I have had my fill.' Seizing a plate, he broke it in pieces, left the room and locked himself in. It is a consoling reflection for more commonplace mortals that such egomaniacs miss the highest prizes of life.

Platon Zuboff, the last of the Favourites, ranks with Orloff and Potemkin in the duration and magnitude of his influence. Selected in 1789 at the age of twenty-two, he bewitched the sexagenarian Empress from the start. Potemkin had not been consulted, but when he demanded his dismissal, she stood firm. Two years later the superman was dead, and for the remainder of her reign the butterfly flapped his brightly tinted wings in the autumn sunshine. He had not been taken seriously at first. 'He is a child, with good manners and little brains,' commented the leading Minister Bezborodko. 'I don't think he will be here long, and in any case it does not interest me.' The Chancellor forgot the maxim *l'appétit vient en mangeant*, and soon the capital was at Zuboff's feet. Next to her grandsons he was the chief consolation of Catherine's closing years, for her heart remained young. He played the same part in her reign as Mme du Barry in the life of Louis XV—the last and perhaps the most contemptible of a long line.

The four Zuboff brothers, like the five Orloffs, joined forces in the scramble for power and wealth. Their father was Governor of a province, and Platon, the second son, was a Lieutenant stationed at Tsarkoe-Selo. 'I have come back to life like a frozen fly,' Catherine reported to Potemkin; 'I am gay and well.' Henceforth her letters were filled with tributes to her playboy who had brought with him a breath of spring. He wanted to give pleasure

F.

to everyone, she testified; it was impossible not to love him. Sometimes she rapturously described him to Potemkin not merely as 'the child' but as 'our child'. Beginning as a plaything he proceeded to exploit his opportunities in the interest of his family. He amassed a fortune, partly, like Talleyrand, by accepting payment for services in promoting other people's careers. He was made a Prince and collected foreign titles. 'Zuboff is everything here,' reported Count Rostopchin a year before Catherine's death. 'His will is supreme. His power exceeds that once enjoyed by Potemkin. He is as careless and incapable as ever, though the Empress tells everyone he is the greatest genius Russia has ever possessed.' He knew little either of civil or military affairs and was too indolent to learn. 'No one at your age', wrote the infatuated ruler, 'was ever better fitted by disposition or opportunity to render services to his country.' His ante-room was crowded, and when, after hours of waiting, his suitors were admitted to the presence-chamber, they found him having his hair dressed and hardly dared speak to him. While Potemkin was at any rate a man of action, Zuboff was like a pampered Sultan, more Oriental than European in type. Pretty faces were too much for him, and he tried his charms without success on the wife of the Grand Duke Alexander and Countess Golovine. Contrary to expectation he was allowed by the Emperor Paul to retain his possessions, and repaid his kindness by joining in his assassination five years later.

In declaring that she could not live even for an hour without love, Catherine was speaking the literal truth; but love is of various kinds, and she had known them all, from the highest to the lowest. She was more than a mere Don Juan in petticoats, and with better luck in her formative years she might have avoided the pitfalls of the flesh. Her life is a story not only of unresisted passions, but of some happy friendships, some lofty ambitions, some enduring achievements. The diary of her last secretary Krapovitsky paints an attractive picture of an elderly lady, cheerful and considerate, natural and laughter-loving, whom it was a pleasure to serve. No one could accuse her of wasting her time. At sixty-three she described herself as working like a horse, her pen never out of her hand. Countess Golovine, her lady-in-waiting, adored her for her 'indescribable kindness', and her household staff wept bitterly

at her death. The Prince de Ligne speaks of her unalterable sweetness of nature. Of no modern ruler can it be said with less exaggeration that she warmed both hands before the fire of life.

## IV. *Voltaire*

AMONG Catherine's aspirations during her hard years of apprenticeship was the integration of Russia into the cultural life of the
West. The virile imagination of Peter the Great had scarcely
soared above the material plane. Literature and the arts meant
nothing to him, and science seemed of use only in fostering the
interests of industry, commerce and defence. Cultivated cosmo-
politans of the eighteenth century, fastidious travellers and elegant
diplomats could hardly be blamed for depicting the greatest of
the Romanoffs as a barbarian of genius, and in regarding his
country—to borrow the formula of Kipling—not as the most
easterly of European, but as the most westerly of Asiatic states.
In her policy of expansion Catherine was merely following pre-
cedents, but in her determination to educate her adopted country
she struck out a line of her own. Here her German blood was a
decisive factor. She carried with her something of the *aura* of
Western civilisation, and her intellectual tastes ripened rapidly as
she grew to womanhood. She had seen enough of German courts
to be appalled by the low standards of the Russian capital. Her
morals were no better than those of Peter, Anne or Elizabeth,
but in the cultural field she was a pioneer. She summoned architects, sculptors and musicians from abroad, filled her palaces with
French *objets d'art*, bought the Walpole collection of pictures for
£40,000, and commissioned Reynolds, whose *Discourses on Art*
she read with delight, to paint a picture of his own choice. His
representation of the Infant Hercules strangling the serpents,
which symbolised Russia surmounting her difficulties, was rewarded by a fee of 1,500 guineas and a gold snuff-box with her
portrait on the lid. She was the first and only occupant of the
Russian throne who might have said with truth: *Homo sum, nihil
humani a me alienum puto.*
Neither Goethe nor Schiller was born when Catherine left

Stettin in 1744. Like other intelligent Continental princesses, young and old, she looked for enlightenment to France. Where else should she turn? England seemed a long way off, and English was an almost unknown tongue. Her French governess had made French her second language and introduced her to Racine and Molière. For the whole of Europe Paris was in literal truth *la ville lumière*, whose flame shone out the more brightly against the squalid background of the Court of Louis XV. While the Monarchy was dissipating the prestige bequeathed by *Le Roi Soleil* and its military prowess was under a cloud, the mind of France was wide awake, exploring the records of the past, questioning the institutions of the present, challenging inherited faiths. It was the age of the *Aufklärung*, in which the bolder thinkers of Germany, France and England resolved to look at life and its problems with open eyes. Though Lessing and Hume fought in the front ranks of the army of emancipation, the main burden of the campaign was borne by the *Philosophes* who enlisted under the banner of Reason. Never since the fierce conflicts of the Reformation era had there been such a stirring of the waters, and never again till the coming of Darwin and Marx was such a ringing challenge thrown down to tradition.

Of this new cult Voltaire was acknowledged by friend and foe to be the High Priest. While the Christian Churches and the upholders of ancient ways like Maria Theresa could hardly bear the sound of his name, the wittiest man in Europe counted his correspondents by the hundred and his readers by the million. Though Frederick the Great despised his character, he saluted his genius to the end of his days. Catherine recognised his towering stature and was in general agreement with his ideology. Democracy meant little more to him than to her, and though she always displayed respect for the ceremonies of the Orthodox Church, she was a sceptic at heart. What could be more natural for one of the vainest of women than to seek contact with the most brilliant writer of the age? And what could be more flattering to one of the vainest of men than to add another ruling sovereign to his list, above all the dazzling Semiramis of the North? Real friendship there could never be, for they never met and never wished to meet; yet each recognised the market value of the relationship, and the stream of correspondence flowed freely and smoothly till the death of the Patriarch of Ferney in 1778 at the age of eighty-four. She had far too much respect for him to submit her own little comedies for his inspection, as Frederick had sent his 'dirty linen' to be washed.

No one has dared to forge letters of Voltaire, for they are inimitable, but doubts have been expressed whether Catherine's letters were drafted for her by another hand. The weight of authority is against the supposition, which is rejected in Reddaway's annotated edition. The best evidence for her authorship is to compare the letters to Voltaire with the far more extensive series to Grimm. Her command of idiomatic French, which strikes every reader of the latter, was quite sufficient to render her independent of substantial literary aid. She apologised to Voltaire for her bad French, which was by no means impeccable. The only difference is that she took far greater pains with her letters to Ferney than with the light-hearted chatter dashed off to her *souffre-douleur* in Paris. Drafts in her own hand have survived, some almost identical with those actually despatched, others differing to a considerable extent. The reason for this deliberation must be sought in the knowledge that her communications were sure to be widely quoted, *verbatim* or in substance, by the flattered recipient; for a letter to Voltaire was potentially a message to the Intelligentsia of Western Europe. That they were corrected by Andrei Schuvaloff and perhaps other assistants is highly probable, but Catherine, who loved letter-writing, probably provided everything except perhaps the final polish. To be a correspondent of the most celebrated writer in the world was a feather in any-one's cap. She eagerly welcomed the opportunity of projecting her personality, boosting her country and presenting her version of events in the only quarter which in some measure anticipated the publicity methods of the twentieth century. If her dominant motive was personal satisfaction, she also aimed in all sincerity at breaking down the barriers between East and West. She was the first Russian ruler to strive for a good press for the little-known country over which she reigned, and Russia meant more to the German princess than France ever signified to the Corsican adventurer.

When the correspondence began in 1763 Voltaire was sixty-nine, Catherine thirty-four. She had long enjoyed his writings, and he had studied the recent history of Russia. His interest was aroused while recording the romantic career of Charles X of Sweden; and many years later he was commissioned by Schuvaloff, one of the leading figures at the Court of the Empress Elizabeth, to compile a biography of her father. Though he could flatter more adroitly than any of his contemporaries, the book is not all incense. Yet he finds more to praise than to blame in the superman, particularly approving his readiness to learn and his system of religious toleration. From praise of Peter to homage to Catherine, who continued his tolerant policy, was but a step. The ties became closer with his election to the Academy of St Petersburg in 1745 and his appointment as Historiographer of the Empire in 1757. The Empress sent him her portrait in a frame of diamonds, but the precious gift was stolen on the way.

A year after Catherine's accession to the throne, contact between Ferney and St Petersburg was established through Pictet, her Genevese secretary. The murder of the Tsar presented no difficulty, for a letter from Pictet, explaining that Peter had been impossible, crossed one from Voltaire to Schuvaloff condoning the incident. 'Like the Jesuits,' he wrote, 'Providence makes use of every means, and a drunkard's death from colic teaches us to be sober.' A letter from Ferney in September, 1762, applauded the new ruler for her offer to print the *Encyclopédie* when the dead hand of authority descended on the massive enterprise in France. To have another large-minded ruler in Europe, in addition to those in Prussia and Sweden, gave him unalloyed satisfaction. While the Jesuits reigned supreme in France, the Empress defied her equally obscurantist ecclesiastics. Pictet reported her as clamouring for his books, adding that she knew almost all of them by heart, and that the Court begged permission to perform his latest plays.

Only one letter from the first three years of the reign has survived. In thanking Voltaire for some verses in October 1763, the Empress begs him to withhold his praise till she has earned it. 'In the immensity of Russia a year is but a day: that is my excuse for not having done as much as I wished. I am grateful for the second volume of *Pierre le Grand*. His genius was astonishing. His best trait was that, despite his hot temper, he was always impressed by the truth. I am collecting and am about to print his letters in which he paints his own portrait. For the first time I regret that I am not a poet and that I must reply to your verse in prose, but I may tell you that since 1746 I have been deeply in your debt. I had only read novels when by chance your books came into my hands. Since then I have never ceased to read them, and have had no craving for anything less well written or less instructive. But where are such writings to be found? So I came back to you. If I possess any knowledge I owe it to you alone. I am now reading the *Essai sur l'Histoire Générale*, and I wish I knew every page by heart.' There is lavish flattery in the letter, but there is genuine admiration as well. Her second surviving letter, written in the summer of 1765, conveys her thanks to 'the nephew of the Abbé Bazin' for dedicating to her *La Philosophie de l'Histoire par feu l'Abbé Bazin*, the work of his 'uncle', which she had read from beginning to end. She feels sure that it will be burned at Paris, which will confer an added lustre. 'Since the nephew of the Abbé Bazin conceals his address, this reply is addressed to M. de Voltaire, so well known for protecting young people whose talents give promise of becoming in due course useful to the human race.'

Voltaire's first surviving letter contains a golden shower of compliments in the fabrication of which he was unapproached. As instructed, he had communicated her letter to the nephew of the Abbé Bazin. 'Retiring and obscure though he be, your glory has found him out. He rejoices in it, knowing the dimensions of your genius, your intelligence, your courage. He admires you for having rendered the priests useful and dependent. The book of the Abbé Bazin has not yet been burned. People believe it was written in your dominions, for truth comes from the North as toys come from the South. He told me that he had been very attached to the mother of Your Majesty. He says that she was very brilliant and intelligent, and that, were she now alive, she would be ready to die of joy in witnessing the success of her daughter. The nephew of the Abbé Bazin has better luck since he has plenty of time to witness it.' The reference to putting priests in their places was inspired by the Synod's deposition and banishment to a monastery of an archbishop who had challenged the policy of secularisation. In this respect the oracle of Ferney looked with envious eyes to Russia, where Peter the Great had broken the

power of the Church by the creation of the State-controlled Holy
Synod; and one of Catherine's first acts was to assert the over-
riding authority of the Crown.

The Empress was delighted with the graceful homage to herself, her mother and her work. 'The attachment of nephew Bazin
to my late mother increases my consideration for him. I find this
young man very amiable, and I beg him to preserve his sentiments
for me. You share my esteem with the nephew, and everything I
say to him is also intended for yourself. In this Empire toleration
is general; only the Jesuits are not allowed.' Her crest, she added,
was a bee which, flying from plant to plant, gathered honey for
the hive, and the inscription on it was *L'Utile*. Voltaire promptly
responded with one of the sparkling little poems which suited his
genius better than the *Henriade* and *La Pucelle*. 'If your crest is a
bee,' he added, 'you have a terrible hive, the biggest in the world.
You fill the world with your name and your gifts. For me the
most precious are the medallions with your likeness, which remind me of your mother. I count another blessing: those who
are honoured by your bounty are my friends. I am grateful for
your generosity to Diderot, d'Alembert and the Calas family.
Every writer in Europe ought to be at your feet. I am older than
the city where you reign, and which you embellish, and older than
your Empire, and I may date its foundations from Peter the Great
whose work you complete. I should take the liberty to pay court
to this astonishing bee if my crushing maladies permitted this poor
drone to leave his cell.'

'I will reply in my bad prose to your pretty verses,' rejoined the
Empress. 'I never wrote any, yet I do not admire yours the less,
and they have spoiled me for others. I immure myself in my big
beehive; one cannot do different things at the same time. I should
never have believed that the purchase of a library would earn so
many compliments. Everyone has commended me for buying
Diderot's books. But confess, you who supported innocence and
virtue in the case of the Calas family, that it would have been cruel
and unjust to separate a scholar from his books.' The mention of
Calas brought her back to the recent incident of the deposition of
a recalcitrant ecclesiastic. 'Toleration is the rule with us, and
persecution is forbidden. True, we have fanatics who, as they
cannot persecute others, consume themselves. If those in other

lands did the same, it would be no harm. The world would be tranquil, and Calas would not have been broken on the wheel. Such are the sentiments we owe to the founder of this city which both you and I admire.' Every letter from both parties brought fresh bouquets. 'I am so much of a prophet', wrote Voltaire, 'that I boldly predict for Your Majesty the greatest measure of glory and happiness. Either men will become completely mad, or they will admire all that you do that is great and useful. This prediction comes, like the rest, a little after the event. If Peter the Great had chosen Kiev or some other more southerly spot, I should now be at your feet, despite my age. I have never wished to go to Rome. I always felt repugnance to seeing monks in the Capitol, and the tombs of the Scipios trampled on by priests. But I die of regret not to see deserts changed into proud cities, and 2,000 leagues of territory civilised by heroines. World history can show nothing comparable. It is the finest of revolutions. My heart is like the lover; it turns always towards the North. D'Alembert is very wrong not to have made the journey, for he is still young.'

Voltaire's letter begged for a little help for the Sirven family— only a little—after her munificence to the Calas. 'The smallest sum will suffice. We only beg the honour of placing your august name at the head of those who are helping us to destroy fanaticism and to make man more tolerant and more human.' The Empress modestly disclaimed praise for helping the Calas family and purchasing Diderot's library. 'It is nothing to give a little to one's neighbour when one has a superfluity; but it is immortality to be the champion of the human race, the defender of oppressed innocence. You have combated the massed enemies of mankind— superstition, fanaticism, ignorance, intrigue, evil judges, and the abuse of power. Many virtues and qualities are needed to surmount these obstacles. You have shown you possess them. You have conquered.' Not to be outdone, Voltaire responded with the most lavish flattery she had ever received. 'You are surely the brightest star of the North; Andromeda, Perseus and Calisto are not your equal. All those luminaries would have let Diderot die of hunger. Louis XIV was less magnificent. He rewarded foreign merit, but his attention was directed to it. You, Madam, seek for it and find it.' The letter was signed 'Le Prêtre de votre temple.' The delicate septuagenarian, who loved his creature comforts, cannot seriously have wished to resume his travels, and the icy climate provided a plausible excuse. 'If you wish to work miracles', he wrote playfully, 'try to make your country less cold. In view of all you have done, it would be pure malice not to effect this change.' Catherine explained that she was striving to improve the air of St Petersburg by draining the marshes, felling trees and settling colonists.

More important than the vain attempt to improve the atrocious climate of the capital was her effort to modernise and humanise the laws of her country, and to bring them up to the standards of the West. She was a prodigious worker, and her studies of Montesquieu and Beccaria were not in vain. 'In June', she reported in the spring of 1767, 'a great assembly will begin its sessions, and will tell us what we need. Then we shall labour at laws which I hope humanity will not disapprove.' Taking the same practical interest in its labours as Napoleon was to show in the fashioning of the Code, she signed one year later the celebrated 'Instructions to the Commissioners for composing a new code of laws', which fill 100 pages in Reddaway's edition, and contain 655 articles. Here was a fresh reason for Voltaire, to whom a copy was sent, to pile fragrant incense on her altar. 'Lycurgus and Solon would have signed your work, but they could not have performed it. It is clear, precise, equitable, firm, human. Legislators occupy the first place in the temple of glory. The conquerors only come after. Assuredly no one will have a greater name in days to come than you.' The flatteries, as usual, were overdone, but his admiration was real. He had always believed in reform from above, and attempts to soften penal laws in any part of the world moved him to enthusiasm. Another cause for compliments was Catherine's patronage of the new hygiene. 'I have been inoculated,' she reported, 'my son too and Orloff, and many of the courtiers, and it has been introduced into schools and hospitals. Indeed, it is becoming quite the fashion.' The innovation was of publicity value in her effort to make the West regard Russia as a civilised state. The mutual admiration of the Empress and Voltaire, if their correspondence may be taken as the test, was now at its height. In December, 1768, she thanked him for the bust of 'the most illustrious man of the century', and despatched a fur coat and a snuff-box adorned by her portrait.

The outbreak of the first of Catherine's two conflicts with Turkey in 1769 provided a fresh pretext for the compliments which gushed forth in a turgid stream. Voltaire detested war, but in this case the Empress was not the agressor. The Turks attacked at a moment when Russian troops were engaged in the Polish civil war which broke out in 1768. The Polish Government, encouraged from St Petersburg and Berlin, had granted equal rights to the Dissident Orthodox and Lutheran Churches. Such toleration was anathema to the stricter Catholics, ecclesiastics and nobility alike, who formed the 'Confederation of Bar', and, with Turkish aid, prolonged the struggle for four years. 'That a Nuncio enlists the Turks in his crusade against you is worthy of an Italian farce,' commented Voltaire. 'Mustafa, the worthy ally of the Pope!' No opportunity of throwing stones at the Vatican was lost.

Voltaire followed the fighting in both countries with deep interest and applauded the triumph of Russian arms. 'You force the Poles to be tolerant and happy despite the Nuncio,' he wrote in November 1768, 'and you seem to be having trouble with the Mussulmans. If they wage war on you, perhaps Peter the Great's idea of making Constantinople the capital of the Russian Empire may take shape. In that case I beg permission to pass a few days there at your Court. I think that if ever the Turks are expelled from Europe it will be by the Russians.' It was not enough to wage successful war against these barbarians, and then to make some sort of peace. 'It is not enough to humiliate them: they must be sent back forever. I am far from desiring a league against the Turks; the Crusades were so ridiculous that they cannot be repeated. But I confess that, if I were a Venetian, I should advise the despatch of an army to Crete while you were beating the Turks at Jassy or elsewhere. If I were a young Emperor, Bosnia and Servia would see me before long. Then I would come and sup at Sofia or Philippopolis and we would arrange an amicable partition.' Fortified by the approval of Voltaire and her own conscience, Catherine snapped her fingers at her critics. 'All your compatriots do not share your opinion of me, and some like to think that I cannot possibly do anything good. As, however, my glory does not depend on them but on my principles and actions, I am consoled for lacking their approbation. As a good Christian

I pardon them, and I pity those who envy me. We are at war, it is true; but that is an old occupation for Russia, which emerges from every struggle more flourishing than at the start. Polish bishops preach a crusade against me to prevent a quarter of the nation enjoying the rights of citizens.'

The visit of Mme Geoffrin to her old *protégé*, King Stanislas, in Warsaw, which became the talk of Europe, led Voltaire to coquet with the idea of a still longer and more arduous pilgrimage. 'Our Mme Geoffrin has been to Warsaw,' he wrote in September, 1769, 'and I do not see what is to prevent me from starting for St Petersburg next April. I should arrive in June and return in September. If I died *en route*, I should put on my little tomb: "Here lies the admirer of the august Catherine, who had the honour to die while journeying to present his profound respect." ' How much of this ardour was genuine in a man of seventy-five may well be doubted, but the prudent Empress promptly poured water into his wine. 'Nothing is more flattering to me than your project, but I should be ungrateful if I allowed my satisfaction to stifle my anxiety about such a long and painful journey. I know you are in delicate health. I admire your courage, but I should be inconsolable if it were to suffer from the effort. Neither myself nor Europe would forgive me. Besides, my presence might be needed in the southern provinces, which would double the distance and the difficulties.' An invitation from the Semiramis of the North, it was clear, would never arrive.

The snub, if such it may be called, left the friendship intact, and every letter from Ferney brought ornate bouquets. 'Madam,' he wrote in October, 1769, 'your Imperial Majesty's very old and unworthy cavalier was oppressed by a thousand false reports. Now comes the consoling news that your army has smashed the slaves of Mustafa on the Dniester. I am born again, rejuvenated; my legislatress is victorious. She who establishes science and makes the arts flourish has punished their enemies. Ah! Madam, this victory was needed, for men judge only by success. Shall I have voice enough to sing your victories?' A brief note from Catherine confirmed the joyful reports. 'You asked me to tell you of the defeat of Mustafa. Well, this victorious Emperor of the Turks has lost the whole of Moldavia.' 'Your Imperial Majesty restores me to life in slaying the Turks,' rejoined Voltaire. 'Your letter made me

jump out of bed, crying *Allah Catherina! Te Catherinam laudamus.*
To add to my happiness, you owe all this glory to the Nuncio. If
he had not launched the Turks against Your Majesty, you would
not have avenged Europe. So there is my legislatress entirely victorious. I do not know if at Paris and Constantinople they have
tried to suppress your Instruction for the code of Russia, but they
certainly ought to hide it from the French. It is too shameful a
reproach for us, with our old and ridiculous and barbarous jurisprudence, almost entirely founded on the Decretals of the Popes
and the Canon Law. If God gives me health I shall certainly come
and place myself at your feet next summer for a few days or a few
hours.' His enthusiasm boiled over when for the first time in history the Russian fleet sailed from Cronstadt through the Baltic,
the North Sea, the English Channel and the Mediterranean to
attack the enemy in flank. 'Your project is the most astonishing
ever formed: that of Hannibal was nothing to it. To write a code
of laws with one hand and to defeat Mustafa with the other is
something so unprecedented.' Peace should be signed by the
Empress herself in Constantinople, and she should be crowned in
the Imperial city. How ardently Catherine longed for the realisa-
tion of her 'Greek project', which would wipe out the stain of
1453, he could hardly have guessed. He was more interested in
Athens than in Constantinople, for ancient Hellas, the mother of
free thought, was his spiritual home. If only the mighty Empress
could liberate Greece from the degrading yoke of the Turks!
Even without this glittering consummation he hailed her as *sans
contredit la première puissance de l'univers.* 'How will you escape from
insupportable pride? How can you condescend to write to an old
dotard like me?'

In 1771 the Turkish conflict was nearly over, and the civil war
in Poland seemed near the end. 'All sensible people', wrote Voltaire, 'agree that Poland will always be the unhappiest country in
Europe so long as anarchy prevails. A little bird whispers to me
that in abating Turkish pride with one hand you will pacify
Poland with the other.' No sooner, however, had the rebellion
been suppressed than Catherine joined her Prussian and Austrian
neighbours in the First Partition. The compliments of the Empress were on the same generous scale. 'Before you no one wrote
like you, and it is very unlikely that anyone will ever be your equal.

After reading you one wishes to re-read and has no taste for other books.' One eulogy always provoked another. When Princess Dashkoff visited Ferney in 1771, 'she recognised your portrait, framed in flowers. Tears came into her eyes. She talked of you for four hours, and I thought it was only four minutes.' In the summer of 1771, when the clouds were clearing, the Empress sang a paean to the greatness of her adopted country. '*Apropos* of pride, I will make my general confession. I have had great successes in this war. Of course I have rejoiced. I have said it will make Russia known. People will see that she is indefatigable; that she possesses men of eminent merit with all the qualities which make heroes; that she does not lack resources; that she can defend herself and can wage war when unjustly attacked. Filled with these ideas I have never thought about Catherine, who at forty-two cannot grow in mind or body but must remain as she is. If her affairs go well, she says: so much the better. If not, she tries her best to put them straight. Such is my ambition, and I have no other. To spare bloodshed I sincerely desire peace, but it is still far off. Equally I desire to pacify unreasonable quarrels in Poland.'

The accession of Clement XIV inspired Voltaire to one of his rare compliments to the Vatican. 'I confess I detest the Papal government,' he wrote in November, 1770. 'I think it ridiculous and abominable: it has stupefied and ensanguined half Europe for too many centuries. But Ganganelli is a man of intelligence, who seems to feel the disgrace of leaving Constantinople to the barbarians, enemies of all the arts, and who prefers the Greeks, schismatics though they be, to the Mohammedans.' His approval grew into admiration when the new Pope dissolved the Jesuit Order. The Empress and Voltaire felt that they were comrades in a great campaign for toleration. 'You, sir, who are such a good Catholic, persuade your co-religionists that the Greek Church under Catherine II has no wish to injure the Latin or any other Church, and that it merely defends itself.' Why she should call her correspondent a good Catholic we cannot guess; but she may well have thought him, as he certainly thought himself, a much better Christian than the ecclesiastics who tortured heretics to death.

Catherine's celebrated Instruction, or draft code, provided Voltaire not only with a new theme for flattery but with a missile against the Government of his native land. 'I have re-read your

Instruction,' he wrote in June 1771. 'I regard it as the finest
monument of the century. It will earn you more glory than ten
battles on the Danube, for it is your work. Your genius conceived it, your pretty hand wrote it. If Your Majesty makes peace,
I beseech you to keep Taganrog, which you say boasts such a fine
climate, so that I can end my days there without always seeing the
snows of the Jura.' The veto on the introduction of the Instruction into France aroused his indignation, though hardly his surprise. 'Your Majesty will think the Old Man of the Mountains
writes too often,' he wrote in July, 1771, 'but my heart is so full
and my feelings must find an outlet on paper. I have read that in
a country of the West, called the land of the Welches, the government has forbidden the entrance of the best and the most reputable
book; in a word, that the sublime and wise Instruction signed by
Catherine is held up by the *douane* of thought. I did not believe it;
this barbaric extravagance seemed too absurd. I inquired, and it
is true. Here are the facts. A publisher in Holland prints this
Instruction which ought to be adopted by all the kings and
tribunals in the world. He despatches 2,000 copies to Paris. It is
submitted to a rascally censor of books, as if it were an ordinary
work, as if a Paris rascal were judge of the orders of a sovereign,
and such a sovereign! This imbecile discovers propositions risky,
ill-sounding, offensive to a Welch ear. He reports to the Chancellor that it is a dangerous book, a work of philosophy, and sends
it back to Holland without further examination. And I am still
among the Welches! I breathe their atmosphere, and I have to
speak their language. No, this insolence would have been impossible in Mustafa's Empire. I am only a mile from the frontier
of the Welches, but I do not wish to die among them. This last
blow will lead me to the temperate zone of Taganrog. Before
finishing my letter I re-read the Instruction and found this sentence: A government must be such that no citizen should fear
another citizen. Are these the divine maxims which the Welches
have not wished to receive? They deserve all they have got.' Any
lingering affection for the land of his birth had long disappeared.
'Les Welches', he complained, wrote many books but not one that
was good. They composed bad music, and there was no money.
'The Parlements which think they are like the English Parliament,
owing to the similarity of name, fight the Government with

printed missiles. The theatres resound with bad pieces which receive applause. All this makes us the first people, the first court, the first monkeys in the world. They carry on a civil war of the pen, like that of rats and frogs.' His eyes were turned no longer to Paris, but to St Petersburg. 'Diderot and I', he wrote in 1773, 'are lay missionaries who preach the cult of Saint Catherine, and we can boast that our church is almost universal.'

The last outstanding theme of the correspondence was the rebellion of Pugatcheff in 1774, which rocked the throne on its foundations. When Voltaire inquired whether the Cossack leader was a fool, Catherine replied that he was not. 'He cannot read or write, but he is extremely bold and determined. There is no evidence that he is the instrument of any Power or any cause. He is a master brigand. I believe that since Tamerlane no one has destroyed so many human lives.' 'Your Majesty does not seem too alarmed about him,' commented Voltaire, who hardly realised how scared she had been. 'I thought the province of Orenburg was the most agreeable portion of your empire, but it seems that it is a dangerous place, full of vagabonds and rogues. Your rays cannot penetrate everywhere at the same moment. The day will come when the town of Orenburg will be more populated than Pekin, and that *opéra-comiques* will be played there.'

Few letters survive from the last three years of Voltaire's life. Though he had passed the eightieth milestone, he could still supply highly-spiced compliments by the score. 'Your subject, half Swiss, half Gaul, named Voltaire, was at death's door a few days ago,' he reported in January, 1777. 'His Catholic Apostolic Roman confessor came to prepare him for the journey.' The sick man said, 'Reverend Father, God may well damn me.' 'Why, good old man?' 'Alas, because I have been accused of ingratitude. I have been overwhelmed with the favours of a lady autocrat who is one of His first images in this world, and I have not written to her for over a year.' 'What is a lady autocrat?' 'Why, an Empress, who does good from Kamchatka to Africa.' 'In that case you have done well. There is no time to lose. The Empress must not be bored, occupied as she is from eve till dawn in beating the Turks, giving them peace, covering the Black Sea with ships, diverting herself with making over a million square leagues fertile.' Catherine replied that she had been reading new Russian translations of Tasso and Homer, but that his letter had given her more pleasure than either. 'Its gaiety and vivacity make me hope that your malady will leave no complications, and that you will reach and pass your full vigour.' There was indeed no decline in his powers, productivity or range of interests. Having created a small watch-making industry in the little village of Ferney, he solicited her patronage. Instead of the few samples which was all he had in mind, a large consignment was despatched from 'ma colonie'. He had scolded these poor artists who had abused her kindness, he explained. He had suggested a package worth three or four thousand roubles, but they had sent one for eight. 'Do not scold your colonists,' came her kindly reply, 'this expenditure will not ruin me. I should indeed be unfortunate if I had not such petty sums at my disposal when I need them.'

The old man's last letter was as sparkling as ever. 'Madame, last night I received one of the pledges of your immortality, your code in German. Today I have started translating it into French. It will appear in Chinese and in every tongue; it will be a gospel of the universe. I was right to say thirteen years ago that the northern star would provide us with everything. A fortnight ago I despatched to Your Majesty the *Prix de la justice et de l'humanité*. It is a little bell proclaiming your boons to the human race. We are two members of the Berne Society who have contributed fifty louis each for a prize for a draft of a criminal code as near as possible to your laws and the most suitable to our own country. I wish someone would propose a prize for the best plan of sending the Turks back to the country whence they came, but I think this is the secret of the first personage of the human race named Catherine II. I prostrate myself at her feet and exclaim on my death-bed, *Allah, Allah, Catherine rezoul, Allah.*'

How much of all this gush was sincere? To answer the question we must think ourselves back into the climate of the eighteenth century, when, as it has been aptly remarked, epistolary compliments to ladies meant little more than a gentleman raising his hat in the street. His homage to Mme de Pompadour was expressed in similar exalted terms. Many thousands of Voltaire's letters have survived, and the references to the Empress when he wrote to his friends sound a much less exalted note. In his exchanges with d'Alembert she was *la belle Cateau*, or simply *Cateau*. No

F

offence was intended, and when these familiarities leaked out in St Petersburg no offence was taken. On both sides the friendship, if such it can be called, was well understood to be an exchange of services, and consequently a limited liability affair. 'Only see your Catherine through the telescope of your imagination,' was the prudent advice of Mme du Deffand to her oldest friend. Catherine's decision never to risk a personal encounter was announced more bluntly in a letter to Grimm than in her rather laboured excuses to Voltaire himself. 'For God's sake,' she wrote a few weeks before his death, 'advise the octogenarian to remain in Paris. What should he do here? He would die, here or at the wayside, of cold, weariness and bad roads. Tell him that *Cateau* is best known at a distance. That *Cateau* tickled me a good deal.' So little did she resent the lively sallies of the man whom she called *la divinité de la gaiété*.

Two letters to Grimm in 1778 may serve as an epilogue. 'May was a bad month for me. I have lost two men I never saw, who liked me and whom I honoured, Voltaire and Milord Chatham. Not for a very long time, perhaps never, will they—especially the former—find their equals and never their superiors. A few weeks ago he was publicly honoured, and now they do not dare to bury him. What a man! The first of his nation. Why did not you take possession of his body in my name? You should have sent it to me embalmed. For the first time in your life your presence of mind deserted you. He would have the most splendid tomb. But if I do not have his body, at any rate he will have a monument here. When I come to town this autumn I will collect the letters this great man wrote me and will forward them to you. If possible buy his library and his papers, including his letters. I will pay his heirs a good price.' A second letter was more intimately auto-biographical. 'He is my master. It was he—or rather his writings—who formed my mind. I am his pupil; in my youth I loved to please him. To be satisfied with any step I took it had to be worthy of telling him. He was so used to this that he scolded me if he heard about my doings from other people. The famous writing-table adorns my Hermitage, and also two busts, especially the one without the wig. Send me a hundred complete copies of the new edition of the works of my master so that I can distribute them. I want them to be studied and learned by heart. They will form citizens, geniuses, heroes, and authors, and will foster a thousand talents.' She requested a plan of the *façade* and of the interior of Ferney, so that she could construct a model in the park of Tsarkoe-Selo. Whatever were Voltaire's real sentiments towards Catherine, her life-long admiration for his genius is not in doubt. Every form of respect was paid to his memory till the French Revolution transformed an enlightened Empress into a frightened reactionary. Though she knew that he would have condemned the opening of the floodgates with scarcely less vigour than herself, she removed Houdon's incomparable bust from her gallery of sages as a sign that she had broken for ever with her liberal past.

## V. *Grimm*

IF Catherine's correspondence with Voltaire presents her in her Sunday best, the letters to Grimm, published by the Imperial Russian Historical Society in 1878, reveal her in her workaday attire. 'Burn them, so that they are not printed in my lifetime,' she wrote in 1787; 'they are in lighter vein than those to Voltaire and might do harm. I tell you, burn them. Do you understand? Or else put them in safe keeping so that no one can unearth them for a century.' Fortunately for posterity as well as for the reputation of the Empress herself, Grimm adopted the latter alternative. Their partial survival is the more welcome since of her correspondence with Diderot not a letter survives, and of the latter's share not more than seven.

While the oracle of Ferney, her equal if not her superior, had to be approached with profound respect and with the careful weighing of words, the relationship to Grimm was that of sovereign to plain citizen, employer to employed, the giver of instructions to her factotum in France. Not that he was merely the fag, the *souffre-douleur*, who carried out her purchases and distributed her largesse, for this Gallicised German gave as much as he received. She needed his services, above all his information, as much as he basked in her smiles. It was both her instinct and her policy to establish cultural contacts with the West, and for this high purpose a rare combination of qualifications was required. Voltaire, Diderot and d'Alembert were all too occupied with authorship as well as too distinguished to play a subordinate role; Montesquieu, of whom she had been a grateful student, was dead, and Rousseau was disqualified not only by his quarrelsome temperament but also by his radical views. In Grimm alone she found exactly what she sought: a man who knew all the stars, who was a welcome guest in every salon, who could assess the latest publications and report the gossip of the capital, who, though himself a professional man of letters, was never too busy to answer inquiries and execute commissions, whose tact, fidelity and financial probity were beyond reproach. Their exchanges reflect credit on them both. Despite the fulsome eulogies of his patron, which in the context of the eighteenth century may be described as merely the customary homage of writers, there was no grovelling on the part of Grimm. If affection is too strong a word—for neither of them was particularly lovable—there was respect and liking on both sides. Long conversations when they met at St Petersburg cemented the friendship, and the stream of correspondence flowed smoothly to the end.

In drafting her letters to Voltaire, Catherine instinctively considered how they would stand up to the scrutiny of those piercing eyes, his friends and posterity. In her far longer and far more frequent exchanges with Grimm she jotted down the first thing that came into her head—the books she was reading, the visitors she received, the pictures she was collecting, the antics of her pampered little dogs. She enjoyed letter-writing, and she wrote as easily as she talked. We derive the impression of a cultivated, industrious, kindly woman, loving all the arts except music, the only Intellectual who has sat on the Russian throne. Till the approach of the French Revolution there is not much about politics, and nobody would guess the part which a score of lovers played in her dazzling career. It is not the whole Catherine, not the woman who poured out her heart to Potemkin, not the ageing ruler who went half crazy about the youthful Zuboff; but without the letters to Grimm we could not have known so fully her many-sidedness, her lightness of touch, her intelligent interest in the things of the mind. The correspondence was conducted in French, but on rare occasions she lapses into her native tongue.

Melchior Grimm, the son of a Lutheran pastor, was born at

Regensburg in 1723, and studied at Leipzig under Gottsched, who encouraged his early efforts in prose and verse. At the age of twenty-five he visited Paris as tutor to the son of Count Schomberg. When his charge returned to Germany he remained in Paris as secretary to a young officer, Count Friesen or Comte de Frise, as Grimm calls him, a son of Countess Cosel, one of the army of illegitimates of Augustus the Strong, and therefore a nephew of the illustrious Marshal Saxe. Living in Count Friesen's house as a comrade rather than a subordinate, he was allowed to give dinner-parties to his literary friends, among them Diderot and Marmontel, Helvétius and Holbach, Raynal and Rousseau. That a foreigner so quickly found his feet in the most brilliant society of the age is sufficient testimony to his social and intellectual gifts. At first his favourite companion was Rousseau, who in his *Confessions* describes the joyous gatherings, and who was attracted to Grimm by their common love of music. 'All my friends became his,' records Jean-Jacques. Who can wonder that he decided to spend his life in France? When the Count Fiesen no longer needed him he recommended him as secretary to the Duke of Orleans. He increased his income by writing on music and literature, and at the age of thirty a satirical comedy, *Le Petit Prophète*, made his name. Yet he lacked the creative touch, and quickly realised that his *métier* was to report on rather than to compete with his contemporaries.

Since everyone in Europe with any pretensions to culture hungered for the latest news from Paris, and since Grimm enjoyed personal contacts with some of the smaller German courts, it occurred to him to offer confidential reports twice a month to whoever cared to subscribe. Inevitably the charge was high. Since the bulletins contained gossip and tit-bits not to be found in the newspapers, every copy had to be written by hand. In 1754 he revisited his native land to work up a connection. Among the original subscribers were the Duchess of Saxe-Coburg and the Landgravine of Hesse, soon to be followed by Stanislas King of Poland, the Margrave of Anspach, the Grand Duke of Tuscany and Karl August of Weimar, who passed on his copy to Goethe. There was no fixed price, for his patrons paid according to their means. The first attempt to enrol Frederick the Great evoked the chilling reply that he was too busy to add to his reading.

What the *Correspondance Littéraire* lacked in circulation it made up in the distinction of its *clientèle*, and every author of a play or a poem, a novel or a treatise, aspired to have his praises sung under the best sounding-board in Europe. The burden was too heavy for one pair of shoulders, and Diderot, the most intimate and faithful of the editor's friends, helped with contributions and advice, particularly in the sphere of the arts. Though the main purpose of the journal was descriptive and critical, space was occasionally found for original work such as Diderot's *La Religieuse*. While literature supplied the larger part of the material, the editor also admitted topics of general interest, such as the dissolution of the Jesuits, Mesmer and his convulsionists, elections to the Academy, and obituaries of famous men. If short of matter he fell back on extracts from new publications, manuscripts submitted to him, or letters he had received. Politics were eschewed, for the editor, in his own words, was resolved to avoid a night in the Bastille. Since ordinary postal communications were liable to the attentions of the *cabinet noir*, the issues were despatched through the Legations in Paris, with the request that the subscribers should not copy the contents.

Though a comrade of the leading *Philosophes*, Grimm differed from most of them both in temperament and opinion. While sharing their repudiation of the dogmas of the Church, he rejected alike the deism of Voltaire and Rousseau, the materialism of Helvétius and Holbach, and the illusion of perfectibility proclaimed by the optimists with Condorcet at their head. His blood was cool and no writer of his time was less of a crusader or an iconoclast. He was too conscious of the complexities of the world's problems to share the burning enthusiasms and the angry phobias of his friends. Though never swept off his feet by flood-tides of emotion, he was ready to assist such good causes as Beccaria's reform of the penal code. He hardly knew Voltaire, but he supported his flaming denunciations of clerical intolerance in the *causes célèbres* of Calas and La Barre.

Compared with the ebullience of Rousseau and Diderot, the principal comrades of his early and middle years, Grimm was singularly reserved. His *liaison* with Mme d'Epinay, like that of Mme du Deffand with President Hénault, was a marriage in all but name. The almost penniless daughter of an officer killed when she was a child was married to a wealthy, selfish and extravagant cousin. With such a husband no woman could be happy, and in the France of Louis XV, where divorce was forbidden, an ill-used wife was expected to console herself with a lover. She had plenty of choice, for she had an excellent heart and her charm attracted a circle of men and women who had made or were making their name. Her first selection was Francueil, who introduced Rousseau, who in turn introduced Grimm. For a time Jean-Jacques was the leading lion in her menagerie, and when he confided to her his wish to live outside Paris she lodged him in a little house on her husband's estate. At first he was in raptures, but the experiment soon proved a failure, as Grimm had warned her that it would. She overdid her attentions to the cantankerous hermit who wanted to be let alone. He proceeded to fall in love with Mme d'Houdetot, the sister-in-law and neighbour of his hostess, while the latter was increasingly drawn to Grimm, who helped her to get rid of Francueil. No aid was required to evict Rousseau himself, whose pathological nature caused him sooner or later to break with all his friends. 'I gave him all my friends,' grumbled Rousseau, 'she has stolen the lot.' The rival versions of the celebrated quarrel may be studied in Rousseau's *Confessions* and in the Memoirs of Mme d'Epinay.

The growth of the friendship with Grimm was duly recorded in her diary for 1751-2. 'I liked him very much. He is pleasant and polite. I think he is shy. He is passionately fond of music; he, Francueil, Rousseau and I, made music all the afternoon. I showed him some of my compositions, which he appeared to like. He is not well off. He is thirty-four. He lives with Comte de Friese. He hopes to make a living with his pen. He is said to be quite unambitious.' A year later the tone is friendly enough though scarcely enthusiastic. 'M. Grimm has returned from Germany. I like him more and more. He comes to see me fairly often. He is young and very talented and amusing in conversation, but I do not think there is much depth in his thought. He should have a future through his writings if he chooses to work, but unfortunately he never sticks to anything. He is undecided, restless and perhaps a little diffident.' She was, however, sufficiently interested to compose a 'Portrait of M. Grimm' which may be given in abridged form. 'Intellectually he is well balanced, keen and profound. Though a poor speaker, no one commands a better hearing. As for taste no one has a more delicate, refined and unerring tact. He is a mixture of truthfulness, gentleness, unsociability, sensitiveness, reserve, melancholy and cheerfulness. He has no natural inclination for society: that of his friends adds to his happiness but is not essential to it. You need to know him intimately to appreciate his worth. Only his friends can do him justice because he is only truly himself with them. Then he blossoms out into humour, gaiety, openness; constraint and unsociability vanish. From this sketch you will see that he is not everyone's idea of an amiable man.' The key sentence in this penetrating analysis is the statement that he had to be intimately known to be appreciated. For a lovable woman who had made a poor start he was the steady comrade whom she deserved to find.

Henceforth Grimm claimed the first place in her life. He was more to her than she to him, for hers was the warmer blood. She was often sacrificed to his work, reported Diderot to his mistress Mlle Volland. 'He has scarcely a minute for friendship, and I know not when he has a moment for love.' Yet, though he was often away for long periods, the partnership of thirty years proved a complete success. He took her out of the rather loose set in which she had moved, and enriched her salon with his distinguished friends. She helped him with the *Correspondance Littéraire* and dabbled in light verse and plays. Her *Conversations d'Émilie*, a manual of education, won an Academy prize in 1783. Diderot, the intimate friend of both, describes their happy *ménage*, and paid Grimm the finest compliment he ever received. 'If ever I were to grumble at my lot, Providence could retort: I gave you Grimm as a friend.' His musical interests revived when the Mozart family visited Paris and were taken under his wing. On his third visit in 1788 the young composer stayed with him and Mme d'Epinay.

Grimm's German birth proved a commerical asset when his reputation began to spread beyond the Rhine. His first diplomatic appointment as representative of the Free City of Frankfurt led Diderot to address him as M. l'Ambassadeur. A year later some criticisms of French commanders discovered in his reports cost him his job, but he soon found other patrons, among them the Court of Saxony and two of the most intelligent women of his time, Louise Dorothea, Duchess of Saxe-Gotha, and Caroline, 'the Great Landgravine'. Of these the former was described as a 'souveraine sans faste et sans faiblesse' by Voltaire, who visited her after shaking the dust of Berlin off his feet, and for whom he compiled the *Annals of the Holy Roman Empire*. After paying her a visit in 1762, Grimm became her unofficial and unpaid *chargé d'affaires* in Paris, transacting all sorts of business and reporting Parisian news and fashions. Equally admired by Frederick the Great, who saluted her as *sexu femina, ingenio vir*, 'the Great Landgravine' loved both French and German literature. No German princess of the eighteenth century possessed a wider circle of devoted friends, and Grimm was regarded as almost a member of the family.

By a curious paradox the German ruler who might have been expected to embrace Grimm with open arms proved the most difficult fish to catch in his net. When the Seven Years War was over the attempt was renewed through Ulrike, sister of Frederick and Queen of Sweden, and through the Duchess of Saxe-Gotha. An approach under such auspices was difficult to decline, but the result hardly satisfied the editor's pride. The busy ruler was bored by the *Correspondance Littéraire*. 'I know he wants petites historiettes de Paris,' complained Grimm, 'but these I would not provide. Moreover, I suffer from the original sin of being German: with a French name I should have better luck.' As a further humiliation the thrifty monarch declined to pay. Grimm was convinced that it was impossible to please him without displeasing other patrons, and after three years he was requested to send no further issues. Despite this disconcerting experience, the two men enjoyed their long talks when Grimm visited Berlin in 1769 and was presented with a gold snuff-box. Few people, declared Frederick, knew mankind so well, and still fewer could win the friendship of the great without compromising their independence.

After the chilling blast from Potsdam the warmer breezes from St Petersburg were particularly welcome. The first item in the correspondence of thirty years was a request to add the Empress to the *clientèle* of the *Correspondance Littéraire*. Grimm had no fear of a refusal, for she was already in friendly contact with Diderot, his bosom friend. 'Madam,' he wrote in 1764, 'since you have heaped favours on one of the most celebrated Philosophes of

France, all who cultivate literature and think, in whatever part of Europe they live, have regarded themselves as your subjects. The most obscure, like the most illustrious, have felt themselves under your protection, and the grace you have just granted me proves that your favours know neither exceptions nor limits. It is therefore with the most entire confidence that I present my homage at your feet. If your exacting duties as sovereign permit you to satisfy the passion which all the great spirits have shown for literature throughout the ages, if you deign to cast a favourable glance at these sheets, you will bear in mind that the regular appearance of a periodical cannot always be guaranteed.' The *Correspondance Littéraire* would be despatched in the diplomatic bag of the Russian Ambassador in Paris. Catherine needed no pressing and responded with 1,500 roubles a year.

Grimm had to wait for nine years before setting eyes on the Semiramis of the North. His opportunity arrived when he accompanied the hereditary Prince of Hesse-Darmstadt to St Petersburg for the marriage of his sister to the Grand Duke Paul in 1773. Welcomed by Frederick at Potsdam and by Prince Henry at Rheinsberg, he found the way prepared for him at St Petersburg by Diderot. The greeting was cordial, and both visitors were promptly made members of the Imperial Academy of Sciences. 'His conversation delights me,' reported the Empress to Voltaire; 'but we have so much to talk about that our exchanges have hitherto had more liveliness than sequence.' Grimm was equally pleased. 'The Empress overwhelmed me with attentions from the start,' he reported to Mme Geoffrin. 'I have had the honour to see her almost every day, to dine with her two or three times, and, best of all, to talk with her for 1½ or 2 hours alone. She is a charming woman. Once or twice a week she dines in the Hermitage, where everyone is equal. There is no hint of the Empress. There are two tables of ten, and the guests sit where they like.' The intimacy increased after the fêtes and the departure of the Landgrave of Hesse. 'Her Majesty often sent for me after supper. She did needlework, and kept me till 10.30 or 11. Soon we were meeting every day, sometimes twice a day. I spend all day from 11 to 11 at the Palace, either in company or in *tête-à-tête*, only withdrawing from 4 to 6. Thus the winter of 1773–4 passed like a continuous intoxication. Her attentions seemed to increase from day to day, and with it her confidence. Mine too was such that I entered her apartment with the same assurance as that of the most intimate friend, certain of finding in her conversation an inexhaustible store of the greatest interest presented in the most piquant form.'

So enchanted was the Empress with Grimm that after the first interview she proposed that he should enter her service. She had always hankered after a tame *Philosophe*, partly for her own entertainment, partly for the prestige of the Crown. On her accession she had invited d'Alembert to teach mathematics to the Grand Duke Paul, and was annoyed by his refusal. She fared no better with Diderot, who was pressed to transfer the direction of the *Encyclopédie* to St Petersburg after its suspension in France. He declined on the ground that it was the property of the publishers, and that the later volumes were being printed at Paris and would probably be published in Switzerland. The real reason was his unwillingness to leave Paris and to entrust his fortunes to the favours of a distant ruler on a rickety throne. Catherine accepted the rebuff in good temper, she purchased his library, when he desired to provide a *dot* for his daughter, left the books in his possession till his death, and appointed him their custodian with a small salary. When he accepted an invitation in 1773, they delighted in each other's company. Diderot was not the man to be overawed by coronets, and he treated her with no more ceremony than his friends at home. He seized her hands, shook her by the arm and rapped on the table to emphasise a point; Catherine humorously observed that she had been compelled to place a table between them to avoid bruises from her exuberant guest. 'He has an inexhaustible imagination,' she reported, 'and I rank him among the most extraordinary people who ever lived.' Feeling himself an emissary of the *Aufklärung*, he wrote memoranda for his hostess, urging her to introduce compulsory education and other needed reforms. He outstayed his welcome, and they parted without regret.

When Grimm received the flattering invitation to settle in Russia, he proposed a compromise. Apart from the precarious nature of the favour of rulers, it was unthinkable that he should leave Paris, abandon the *Correspondance Littéraire*, and, above all, desert Mme d'Epinay. Accordingly, he promised a second visit and the frequent despatch of news. The Empress understood his dilemma, and her first letter after his departure, dated 25th April, 1774, shows the easy terms on which they stood. 'M. de Grimm, I received your letter from Riga. You say: How can I manage to escape from your empire? I can only reply with Molière: *Georges Dandin, vous l'avez bien voulu.* It is for you to decide about your return. I congratulate you on your pleasure in celebrating my forty-sixth birthday in Courland. I hate this day like the plague, for every time I am a year older, with which I could well dispense. It would be charming to have an Empress who would always remain fifteen. But adieu, M. de Grimm, this begins to resemble a gossip at Tsarkoe-Selo, and the fools who will read it before you may well think it improper that persons so grave as you and I should write such letters.' Many years later she expressed her abiding satisfaction at their partnership. 'My dear factotum, I think it is ordained on high that we are both created to have a pen in our hand in order to write to one another without pause. Almost always I write in haste, holding your letters in my left hand.' Another time she spoke of *le démon de griffonage* which had tempted her. She disliked dictating, and the mere physical action of writing served as a welcome outlet for her inexhaustible vitality.

After receiving a further letter from Grimm on his way home, the Empress explained that her time was fully occupied. 'Do not imagine, M. le Philosophe, that you will get a twelve-page reply. *Das ist eine pure unmöglichkeit.* I love to receive letters of twelve pages when they are as agreeable as yours from Dresden, but I have not much taste for my replies. I was sorry I could not give better news of your health to your friend Diderot. I do not like these frequent consultations of doctors. These charlatans always do you more harm than good, as we see with Louis XV, who had ten at his bedside and yet is dead. I ought to take up many points in your letter, but that would fill twelve pages, and I only want you to have six, to prove that you are not writing to an image.' That Grimm's early bulletins, not one of which survives, gave pleasure is clear. 'Thanks for the letter from Berlin of June 30th. I am enchanted at your welcome by the King of Prussia. I am not astonished by what occurred at Rheinsberg; I know the friendship of Prince Henry. Since September I have not ceased to repeat that M. Georges Dandin was the most absolute master of his destiny as to remaining, leaving and returning. I hope with all my heart that the waters of Carlsbad will clean you out and that you will increase in virtue, knowledge and good humour to the end of time, or the end of the century at your choice.' Three weeks later she wrote again by return of post. 'Your letter of this morning is only eight pages. Allow me to say it is the maddest of all your scrawls; but, lengthy though they are, I like to read them two or three times, for they are most entertaining, though not very wise. I do not possess either the failings or the qualities you ascribe to me. Perhaps I am good, ordinarily I am gentle, but occasionally I have to wish terribly what I wish, and that is about all I am worth.' Her names for her new friend suggest a pleasing absence of etiquette: M. l'encyclopédiste, M. le philosophe, M. le souffre-douleur, Marchese del Grimmo, M. le Baron, the last-named title having been conferred on him by the Emperor Joseph II. Her friends in the West were kept in mind, not only by visits and corre-spondence, but by her well-thumbed copy of the *Encyclopédie*. 'I cannot dispense with it for a single day,' she wrote in December, 1774; 'despite all its faults it is an essential and excellent work.'

Grimm's second visit to Russia strengthened the ties. He had much of interest to tell her, for on his way he had visited Voltaire at Ferney, the witty little Abbé Galiani in Naples, Frederick and Prince Henry in Berlin. Arriving at St Petersburg in September, 1776, and remaining for almost a year, he saw her daily, both in company and in private talk. Two, three, four, once seven hours, were spent in conversation that never flagged. Once again the question arose whether a closer partnership could not be arranged. She would have dearly liked him not only to enter her service but to settle in her dominions and supervise the educational system. He had grown rather tired of the burden of the *Correspondance Littér-aire*, had handed over part of the work to his Swiss colleague Meister, and would have been glad of a settled income. Yet the lure of Paris was too strong. He reflected that she might tire of him and that his privileged position might provoke jealousy. Finally it was agreed that he should act as her Paris agent for con-fidential missions and the purchase of works of art at a salary of 2,000 roubles. He left Russia a happy man, and after visiting Gustavus III at Stockholm reached home after an absence of two years. Henceforth, next to Mme d'Epinay, Catherine occupied the chief place in his life. While most of her letters have survived, only enough of his voluminous bulletins have been found to fill a volume of moderate size in the publications of the Imperial Russian Historical Society.

The partnership lasted till her death twenty years later, untroubled by a single cloud. He had blended his existence with hers, declared Grimm, separate yet inseparable. Her confidence in him was impregnable. 'I never wrote to anyone as I do to you. I jot down everything that comes into my head. You are quite right to call it *olla podrida imperiale*. I know how deeply you are attached to me, so I tell you everything.' He was a factotum in the fullest sense of the word, charged both with the greatest and the smallest commissions—from arranging the purchase of the libraries of Voltaire and Diderot to the selection of toilettes, bonbons and rouge. He supplied architects for her buildings, actors for her theatres, plays specially written by Sedaine and other dramatists. When Russians visited Paris he played the host; when they got into bad company and debt, like Bobrinsky, the son of Catherine and Orloff, he helped with advice and cash. As the agent for such commissions and the distributor of her lavish gifts he was overwhelmed with correspondence and visitors and complained that no time was left for reading. Since his contacts with the Empress were known to the French Government, he was occasionally employed for semi-official purposes. He was the perfect cosmopolitan: German by birth, domiciled in France, a Baron of the Holy Roman Empire, a man worth cultivating and impossible to distrust.

Henceforth Grimm could hardly call his life his own. 'Since the favours of your Imperial Majesty have made me a celebrity,' he wrote in 1780, 'God alone knows all I have had to suffer. All the idlers and importunates feel entitled to rob me of my time, the most precious of my possessions.' Never had a man been more cruelly divided, he complained. 'Half, three-quarters, of me are at St Petersburg, while the rest vegetates here. Not a day passes that I am not overwhelmed by visits, letters, proposals of every kind. I spend my life in useless interviews, listening, reading letters, answering, refusing. Oh! these deplorable distractions.' It was the price of his promotion; yet though an occasional sigh escaped him, he would not have exchanged his yoke for a king's ransom.

'Being mentioned in a published letter of Your Majesty, my glory
has reached the summit, but my time and my repose have fallen into
the power of other people. I am complaining at the moment when
my admired sovereign fills the universe with the glory of her immortal name, and when she deigns to cast a kind glance at me just
when the eyes of all Europe are fixed on her. Your Majesty has
made the happiness of a good fellow who since the beginning of
1778 has dedicated himself almost entirely to your service with a
zeal as indefatigable as the favours of our Empress are inexhaustible. If Your Majesty desires to make me perfectly happy,
she will confer on me the title of her agent or her councillor, so
that he can say in public: 'Our august sovereign'.

Grimm would have been more than human had he not endeavoured to enlist the sympathy of his patron in Mme d'Epinay and
her family. 'No palpitating heart ever approaches your great heart
without being comforted,' he wrote in 1780. She had been deprived of her allowance by Necker's reforms. 'This woman has
been in a miserable state of health and suffering for seven or eight
years, two or three times in sight of death. Yet her resilience is
astonishing, and she has convinced me of the truth of M. de
Buffon's axiom that one dies only when one consents to die. She
had a small grant from the state all her life, and her children a little
more. Her daughter has three charming children. At this moment
of infirmity and of need for the education of the children M.
Necker suppresses all these pensions and the whole family is reduced to misery. One cannot blame him. He knows her and is
interested in her case, and pleaded her cause when Mme du Barry
and Abbé Terray tried to seize her portion. But now he has seized
what he then saved. All this is to justify inducing you to buy the
diamonds.'

Grimm's bouquets were often of super size. The first long letter
which has been preserved, written in July, 1779, addresses her as
'our great and immortal Empress,' and ends in German: 'Der
Himmel beschutze seine Gesalbte, Deutschlands Ruhm, Russ-
lands Freude und Europens Wunder, Amen.' The earthquake of
Lisbon, he declares, was a dance of marionettes compared with his
transports when a letter arrived. To the imperial dog-lover he
described himself as 'one of your dogs,' a worm crawling at her
feet. His friends, he reported, used to say that if they were looking

for him they would find him at her feet. 'If anyone, I will not say in your Empire, but in the whole world, boasts of surpassing me in attachment to my Empress, let him come forward and I will assert that he has lied, and will prove it if necessary at Riga or at Narva.' When the courier arrived he nearly died of happiness and gratitude. Even Diderot, who was much less of a courtier, declared that the Empress combined the soul of Brutus with the charms of Cleopatra.

Catherine's phraseology is more restrained. 'Here are two of your letters demanding a reply,' she wrote in 1778. 'True there are two from the King of Prussia, three from the King of Sweden, two from Voltaire, several more from God knows who, all arrived before yours. But as they do not amuse me, because they must be written to, whereas with you I chat, I prefer to amuse myself and to let my hand, my pen and my head run on as they like. Bombard me with letters, for it amuses me. I read and re-read them, and say to myself: Comme il me comprend! ah ciel! Il n'y a que lui qui me comprenne bien.' Two months later she wrote: 'Let us have a little gossip. Do you know why I dread royal visits? Because they are usually boring and insipid folk and one has to stand stiffly at attention. As I like chatting, silence bores me.' She excused her bad writing, as one of her pet dogs had put his paw on the paper.

The Empress derived greater pleasure from Grimm than from her children. With Paul she stood on a footing of armed neutrality, well aware not only that he had a better claim to the throne but that he was always brooding over the theft of his rights. Mother and son were tormented by fear of each other, the Empress dreading that he might hurl her from the throne by a bold *coup* similar to that by which she had seized it, the Grand Duke that he might be disinherited in favour of his precocious eldest son. Count Bobrinsky was more trouble than he was worth, as she admits to Grimm in 1785. 'This young man is singularly nonchalant, but I don't think he is ill-meaning or dishonest. He is young and may be led into very bad company. He has disgusted his entourage. He wanted to be on his own and so he is. He is quite capable of paying up. I should be glad if you knew the state of his affairs at Paris. Has he debts? It would not be a bad idea to have him watched, but if he noticed anything it might make things worse.

*Das ist ein wenig ein sonderlicher kopf.* But he is not lacking in brains, knowledge, and even talents.' Two years later she informed Grimm that she had received two letters from 'young Bobrinsky'. 'Please do not let him go short. He can count on 37 or 38 thousand roubles, over which no one else has any claim.'

Catherine found compensation in her eldest grandson, whose charm and friendliness seemed to justify the highest hopes. 'He begins to show a singular intelligence for a child of his age,' reported the adoring grandmother when he was three. 'He would spend his life with me if he were allowed. He is always the same, because he is well—always gay, friendly, considerate, fearless, beautiful as love. He is the delight of everyone, especially myself. I can do what I like with him. He understands everything one says to him. This child loves me instinctively. If he is crying and I come in, he stops. God bless M. Alexandre. He is always asking: Why? He wants to know everything.' Writing at midnight on September 7, 1780, she informs Grimm that she has asked Buffon questions about nature. 'I am like M. Alexandre: *le pourquoi du pourquoi serait fort agréable à savoir.*' She was using the educational methods recommended in Mme d'Epinay's *Conversations d'Émilie*, she reported to Grimm, and it was succeeding well. His tutor, La Harpe, had the greatest expectations, she reported in 1787. 'He is Swiss and he is not a flatterer. *Der Junge ist gut und sehr schön und glücklich erschaffen.* His brother (Constantine) is very intelligent, but he has faults from which the elder is free. Both are full of the ambition and desire to do good and they possess the qualifications for success, for they are open minds and the elder has as much *flair* as anyone can possess.'

The fullest description of these clever lads occurs in a letter to Grimm in September, 1790. 'M. Alexandre, in body, heart and mind, is exceptional in goodness and understanding. He is lively but sedate, prompt and reflective, with profound ideas, and finds everything easy. One would think he had been nothing else all his life. He is tall and strong for his age, yet agile. In a word, he is a combination of contradictions, which results in his being greatly loved by his entourage. Those of his age adopt his opinions and follow his lead. I fear only one danger: women will run after him. He is unaware of his good looks. He is very well informed for his age. He speaks four languages. He likes reading

G

and is never idle. He enjoys all the amusements of his age. If I talk seriously he listens and replies with equal courtesy. Everyone is pleased, including myself. La Harpe, his tutor, says he is exceptional. Now he is doing mathematics, which are as easy to him as everything else. If he does not succeed, I do not know who could. When he is ill or tired, or in the evening, he surrounds himself with engravings and objects of art. Constantine is vivacious to the point of petulance. He has a good heart and is very intelligent. He has less consistency of character than his elder brother. He will make his name. He speaks four languages. The elder speaks English, the younger knows all the Greek dialects. Seeing Plutarch in my room, he says to me: 'That passage is mistranslated: I will do it better.' So he brought me several versions. I enjoy his conversation. He likes military things, especially the navy, and loves heroic actions. In a word, he is a joy.'

In her dreams the Empress already saw her eldest grandson seated on a throne in Constantinople from which the intruding Turks had been expelled by Russian arms. In her eyes the highest compliment he received was the affectionate admiration of her greatest friend. 'M. Alexandre has conquered Prince Potemkin,' she reported in April, 1791. 'He calls him the prince of his heart. He finds in him the figure of Apollo combined with great modesty and unusual intelligence, thoughtful, courteous, well-informed. If one had chosen someone for his place, it would have been difficult to find his equal, and impossible to discover his superior. And he is only in his fourteenth year.' It was indirectly through Grimm that La Harpe became Alexander's tutor, for he had recommended the Swiss writer as a teacher to the son of a Russian nobleman in St Petersburg. The Empress saw both her grandsons married, and lived just long enough to hold the future Emperor Nicholas in her arms. 'Maman (the Grand Duchess Paul) has given birth to an enormous boy,' she reported to Grimm. 'He has a bass voice with which he cries in an astonishing way. His hands are almost as big as mine. I never set eyes on such a chevalier. If he goes on like this, his brothers will be dwarfs in comparison.'

Among Catherine's reigning visitors no one gave her so much pleasure as the Emperor Joseph, who travelled as Count Falkenstein. 'We talked all day and he did not seem bored,' she reported

to Grimm after meeting him at Mohile in 1780. 'I find him very
well informed; he likes talking and talks well. He said things worth
printing and uttered thoughts which would assuredly do him
great honour if they were put in practice.' During the long drive
to Smolensk 'we talked about the whole world, yourself included.' The impression deepened from day to day. 'I should
never stop if I were to sing his praises,' she wrote after his departure. 'He possesses the most solid, profound and best-in-
formed mind I ever met. To catch him out one would have to
get up very early.' Joseph's personality left an ineffaceable impression, and she mourned his early death in 1790. 'I could not
see the Ambassador for some time,' she wrote to Grimm, 'because
we were both in tears. I have also pitied the Queen of France,
but she has the courage of her mother and the family. Joseph
blundered, if I may say so, by this same intrepidity which I
observed in news of the troubles in the Netherlands received in
the Tauris.' A year later, when the Emperor Leopold had
cancelled some of his elder brother's unpopular improvisations,
she pronounced her final verdict: 'I can never get over my
astonishment that he, born and trained for this post, full of intelligence, talent and knowledge, not merely ruled so badly but
was reduced to the misery in which he died.' The Empress was
as much his superior in *flair* as he surpassed her in character. His
virtues shone in a still brighter light by contrast to the hulking
heir to the Prussian throne who paid a State visit soon afterwards. Even less welcome than Prince Frederick William was
'the charlatan' Cagliostro. 'He says he is a colonel in the service
of Spain—Spanish by birth, and pretends he is a master-sorcerer,
seeing spirits who awaits his commands. When I heard all this I
remarked that he made a great mistake in coming here. Nowhere
will he score less than in Russia, where there is no enthusiasm for
sorcerers.'

Catherine's fulminations against the French Revolution in her
letters to Grimm are reserved for a further chapter. The sombre
drama was equally hateful to both; but whereas it facilitated her
fresh spoliations of Poland, it wrecked his career in France.
Suspect as a friend of the Empress, he left Paris in February, 1792.
His kindly patroness nominated him her representative at Hamburg and Gotha, but the invitation to Russia for which he had

hoped never came. The appointment was confirmed by Paul, who also continued the pension granted by his mother to Mme de Bueil, the daughter of Mme d'Epinay, for whose welfare Grimm had assumed responsibility. His closing years were spent at Gotha with his adopted family in a house provided by the Duke, but he was never to know happiness again. 'I am pushed around, persecuted, tormented without respite,' he complained in his last letter to Catherine, 'and one has only a certain allowance of strength.' Goethe, who was almost a neighbour and occasionally dined with him, records that he could not always conceal his bitterness at the decline of his fortunes. He lived till the age of eighty-four, long enough to see Napoleon the master of France and Alexander on the throne of his grandmother. Old and disillusioned, he had lost his zest for life, literature and travel. Yet his career was in no sense a failure, for he had been the valued friend of men and women greater than himself.


VI. *The Autocrat*

At the age of thirty-three Catherine ascended the throne of the Romanoffs with the resolve not merely to reign, but to rule. Peter the Great, whom she took as her model, had hoisted Russia into the rank of the Great Powers, and it was her mission to build on his foundations. Having been deliberately excluded from affairs of state, she had everything to learn, and she threw herself into her task with unflagging zeal. She attended debates in the Senate, asked questions of officials and private citizens, and recorded her impressions. It was not a pretty picture. Ever since the firm hand of the superman had been removed in 1725 the machinery of government had been running down. The pay of the troops fighting on Prussian soil was many months in arrears; the navy had been so grossly neglected that, in her own words, it was only fit to catch herrings; the national credit had declined, nearly half the revenues of the State failing to reach the Exchequer, and the administration of justice cried aloud for reform. A new broom was urgently required. Knowing little of her vast dominions, she undertook long journeys during the opening years of her reign, and studied the problems of local administration on the spot.

The new ruler was as tireless a worker as Peter himself. Only when the executive had regained its authority and was functioning efficiently could she turn to the second item on her programme—the aggrandisement of the empire. How well she was to implement it is indicated by the addition of Courland, Eastern Poland, and the northern littoral of the Black Sea. Unfettered by moral scruples, she adopted the simple maxim formulated by Frederick the Great when he seized Silesia: 'If an opportunity is offered me, shall I let it slip?' Why should she not combine with Russia and Austria to cut substantial slices off the Polish joint? And why should she not secure fertile provinces in the south which the Turks were too weak to defend? *Raison d'état* has always been the religion of rulers, and the maxim that the end justifies the means is older than the Jesuits.

Tradition and conviction combined to make Catherine an adherent of the doctrine of enlightened autocracy which dominated the political thinking of the Continent during the eighteenth century. She reached adolescence in the years when Frederick the Great was filling Europe with his fame, and her father was proud to serve as a Prussian officer. Nowhere in Germany could she discover any alternative to the principle of dynastic omnipotence: *Sic volo, sic jubeo.* The conception of self-government, even of a sharing of responsibility, was beyond the range not only of princes, but of nearly all the Intelligentsia. The stage was occupied by the Cameralists, who accepted the Absolute State as an axiom. Cameralism, as expounded by Seckendorf and Justi, was the theory and practice of administration: though its interpreters hoped to raise the standard, they suggested no sanctions except an appeal to the conscience of the ruler. Instead of proceeding from the needs of the community, the State was their starting-point, its power and opulence their aim. The commonweal is presented sincerely enough as the goal of endeavour, and the happiness of the subject receives lip homage, but they assume that it is secured—and can only be secured—by the will of the prince. He is exhorted to respect property and the law, and is warned not to overtax his subjects, but they are not to co-operate in the making of laws, nor in resisting oppressors. Unlike Hobbes, who demanded nothing beyond the maintenance of order, the Cameralists assume the wisdom and benevolence of the ruler. Thus the difference was not between rival conceptions of the State, but between good and bad exponents of the prevailing creed. The Estates, where they still existed, were rather obstacles to progress than instruments of reform. That a Limited Monarchy worked well in England aroused merely academic interest, since the long Parliamentary experience of the island kingdom and the majestic tradition of the Common Law found no counterpart abroad.

The political ideology imbibed by the little princess in her parents' home was enlarged but not substantially modified when she exchanged the narrow horizon of Stettin for the ampler vistas of the Neva. Not even professional flatterers could have described the disreputable régime of the Empress Elizabeth as a model of paternal government, but behind the Tsarina stood the towering figure of her father. From the moment of her arrival, the Grand Duchess had been thrilled by the magnificence of his achievements. No name occurs more frequently in her correspondence, and to the end of her days he was rarely out of her thoughts. Here was the superman, *pater patriae*, the first servant of the State, the practical idealist, untiring and resourceful, who built a new capital, opened a window to the West, created a navy, reformed the Army, developed trade, dug canals, exploited minerals, introduced religious toleration and shattered the yoke of a reactionary Church. Her mission, as she realised every year more clearly while she waited for the clock to strike, was to strengthen and enlarge the edifice of which he was the architect, never doubting that she possessed the necessary brains and will. Her self-assurance was fostered by her observation of the third-rate actors on the St Petersburg stage. On her accession she was ready with a programme of administrative and judicial reform. Peter had made his country a Great Power: it was her task to provide the blessings of civilisation. No minister, no class, no political or ecclesiastical institution stood in her way. The Senate, a legacy of Peter the Great, possessed dignity without power. The Holy Synod, another of his legacies, was merely a department of state. Thirty-four years later she could point with pride to the fulfilment of the larger portion of her plans. The only unanswerable indictment that could be brought against her as a ruler in the context of eighteenth-century political ideology was her shameless extravagance towards her lovers, not only during their term of office, but when they were successively hustled off the stage. Shirking labour and responsibility as little as Frederick and Joseph she left Russia larger and stronger, more respected and more feared, more prosperous and more civilised, than she had found it when she eliminated her feeble husband and seized the throne in 1762.

Catherine was an eager student of *L'Esprit des Lois*, which she described as a breviary for rulers: if she were the Pope, she declared, she would canonise Montesquieu. From its pages she learned the merits of the English Constitution, and she told Diderot that she would gladly have copied it had the conditions of its successful operation prevailed. But how could the principle of the division of power be adopted in a state mainly composed of illiterate serfs? Since any form of constitutional government was recognised to be impracticable, the first step was to introduce the rudiments of the reign of law. Law, once described by Hooker in a noble passage as the voice of God, came before liberty, which demanded a minimum standard of education and self-control. Peter had issued instructions for the drafting of a code, but nothing had come of it. The plan was revived under Elizabeth, but a driving force was lacking. During the six years of peace which followed her accession, Catherine's abounding energies were largely concentrated on the project of a code which, not only in its broad conception but in its details, could hold its own with the jurisprudence of the West. Three hours of her busy day were set aside for the purpose. She interviewed experts, drafted memoranda and devoted more thought to her ambitious scheme than Napoleon gave to the French Code. The so-called *Institute* has been described by Kluchevsky, the greatest of Russian historians, as her Political Testament. Though narrower in scope than the Political Testaments of Frederick the Great, it bears in almost equal degree the impress of her personality during the early phase of her reign, and registers the high-water mark of her liberal ideology.

The first result of her efforts was the Code, and a memorandum of 1779 described its gestation: 'For two years I read and wrote, and for eighteen months consulted no one, being guided solely by my heart and reason. When I thought I had reached my goal I began to show parts to various people, including Prince Orloff and Count Nikita Panin. The latter remarked: 'These maxims are high explosives.' Prince Orloff praised my work and often wished to show it to others; but I never presented more than a sheet or two at once. Finally I composed the manifesto summoning delegates from the whole Empire in order to learn the conditions of every section of the realm. They assembled in Moscow in 1767. I summoned several persons of different views to hear the Instruction read. Every part provoked disagreement. I allowed them to cancel what they pleased, and they omitted over half of my draft. I bade them take the rest as rules on which opinion could be based, not as a law.' These rules were to be read monthly as a guide to the deputies in their law-making activities: they neither formed a code nor created a Parliament, though many foreigners believed that they did.

The experiment of administrative reform aroused wide interest. Frederick the Great applauded its humanitarian spirit and made the Empress a member of the Berlin Academy. The French Consul in Moscow cynically reported that the meetings were reputed to be a comedy staged by despotism masquerading as humanity. The British Secretary of Legation was equally unimpressed. 'Knowing the restless disposition of her subjects, the great object of her policy is to occupy them at home and abroad as much as possible. This motive, sharpened by her vanity, has made her undertake to be the legislator of this Empire. But to do it safely she has taken care to have in the Commission only those who will follow her dictates and pay tribute to her generosity, justice and moderation. If these laws were to be brought to a certain level of perfection, the extreme deficiency of respected and disinterested magistrates would prevent success.' The latter criticism was only too well justified, but for the backward condition of Russia on her accession she could not be held responsible. After years of reflection and discussion, she ordered the election of 564 deputies and the drafting of *cahiers* setting forth grievances. The conference opened on August 4, 1767, in Moscow, where her draft was laid before them. In addition to the plenary sessions, nineteen special committees were appointed for the consideration of details. The meeting-place was transferred to St Petersburg in February, 1768, and the Instructions to the Commissioners, containing 655 articles, were signed by the Empress on April 8, 1768.

She was proud of her work, half code, half gazetteer, and desired that it should be widely read by her subjects and in the schools. The more people read it, she added complacently, the less crime there would be. Frequent references to the practices of Greece and Rome jostle moral precepts, disquisitions on the Russian people and proposals for the reform of the criminal law. Peter the Great, we are reminded, introduced the manners and customs of Europe, but the new work suggests how much remained to be done.

The opening articles breathe the crisp ideology of Enlightened Autocracy. 'The sovereign is absolute. The extent of the empire necessitates absolute power in the ruler. Any other form of government would have ruined it. The aim of monarchy is the glory of the citizen, the state, and the sovereign.' For the first time in a Russian official document the inhabitants are described as 'citizens', a term tacitly involving a right to be governed by the Rule of Law. 'The equality of the citizens consists in this: that they shall all be subject to the same laws. No citizen should stand in fear of another.' The execution of the laws is entrusted to the Senate. The larger portion of the document is devoted to the reform of the criminal law, where the influence of Beccaria's epoch-making treatise on Crimes and Punishments, published in 1764, is felt in every clause, above all in the injunction: 'All maiming ought to be abolished.' One of the most striking features of the Instructions is the regret that such a spacious empire was largely an empty land. 'Russia is greatly deficient in population and at the same time increases her dominions. Therefore too much encouragement can never be given to the propagation of the human species. The peasants usually have twelve, fifteen, or twenty children by one marriage, but only rarely do a quarter reach maturity.' Like Frederick, who welcomed every able-bodied immigrant, she recognised that man-power was the foundation of national strength.

No reference occurs to the most pressing of domestic issues. If the teaching of the West were to be taken seriously, as Catherine took it, serfdom would have to disappear. But such a drastic social and economic revolution would have been fiercely resented by the gentry, and without their acquiescence it was impracticable. Moreover, serfdom lingered on in various forms in several Central

European states which were usually regarded as more civilised than Russia. In Prussia abolition had to wait for Stein and Hardenberg, in Austria till the Year of Revolution, in Russia till 1861. Representative institutions, equally ignored in the Instructions, were only grudgingly granted by the last of the Tsars at the opening of the twentieth century and speedily withdrawn. Thus both the caste system and the technique of autocracy inherited by Catherine were transmitted without significant modifications to her son and his children. Diderot, the most democratic of the *Philosophes* with the exception of Rousseau, argued in his critical analysis of the Instruction that the only true sovereign was the nation, and that a good code must begin by compelling the ruler to swear to the law. This idea, however, remained wishful thinking even in the country of his birth till the French Revolution destroyed the *mystique* of the Crown and brought the Tiers État to the centre of the stage.

The project of comprehensive reform of the law was held up and finally abandoned owing to the Polish rebellion and the Turkish war. Committees worked at details for several years, but the results of their labours were not embodied in the law of the land. Yet the zeal of the Empress for a more civilised jurisprudence was not wholly in vain, and the summoning of a partially representative Assembly to confer with the sovereign for seventeen months on high matters of state remained a bracing precedent. Catherine made no attempt to conceal her indebtedness to Montesquieu and Beccaria. In presenting a German translation to Frederick, she compared himself to a crow in peacock's feathers, merely claiming the merit of arrangement with a few words or lines of her own thrown in. Though Pokrovsky, the outstanding Communist historian of Russia, complained that she summarised Montesquieu without understanding him, he conceded her energy and good will. Within four years of its completion the Instructions appeared in twenty-four foreign versions, and Voltaire dutifully hailed them as the finest monument of the century. The greatest compliment they received was the refusal of the French Government to allow the entry of 2,000 copies, and a generation later the Emperor Paul forbade their circulation in Russia. Portions of the code, indeed, were in advance of most European states. Declarations of rights and projects of reform are not necessarily useless because they have to wait for the flowing tide. Diderot, who was no courtier, described his friend as 'L'Impératrice a l'âme grande, de la pénétration, des lumières, un génie tres étendu, de la justice, de la bonté, de la patience, et de la fermeté'. The 'only begetter' of the Instructions is the Empress at her best, sharing the belief of the *Aufklärung* in the authority of reason and genuinely anxious to help her backward subjects so far as circumstances allowed.

Catherine's liberal instincts received the first shock in 1773, when Pugatcheff, an illiterate Cossack adventurer, gathered a motley following and marched on Moscow. Asia, it was remarked, had challenged Europe. Though he arrived in chains and was speedily executed, it was the most critical moment of her reign, and its memories haunted her to the end. 'They are only a collection of coquins with an impostor at their head,' was her first comment; but as the news of massacre and desolation poured in she was undeceived. 'Hurry up and exterminate these criminals who disgrace us in the eyes of the world,' she wrote to Bibikoff; but the General doubted if the revolt could be suppressed by arms alone, since reforms were needed to remove discontent. The slogan of liberty for the peasants and extermination of the nobility had rallied multitudes to the rebel flag. It seemed as if the crust of the earth had suddenly opened and she gazed with horror into the bottomless pit. Of palace revolutions she had experience, but now she became aware that volcanic passions were seething in the mob. Her primary duty, she decided, was to affirm the authority of the Crown: since the fabric of empire had proved so brittle, it required bonds of steel. The Cossack revolt was the turning-point in her ideological development: henceforth she frowned on popular movements wherever they occurred. The ruler who had saluted Paoli's rebellion in Corsica denounced the revolt of the American Colonies.

The superman—or the superwoman—ought to look as well as to act the part, and this qualification was possessed by Catherine the Great. 'I was at first extremely surprised to find her very short,' reported Mme Vigée le Brun, who spent several years painting portraits in Russia. 'I had fancied her prodigiously tall, as high as her grandeur. She was very stout, but still had a handsome face, beautifully set off by white curly hair. Genius seemed seated on her lofty forehead. Her eyes were soft and sweet, her nose quite Grecian, her complexion florid, her features very animated.' Whatever the *Corps Diplomatique* thought of her policy and her morals, there was no disagreement about her capacity to rule. 'Prepared even as I was for the magnificence and parade of this court,' reported Sir James Harris, the British Ambassador in 1778, 'it exceeds in everything my ideas. To this is joined the most perfect order and decorum. The Empress herself unites in the most wonderful manner the talents of putting those she honours with her conversation at their ease, and of keeping up her own dignity. Her character extends throughout her whole administration; and although she is rigidly obeyed, she had introduced a lenity in the mode of government to which this country was a stranger.'

Closer observation revealed that all is not gold which glitters. Only a few weeks later, Sir James struck a very different note. 'The system of the Court goes on here in its old train; immense prodigality, and a habit of indolence and procrastination reigns from the first to the last. The incredible vanity of the Sovereign gets the better of her fine parts; she is willing to give credit to any assertion that she supposes to be in consequence of her own greatness and power.' The Ambassador was at a disadvantage, for he could not stoop to such flattery as his diplomatic competitors. 'My adversaries ever addressed her as a being of a superior nature; and, as she goes near to think herself infallible, she expects to be approached with all the reverence due to a divinity. She is spoiled by flattery and success. Levity and want of precision in her ideas are the weak side of her character, and these increase as she gets older.' A similar verdict was passed by the Emperor Joseph after his first visit in 1780 when he impressed her far more favourably than she impressed him. On his return he drafted a letter to his hostess which he sent for approval to Kaunitz, the Foreign Secretary. 'Herewith my letter; add or omit as you like. Remember we are dealing with a woman who cares only for herself, and no more for Russia than I do; so we must tickle her. Vanity is her idol; luck and exaggerated compliments have spoiled her. Now we must bay with the wolves.' That she cared nothing for her country was a libel, but it was true enough that her vanity grew with advancing years. Ségur, the French

Ambassador appointed in 1785, was equally impressed by his first sight of the sovereign. 'She stood there richly attired, her hand resting on a column. Her majestic air, the pride in her countenance, her slightly theatrical pose, clouded my memory.' With great presence of mind he improvised an address completely different from that which had been handed in, and to which she had prepared a reply. She seemed surprised, and at a later date asked why he had altered the text. At the moment, he replied, he was upset in the presence of such glory and majesty. This was not mere flattery, for closer acquaintance increased their mutual liking, and he was invited to accompany her on her historic visit to the South in 1787. Nor till he showed signs of approval of the ideas of 1789 did her liking for the witty Frenchman begin to wane.

## VII. *The French Revolution*

WHILE Catherine delighted in French culture, she had no cause to envy the political practice of France. Dynastic absolutism, she realised no less fully than Frederick and Joseph, must justify itself or take the consequences. That France had been in financial trouble ever since the later wars of Louis XIV was no secret, but it was not till Turgot and Necker had tried and failed that forecasts of revolution began to circulate. The former was evicted after two years of office, the latter after five, and henceforth no real attempt was made to avert the rush of the avalanche. Both were men of outstanding ability and lofty character, but their virtues increased the number of their foes. Necker's comprehensive *Compte Rendu*, published on the eve of his fall in 1781, was read all over Europe, and Catherine, to whom Grimm forwarded a copy, was unstinted in her praise. 'Please thank him,' she wrote, 'and tell him of my infinite admiration of his book and above all of his talents. I do not doubt that heaven has destined him to rescue France from her financial embarrassments, but that, I know from experience, is not the task of a day or a year.'

Unhappy France, like the Rome of Tacitus, could bear neither her ills nor their remedies, and two months after the Empress had despatched her eulogy Necker lost his post. Grimm felt that he, like Turgot, had tried to do too much. 'Your Majesty will have learned of the fall of this celebrated man,' he wrote on June 6, 1781. 'This may have come as a surprise at a distance, but those on the spot have seen this misfortune slowly approaching for months and felt it to be inevitable. M. Necker was marvellous in his control of the finances, but in trying to go too fast he came to grief. If he had gone slower he would certainly have reached his goal. He decided to rush to his ruin, and perhaps he will have dragged France down too. I regard him as finished: he will not recover from this great catastrophe. He is born for great affairs. He was only well when in office, and unless he has an empire to govern I see no future for him. The danger remains that everything will topple back into disorder and that all the old abuses will insensibly return. Then he will have the grief of seeing his Ministry as one of the luminous meteors which dazzle for a moment but whose passage is too rapid to leave a lasting impression.' Catherine was no less distressed and equally pessimistic. 'So Necker is gone; it was just a beautiful dream for France and a great victory for his enemies. The character of this exceptional man is to be admired in his two works, for the *Memorandum* is as good as the *Compte Rendu*. He displayed the height of disinterestedness, for he resisted the claims of his friends.'

During the six years following the fall of Necker, France staggered towards the abyss: not till the Assembly of Notables met in 1787 was there any attempt to grapple with the growing deficit. Catherine's correspondence with Grimm now becomes predominantly political. Though she had little hope of success, she did not think a great revolution was at hand. 'Though it does honour to the good intentions of the King,' she wrote in April, 1787, 'so far we do not think much of it here. The idea is excellent. What makes my assembly of deputies a success is that I say: Here are my principles. Tell me your grievances. Where does the shoe pinch? Put things right. I have no system. I desire the common good, which is also mine. Get to work, make plans! So they started looking about, collecting material, talking, dreaming, disputing, and your humble servant listens and is indifferent to everything except the common good.' When the news arrived of the fall of Calonne she commented: 'What will these

Notables do? The floor is slippery, for everybody slips. Gott segne die armen Leute.' Two months later she let herself go. 'Away with your Notables! Neither your M. de Calonne nor anyone else in France impresses me. Keep them for yourselves. They know ten times more than I and do ten times more harm than myself and my employés who do not indulge in such fine phrases.' Nowhere could she discover a pilot to weather the storm. 'What you say of the Marquis Lafayette does not surprise me. He seems to like revolutions.'

The fall of the Bastille was not merely a shock but a surprise. 'How times are changed!' she wrote to Grimm in November, 1789. 'Henri IV and Louis XIV called themselves the first gentlemen of their kingdom and thought themselves invincible at the head of their nobility. The Bishops and preachers chose texts which affirmed the royal authority. The splendour of the reign of Louis XIV survived abroad till our days. I confess I do not like "justice" without justice. These barbarous lamp-post executions! I cannot believe in the superior talents of the cobblers and shoemakers for government and legislation.' She describes the deputies as Pugatcheffs, adding that if a few of them were to be strung up the others would reform. Necker's recall to office had come too late. At the close of Ségur's mission in the autumn of 1789 the Empress charged him with friendly messages for the King. 'I regret your departure,' she added. 'You would do better to stay with me and not expose yourself to the tempests which may rage more fiercely than you anticipate. Your *penchant* for the new philosophy and for liberty will probably lead you to support the popular cause. I shall be sorry. I shall remain an aristocrat: that is my *métier*. Remember, you will find France with a temperature and very sick.' That the bourgeoisie and the peasants were reinforced by a section of the *Noblesse* and were determined to end both the political and social institutions of the *Ancien Régime* was beyond her grasp. 'Colonel,' remarked Potemkin to Langeron, a French officer of Royalist sympathies, 'I should only need my grooms to deal with your Jacobins.' 'Prince,' was the reply, 'I doubt if you could succeed with the whole of your army.'

'I sincerely desire that the misfortunes of France should end and that she should count in Europe again,' wrote Catherine, who was growing more and more anxious, in June, 1790. 'Above all I hope that the situation of the Queen will match my lively interest in her. Great courage triumphs in great perils. I see you share my opinion of M. de Lafayette. As for M. Necker, I have long ceased to hold him in regard, and I think it would have been better for France had he never meddled in her affairs.' Grimm's view, which was much the same, was expressed after the financial wizard's third and final resignation. 'This unhappy country draws nearer every day to destruction and one sees no sign of salvation. M. Necker has closed his ministerial career, and his reputation is buried in the ruins of the Monarchy. I fear the same fate awaits M. de Lafayette. I discern only people who set in motion a machine which they lack the talent and skill to control, have been carried away themselves, and are at any rate the innocent cause of the fall of France. France is the prey of a crowd of lawyers, fools masquerading as philosophers, rascals, young prigs destitute of common sense, puppets of a few bandits who do not even deserve the title of illustrious criminals.'

The more Grimm reflected on the mounting catastrophe the less he thought of Necker. 'It was his unpardonable error,' he wrote in December, 1790, 'not to double the representation of the Tiers État, which was quite right and which he could not prevent, but to have imagined that a Minister could convoke the States-General without troubling about their composition, guiding the elections, and arranging for a preponderating influence. The King could have demanded two essentials in a deputy: a minimum age of forty, since reason and reflection develop later in France than elsewhere, and the possession of property. These two conditions would have saved the Monarchy from falling into the hands of lawyers and clowns. When I recall the occasions on which this nation has aspired to govern itself, I am tempted to believe that its doom was settled when the name of the States-General was pronounced. It has manifested the same character of passion, ferocity, extravagance and puerility as on all occasions since it began to exist. We were wrong to believe that a brilliant reign of success, pride and glory had eradicated its primitive character. When, in the winter before the States-General, I detected amidst the effervescence the first germs of public madness, I used to tell them sometimes in jest: I see you wish to surpass the English and Americans; try not to fall behind the Poles! Then I thought I was making a joke. Now I would not insult a Polish Diet by comparing it to the National Assembly.' Though Grimm had never admired Mirabeau, he was shocked by his sudden death in April, 1791. 'It is generally regarded as a public misfortune,' he reported. 'Despite all the mischief he caused, the people hoped that he would preserve us from those who the Jacobins hoped would give the Monarchy its *coup de grâce*. We shall see if heaven sends some other monster as successor to save it. As for some great man, some hero to whom France might owe her salvation, I fear there is no chance. Nothing proves the madness of the nation more than the incredible honours rendered to a man generally despised during his life and who indeed could be regarded as a gaol-bird.'

Catherine was deeply grieved by the plight of Marie Antoinette. 'No one feels her sufferings more than myself,' she confided to Grimm in June, 1790. 'I love her as the dear sister of my best friend Joseph II, and I admire her courage.' Three months later she added: 'Your news of the unhappy situation of the Queen of France confirms what I knew. Much prudence is all we can advise at present. She may be sure that if I can ever be of use to her I shall do my duty. The friend and faithful ally of her brothers could have no other thought.' She knew too little of the sufferer to understand that prudence had never been one of the Queen's virtues and that she had helped to dig the grave of the French Monarchy. 'I read and re-read the *Henriade* during these troubles in France,' she added, 'and I advise the French to read it too so that these ragamuffins may learn to think.'

The Empress, like other autocrats, never realised that the *Ancien Régime* had lost its hold on the people and forfeited its claim to survive. She made no difference between the moderate reformers of 1789—ordinary men confronted by an extraordinary task, as Acton put it—and the fanatics of 1792. For her, as for Burke, the whole drama was a brutal assault on the continuity of civilisation, a monstrous rebellion against law and order, an outbreak of anarchy, the Chamber a hydra with seven hundred heads. All that was needed, she believed, was a strong hand at the helm: until the man of destiny emerged there was little hope for France. The flabbiness of the King, revealed above all in his acceptance of the Constitution of 1791, filled her with dismay. While *Régner ou*

H

*Mourir* was her watchword, Louis XVI knew how to die but not how to rule. 'One never knows if you are alive in the midst of murders and carnage,' she wrote to Grimm in January, 1791, 'now that brigands have seized power in France and are making it like Gaul in the time of Caesar. But Caesar subdued them. When will this Caesar come? Oh! he will come, you may be sure. If I were M. d'Artois or M. de Condé I would utilise these 300,000 French knights: they would save the country or I would die. All these reflections are only for your ear, for I do not want them to injure the King or Queen, whom I pity with all my heart.' The writer was a better prophet than interpreter, for as early as 1791, while France was still governed by the Constituent Assembly with its monarchist majority, she sensed the coming of Napoleon. She was equally correct in a further expectation. 'Do you know what will happen in France if they have a republic?' she wrote in April, 1791. 'Everyone will desire the return of the Monarchy. Believe me, no one likes a Court more than republicans. From what I know of France I regard her as demented, but her nimbleness of mind will throw off this malady quicker than in any other country. It seems to attack them every 200 years.' If only Henri IV could come to life again!

Catherine's friendly interest in Grimm extended to his adopted family, above all to Mme de Bueil, daughter of Mme d'Epinay. 'I see she is profoundly distressed by the misfortunes of her country. Tell her, please, that no one desires more than myself that France should regain her place in Europe; that I am tenderly attached to the King, the Queen and their fortunes; that by my calling and my duty I am royalist; that I have never seen a National Assembly or Diet do anything except make mistakes, and it certainly does little honour to human nature *en masse*. Your Gauls must have hearts of stone. How can it be that this Queen, with tears in her eyes, dares speak to no one; that this royal prisoner is forced to utter indignities which degrade him and his nation in the eyes of Europe; that there are no more liberators, no hearts moved to deliver them? Some people suggest that through Count Fersen some consoling words could be sent to the Queen, but you must judge if it would be wise.' The Empress, like many others, expected an attempt by the caged birds to escape. 'Though we have never for a moment trembled about ourselves,' she wrote on

June 1st, 1791, 'we trembled every day for almost three years for our great friend Louis XVI, for the Queen, and for the dear children whom we would like to see out of Paris. Tell me how it is that they are left there exposed to every misfortune. They must get away, for it is unbearable. Not even Charles I, I think, was exposed to such humiliation.'

The ink was hardly dry when the news of the flight to Varennes reached St Petersburg. 'The ingratitude of the nation or rather of the French populace towards the King is the most striking part of the story,' commented the Empress. 'Instinctively I feel the greatest contempt for all popular movements, and I believe that a couple of hovels seized by anyone you care to name would send all these sheep flying, and that the maddest of them would be the first to submit. I fear that the greatest obstacle to the escape of the King is in himself. Knowing her husband the Queen does not leave him, and she is right, but it complicates the problem. I have never regarded his cause as a matter of indifference to crowned heads and indeed to all established governments. You should remove your pupil and her children and husband if you can from this gulf of hell called France. To all the Frenchmen I meet I preach reunion on this one point—perfect fidelity to the King and the Monarchy, to live or die for it. Here are my parting words: I will befriend and support all who share my view.' After his acceptance of the Constitution three representatives of France were in the Russian capital at the same time—Genet, the voice of the new Constitutional Monarchy; the Marquis de Bombelles, representing the Court; Count Esterhazy, speaking for the *Émigrés*. The first, after being insulted, boycotted and spied upon, was expelled after the invasion of the Tuileries by the mob, and Bombelles was coldly treated as representing a captive King. Russian travellers in France were recalled, and French residents in Russia had to swear hatred of the Revolution and fidelity to the King. Catherine's policy, however, was to preach a crusade without the slightest intention of joining the crusaders.

Her diagnosis of the agony of a great nation and her prescription for its cure were set forth in an elaborate Memorandum in the early part of 1792, first published in its entirety in 1895. The cause of the King of France, she began, was the cause of all rulers. It was in the interest of Europe to see France resume her position as a great kingdom. Ten thousand men would suffice to march from one end of the country to the other. The modest sum it would cost could be borrowed in Genoa and repaid after the victory. The best recruiting ground for this corps would be the Rhineland, and Swiss mercenaries were easy to obtain. The expatriated knights would co-operate, and perhaps troops of some German princes might help. This corps would deliver France from bandits, restore the Monarchy, eject the impostors, punish some of the criminals, deliver the kingdom from oppression, and issue an amnesty for all who submitted. Moderation and the *juste milieu* must be observed. A fortified place, however small, might be needed as a *point d'appui*. The property of the clergy should be restored to them, the *noblesse* regain their privileges. Force should be used only in case of resistance. Many Deputies would probably come out on the side of authority and justice. Oaths imposed by force would be declared null and void as infringing the pledge of fidelity to the King. The Bishops and the Pope would relieve the kingdom from the excommunication incurred by unauthorised oaths. The authority of the Pope should be carefully respected. Foreign troops would be best to start with, though many French nobles, sword in hand, would form a squadron called *Maison du Roi*. Did not Henri IV and Louis XIV, after the gravest misfortunes, restore the national prestige? A hero prince at the head of an army easily commanded obedience. Complete anarchy never lasted long. The only solution was the restoration of the Monarchy which had existed since Clovis and which the *Cahiers* of 1789 had desired to preserve. The first and most difficult task was the liberation of the Royal Family: one shuddered to think of their plight. When the troops entered France there would be danger in the capital, which would be the last city to surrender: the war would have to be won in the provinces. The *Émigré* Princes were weary and disheartened, but the Powers must make a treaty with them. A noble and assured countenance was essential to victory. The whole of France was sick with discouragement. The restored Monarchy would revive the Parlements and the Church. The slogan of Liberty was a force to which concessions must be made, but class differences must remain. The Memorandum revealed Catherine's incorrigible ignorance of the new France: that the familiar landmarks—Crown, the *Noblesse* and the Church—had lost their prestige she was unable to believe. Ageing in mind and body, she could no longer assimilate new ideas. Montesquieu was forgotten, and Burke reigned in his place.

The letters to Grimm during the last convulsions of the Monarchy are lost, but Catherine's actions speak for themselves. She broke off official relations and ordered six weeks' mourning at Court when the King perished on the scaffold, and she received the Comte d'Artois a few weeks later. For old acquaintances like Prince Henry of Prussia who refused to condemn the revolution root and branch, she expressed her anger and contempt. Her invective invited retaliation and the Semiramis became for the *Moniteur* 'the Messalina of the North'. Yet while proclaiming the need of an organised counter-revolution and promising financial support, she took good care to limit her commitments to words, welcoming the opportunity of carving up Poland again while Austria and Prussia were fighting the Jacobins in the West. Though she closed her ports to the tricolour flag and subsidised the *Émigrés*, she never ordered a soldier to the front. She was playing a double game with consummate skill. 'I rack my brains', she frankly confessed to her private secretary Krapovitsky, 'to engage the Courts of Vienna and Berlin in the affairs of France in order to have my hands free.' The publication of her correspondence with her Ministers and Generals has revealed that her main attention was focused on Poland, Sweden and Turkey, and, at the end of her reign, on Persia. For all her loud talk about combating revolution in Western Europe, she found a more rewarding outlet for her energies by extending her dominions in the East. The more she saw of the French *Émigrés* the more she despised their quarrels and their incapacity. A vague plan for combining with Sweden to land troops in Normandy, never very seriously entertained, was abandoned when Gustavus III was murdered early in 1792. Her detestation of the Jacobins was perfectly genuine, but Warsaw and Constantinople were nearer than Paris. Not till her son mounted the throne did Russia despatch troops to the West.

The régime during Catherine's closing years was as repressive as any in Europe, and the few Russian Intellectuals fared badly. Never again did she speak of her *âme républicaine*. Novikoff, Russia's leading publicist, the founder of the popular Press and the outstanding figure among Russian Freemasons, was arrested and imprisoned. Raditcheff, author of the celebrated *Voyage de St. Petersbourg à Moscou*, which complained that there was no liberty in Russia and forecast an insurrection, was banished to Siberia. Only La Harpe, the Swiss tutor of her grandsons, was spared for a time, despite the efforts of the *Émigrés* to dislodge him. Though she called him M. Le Jacobin, she believed that he would do no harm. But he too was soon packed off with a gift of 10,000 roubles and a decoration. It required an effort to remember that she had ever sat at the feet of the *Philosophes*.

The withdrawal of Prussia from the unprofitable conflict with the new France of the *Marseillaise* infuriated her no less than Burke. 'Here is the King of Prussia about to conclude an infamous peace with the regicides,' she wrote bitterly in April, 1795. 'If he does, one may say that next to Jesus Christ no one has made a greater sacrifice, for he loses reputation, honour, good faith, perhaps his repose, and will become the first dupe in Europe.' Her only comfort was that the republican experiment could not possibly endure. 'I maintain that only absolute power will please the French people, and that any other kind of government could not end the troubles. France is sick of republicanism which has done her so much harm. And then a republic always ends up in monarchy.' A few days later came the expected news of the great surrender. 'A courier brings a letter from the King of Prussia announcing peace with the regicide bandits and the scum of the human race. The great Henry has pushed his nephew into breaking his treaties with the Emperor, England and myself.' She was scarcely less incensed with the Princes and the *Émigrés*, whom she accused of wasting her subsidies. The Comte de Provence was a pedant, Artois a mere stage hero, Calonne a windbag. Her last letter to Grimm, dated October 20, 1796, only a few weeks before her death, was as full as ever of vigour and vituperation. The King of Prussia, whom she had disliked and despised ever since his visit in 1780, is denounced as the friend of the regicides. 'I preach and shall continue to preach common cause among all kings against the destroyers of thrones and society, despite all the adherents of the miserable rival system, and we shall see which side wins.'

Catherine lived and died in the conviction that the best form of government was Enlightened Autocracy as practised by Frederick, Joseph and herself. In the middle of her reign she had drawn up what she deemed a suitable inscription for her grave. 'In 1744 she went to Russia to marry Peter III. Eighteen years of tedium and solitude caused her to read many books. When she came to the throne she wished to do good and strove to introduce happiness, freedom and prosperity.' It was the truth but not the whole truth. Never for a moment was she assailed by doubts as to the excellence of her work or by apprehensions that it might not endure. She could never have enough compliments, but she felt they were fully deserved. She was the only human being ever flattered by Frederick the Great, but he rated her political judgment far above that of the impulsive Joseph II. Looking back on her eventful career, she might well feel that she had been a success, a sentiment widely shared beyond the frontiers of her realm. 'Obviously the country has changed out of all recognition since the beginning of the century,' wrote the Emperor Joseph II on his first visit in 1780. 'It has so to speak been reborn. It is rich in territory and resources, and its situation is impregnable.' Yet like most of her contemporaries she could not see far ahead. She expected the emergence of a Caesar in France and the ultimate restoration of the Bourbon monarchy, but her vision was too circumscribed to anticipate a political and social earthquake in her own land. No one need blame her for accepting the prevailing ideology of her time, and she deserves a place among the rulers who honestly tried to play the exacting part of *le premier domestique de l'état*. What she overlooked was the extreme improbability of their respective countries throwing up a never-failing supply of such gifted persons as themselves, and the dire results of the concentration of authority if power should fall into unworthy hands. With her death the era of Enlightened Autocracy passed into history and the era of the common man came within sight.

*Bibliographical Note.*—The serious study of the reign became possible towards the close of the nineteenth century with the voluminous publications of the Imperial Russian Historical Society, supplemented by the revelations from the rich Woronzoff archives. The imposing torso of Bilbassoff ends in 1764. The first critical survey of the whole period was supplied by Alexander

Brückner's *Catherina die Zweite*. Waliszewski's better known
volumes, *Le Roman d'une Impératrice* and *Autour d'un Trône*, are
more readable but somewhat less scholarly. Of the smaller biographies Miss Gladys Scott Thompson's *Catherine the Great and the
Expansion of Russia* is the latest and best. No critical edition has
appeared of the *Mémoires* published by Alexander Herzen in
London in 1859. The correspondence with Grimm fills Vols. 13
and 23 of the Imperial Russian Historical Society's series. The
correspondence with Voltaire and the Instructions for a Code
should be read in Reddaway's annotated edition, *Documents of
Catherine the Great*. The correspondence with Potemkin appeared
in 1934, with the Prince de Ligne in 1936, with Sir Charles Hanbury-Williams in 1928. The best introduction to Russian studies
is Sumner's *Survey of Russian History*. The eighteenth-century
background may be studied in Kluchevsky, *History of Russia*
(English translation, Vol. 5); Sumner; *Peter the Great*; Waliszew-
ski, *Pierre le Grand*; Waliszewski, *L'Héritage de Pierre le Grand*;
Waliszewski, *La Dernière des Romanoff, Elizabeth I*; Nisbet Bain,
*The Daughter of Peter the Great*; Nisbet Bain, *Peter the Third*.
Among the biographies of Catherine's friends may be noted
George Soloveytchik, *Potemkin*; Montgomery Hyde, *Princess
Dashkow*; Edmond Scherer, *Melchior Grimm*; and Perey et Maugras,
*Mme d'Epinay*. Light was thrown on the little known closing
years of Grimm by the *Correspondance Inédite (1794–1801) du Baron
Grimm au Comte de Findlater*, 1934. For Paul see Morane, *Paul
avant l'Avenement*; Waliszewski, *Paul the First*; and Rappoport,
*The Curse of the Romanoffs*.

# 2

## FOUR FRENCH SALONS

### I. *Mme Geoffrin*

THE salon, a typical French institution, was invented by Mme de Rambouillet in the first half of the seventeenth century and reached the summit of its influence in the second half of the eighteenth. In no other land was the intellectual life of a great nation so concentrated in the capital, and nowhere was the desire for the exchange of ideas so deeply felt. French, declared the witty Abbé Galiani, was the language of the most sociable people in the world, who talked more than they thought, who had to talk in order to think and only thought in order to talk. Paris, he added, was the café of Europe. The time was long past when Molière could rely on applause in poking fun at the *Précieuses Ridicules*. To create a salon two conditions were essential: a tactful hostess and one or two literary lions who could be relied on for regular attendance. If the *salonnière* had room to entertain a large number of guests and could afford well-served dinners, so much the better, but the experience of Mlle de Lespinasse proved that money and good food were not indispensable. Everything depended on the intelligence and the good sense of the lady herself. Hostesses, like poets, are born, not made.

The vogue of the salon in eighteenth-century France was not due exclusively to the synchronisation of a galaxy of gifted women and an exceptional supply of master minds. France was governed by a lazy and dissolute monarch who lived on the rapidly diminishing capital bequeathed by the *Roi Soleil*. The bourgeoisie were advancing to the centre of the stage, criticising traditional institutions, ridiculing inherited beliefs and dreaming of a brave new world. The France of the nineteenth and twentieth centuries—sceptical, empirical, equalitarian—was born in Paris between the death of Louis XIV in 1715 and the meeting of the States-General in 1789; and the *Philosophes* and *beaux esprits* who adorned the salons stood round its cradle. For the Revolution began in the world of thought several decades before it took shape in institutional changes and social reform. Though the Press was fairly free and arrests were relatively infrequent, critics of the Court and the Church lived under the shadow of imprisonment. In Russia, to quote the familiar witticism, it was a case of despotism tempered by assassination, in France of despotism tempered by epigram. Voltaire had been in the Bastille, Diderot spent three weeks at Vincennes, and Marmontel was locked up for eleven days for a satire which he had not composed. While the Intelligentsia in the France of Richelieu and Colbert busied themselves mainly with *belles-lettres*, the subjects of Louis XV and Louis XVI added philosophy and sociology, economics and politics to poetry and drama. The men and women who foregathered in Paris every week and sometimes almost every day talked of everything in heaven and earth, and could let off steam without fear of betrayal or espionage. With the cool breeze of the *Aufklärung* sweeping across Eruope, visitors from many lands who flocked to *la ville lumière* coveted invitations to the circles where they could listen to the most brilliant talkers in the world. In the seventeenth century the Court of Versailles was the magnet, in the eighteenth the salons of Paris. 'Paris est ma patrie' wrote the Abbé Galiani at the close of his diplomatic service. A visit to France was an essential part of the education of every young aristocrat.

Mme Geoffrin and Mme du Deffand, Mlle de Lespinasse and Mme Necker differed more widely than their respective *clientèles*, for most of the star performers frequented more than one drawing-room. A certain rivalry was inevitable, but it was generally conceded that the name of Mme Geoffrin, the least intellectual of the four, stood at the head of the list. How this plain, reserved and rather conventional bourgeoise, whose father was *valet de chambre* to the Dauphine, who never learned to spell correctly, who rarely opened a book, who displayed no obvious charm, who talked little and had not much to say, attracted the most eminent writers in France and in almost every case retained their friendship till the end of her life is one of the romances of social and literary history. Her wealth was a great help, but money never made a salon. Alone of the four she became a European figure, and no subsequent *salonnière* has equalled her fame. That she owed a large part of her celebrity to the fact that she was the Egeria of the *Encyclopédistes* is the more surprising since she took little interest in politics and philosophy, and her religious convictions were mildly conservative. Though too cool a nature to inspire ardent sentiments, she earned a measure of affection and enjoyed universal respect. No prominent woman of her time was less colourful or had fewer faults.

Losing her parents in early childhood, Marie Thérèse Rodet was brought up by a devout grandmother, who treated her kindly but neglected her education and married her in her fifteenth year to a dull, good-tempered and wealthy business man of forty-eight. M. Geoffrin inherited money and a roomy house from his first wife and increased his fortunes in the glass trade. Two children were born, a daughter who meant little to her mother throughout life, and a son who died in childhood. He was a blameless husband, but there was not the slightest pretence of love on either side, and his mental horizon was strictly bounded by his business interests. When his child-wife grew to maturity she felt a great void and looked round for some means of filling it. Since visitors rarely came to the house, she starved for companionship and mental stimulus, but not till she was over forty was there a prospect of escape from her gilded cage.

A near neighbour was the Marquise de Tencin, like Mme du Deffand an ex-mistress of the Regent, who after the years of gallantry collected a little 'menagerie' of celebrities with the aged Fontenelle, Montesquieu and Marmontel at their head. No one was less likely to attract Mme Geoffrin than the woman who had abandoned her illegitimate son, afterwards the celebrated d'Alembert, on the steps of a church and left his father, the Chevalier Destouches, to provide for his maintenance and education. Though there could be no intimacy between them, the strict-living bourgeoise felt grateful for her invitations and for unlocking the door to a wider world. She studied the technique of the hostess and before long she was planning a salon of her own. 'Never repulse a man', she was advised; 'nine out of ten do not

care a halfpenny for you, but the tenth may prove useful'. Soon,
however, she was able to pick and choose, for the material was
ready to hand. Since Mme de Tencin was growing old, why
should she not induce the *habitués* to transfer their patronage to
her own spacious mansion when the hour should strike? Why,
indeed, should she wait for a funeral? She invited a few writers
and artists to drop in till her circle grew large enough to start
weekly dinners. Mme de Tencin noted what was going on without resenting it, for her old friends continued their visits. *Savez-
vous ce que la Geoffrin vient faire ici? Elle vient voir ce qu'elle pourra
recueillir de mon inventaire.* When she died in 1749 there was nothing
to prevent them migrating *en masse*. At the age of ninety, drained
of all emotions yet full of wit, Fontenelle became the *doyen* of the
new salon as he had long been of the old, entertaining the guests
for a further decade with lively reminiscences of the France of
Louis XIV.

Mme Geoffrin neither found nor expected encouragement from
her family. Her husband, who had disapproved her visits to
Mme de Tencin and disliked still more an invasion of intellectuals with whom he had nothing in common, resented the
expense of entertaining a lot of 'parasites'. 'Every time my mother
asked for money,' relates the daughter, 'there were terrible scenes
and I feared for her life.' The stronger will prevailed, and M.
Geoffrin finally accepted his defeat with a good grace, helped to
prepare the menus, and appeared at the weekly dinners. When
a newcomer noticed his continued absence he innocently interrogated the hostess. 'Qui était ce vieux monsieur qui se plaçait au
bout de la table et ne disait rien?' 'C'était mon mari,' replied the
widow without a trace of emotion; 'il est mort.' The subject was
dropped and the old man of eighty-four faded out of the picture,
leaving behind him a roomy mansion and a substantial fortune
which was put to good account.

The new *salonnière* had a harder and longer struggle with her
clever daughter. Mme de la Ferté-Imbault was little more than
a shadow till the Marquis de Ségur utilised the family papers in
his delightful book *Le Royaume de la Rue St Honoré*. Though
differing as widely in temperament as in opinion, they were alike
in their high moral standards and were equally deserving of
respect. Since Mme Geoffrin had been assigned as a child to a

man for whom she never cared, she and her husband saw nothing amiss in compelling their wealthy daughter at an almost equally early age to marry a poor, elderly, ugly and disagreeable Marquis. After a few years of loveless partnership he died, but the attractive young widow never tried again. She returned to her parent's home, where she lived her independent life in her own apartments. While the mother welcomed the *Encyclopédistes* to her table without sharing their anti-clerical ideology, the daughter, as conservative in religion as in politics, hated the sound of their names. Though there was little open friction, the lack of domestic warmth increased Mme Geoffrin's dependence on the salon which became the main purpose of her life.

She differed from the other *salonnières* in her liking for the arts. In the field of literature and philosophy she could do little but listen, but in the world of art she had a mind of her own. When she noticed that the artists always drew apart at her receptions she arranged a weekly dinner for them on Monday. She was fond of china, bronzes, tapestries, sculpture and furniture, but pictures appealed to her still more. Vanloo, Vernet, Boucher, Latour and many others met at her table and found in her a generous patron no less than a faithful friend. She was ready to criticise as well as to praise. When she complained of a picture by Greuze in the Salon of 1769, the irate artist threatened to immortalise her as a schoolmarm with a whip.

Of the four leading salons hers alone possessed a distinct ideological tinge. The dominant influence in the intellectual life of France was embodied in the *Encyclopédie*, the first instalment of which appeared in 1751. The object of this manifesto in seventeen volumes was to present the whole range of science, history and philosophy as visualised by the *Aufklärung*. Voltaire, the most celebrated of the contributors, had made the capital too hot for him and thought it wiser to live abroad, but the other standardbearers were *habitués*. Among the lions were Diderot, the editor, and d'Alembert, his chief of staff, both of them brilliant conversationalists. If Bayle's *Dictionnaire Critique* may be said to have inaugurated the *Aufklärung* in France and the *saeculum rationalisticum* in Europe by its challenge to tradition, the *Encyclopédie* was its most imposing achievement. Politics were kept in the background, not merely for fear of the long arm of the State but because the attack on orthodoxy and the Jesuits, then at the height of their influence, exposed quite sufficient surface to retaliation. The public burning of eight volumes in 1759 reminded the team that they were skating on very thin ice.

It is one of the paradoxes of Mme Geoffrin's career that, despite her own conventional church-going, she helped to finance and indeed saved from collapse an enterprise which preached philosophic materialism. The explanation is to be found in the fact that she was far more interested in her *bêtes* than in their ideas. Moreover, a *salonnière* in quest of celebrities had no choice, for the age of Bossuet and Fénelon was over and most of the *Intelligentsia* had abandoned dogmatic Christianity. Voltaire and Rousseau were Deists, but the most fashionable philosophy was the crude materialism of d'Holbach and Helvétius. She stood by the *habitués* of her salon, from which no one was banished if he observed her simple rules of *bon ton*. When the vicious Duc de Richelieu, who loved to boast of his latest conquests, tried to enter the magic circle, he found his match. '*Soyons aimables*' was the order of the day. The queen of the highbrows frowned on scandalous talk. No one knew better how to keep her guests within bounds of decorum and to prevent anyone from monopolising the conversation. In the words of Sainte-Beuve, it was the best administered salon of the time. She possessed the secret of getting the best out of her circle and giving everyone his chance. 'I compare myself to a little round tree with branches on all sides,' she remarked; 'I share a little of everything and know a little of everything.' She was a blend of kindliness, caution and good sense. In a pasage of humorous exaggeration Grimm enumerated a formidable list of subjects which were taboo. 'She desires it to be known that she cannot permit conversation about internal affairs, or foreign affairs, or affairs of the Court or the town, nor of the affairs of North or South, East or West, nor of politics or finance, or peace or war, or religion or government, or theology or metaphysics, or grammar or music, or, in fact, of any other matter.' Despite such limitations it was a tolerant autocracy. Abbé Galiani, the witty little secretary of the Neopolitan Legation, who called himself 'votre petite chose,' described by Marmontel as the head of Machiavelli on the shoulders of Harlequin, kept the table in a ripple of laughter, while Count

Creutz, the popular Swedish Ambassador, and other diplomats opened windows on a wider world. In the words of Abbé Morellet foreigners felt that they would not have known Paris if they had not been her guests. King Gustavus of Sweden and Catherine the Great corresponded with her, but as a bourgeoise she was ignored by the dull French Court. Only men were present at the Monday and Wednesday dinners, but women were admitted to the *petits soupers*.

The memoirs and correspondence of the time help us to visualise the celebrated salon. A vivid portrait of the hostess was painted by Lady Hervey, widow of Queen Caroline's clever friend, in a letter to Hume on his first visit to Paris. 'There are few heads naturally better than hers; there is no heart that can surpass the friendly warmth of hers. Unimproved by books, of which she has read but few, her strong natural sense and uncommon sagacity owes all its experience to her knowledge of the world. I never knew anyone seize every part of a character so soon or paint it so strongly. She has a great deal of wit, and particularly excels in the narrative, which is always short and lively. The vain, the affected, the worthless may fear her, but the foibles of her friends and even of those acquaintances who frequent her are safe. Nothing escapes her observation, but nothing transpires from her to their prejudice; if she once loves anyone (and when she says she does, she may be believed), she never gives them time to apply to her to be of any use to them. Her attention and sagacity soon make her perceive how she may be so, and that perception is immediately followed by her endeavours to serve her friend, which from her address, abilities and perseverance seldom prove ineffectual.' Horace Walpole, to whom Lady Hervey also gave an introduction, was no less impressed. 'I have been with Mme Geoffrin several times,' he reported, 'and I think she has one of the best understandings I ever met, and more knowledge of the world.' A few days later she visited him during a bad attack of gout. 'I could have sworn it had been my Lady Hervey, she was so good to me. It was with so much sense, information, instruction and correction. The manner of the latter charms me. I never saw anybody that catches one's faults and impositions so quick, explains them to one so clearly, and convinces one so easily. I never liked to be set right before.' Walpole, however, never felt quite at home in the company of the *Philosophes*, and soon transferred his favours to the rival salon of Mme du Deffand.

Mme Geoffrin, testifies Garat, lacked cultivation and education but not information, which she derived from her thoughts and heart. Amidst all the currents and agitations of the most tumultuous of European capitals, with all its enthusiasms and animosities, she retained the full flavour of her character and the mastery of her soul. Surrounded by men of genius who dominated European thought, she kept her independence intact. She whom a king called his *maman* and celebrities their mother, with so many means of indulging in ostentation and even a kind of glory, preferred the ways of simplicity. She used her fortune as a trust for the unfortunate for whose needs she was always on the look-out— artists and men of letters so often impoverished by the very talents which contribute to the capital of nations and the treasure of kings. It was the art and the occupation of her life to discover the real needs of men of merit and to assist without injuring their pride. She put aside her personal affairs in order to devote herself wholly to her secret charities, which she managed with skill. Here she wrote well and spoke with eloquence, abandoning the reserve which formed her first rule of conduct and was doubtless the most trying, since she had to keep in check both a great impetuosity of reason and a great sensibility of heart. Though a salon of writers and artists, savants and foreigners was, like a democracy, always apt to get out of hand, hers had no need to be governed, as some have suggested, by Fontenelle. Though in the heat of discussions she intervened when her guests raised their voices, it was unnecessary to restore order for she averted disorder.

The most finished portrait is to be found in the entertaining Memoirs of Marmontel, Editor of the official *Mercure*, Historiographer of France, Secrétaire Perpétuel of the Académie Française, an ever welcome guest in Parisian drawing-rooms. There is little warmth in the colouring, for he was never one of her closest friends, though he lodged in her spacious mansion for twelve years; but there is full recognition of her solid qualities, which earned the respect of her circle and the affection of those who knew her best. 'Possessing sufficient means to make her home the rendezvous of literature and the arts, Mme Geoffrin instituted two weekly dinners, on Monday for the artists, on Wednesday for the men of letters. Though she possessed no inkling either of art or of literature and had never read nor learned anything except at random she felt no embarrassment in their company. She had the tact only to join in the conversation on matters she thoroughly understood; listening politely and without signs of boredom when it strayed beyond her range. She excelled in the art of presiding over and controlling these two groups, setting limits to their liberty and reining them back in case of need by a word, a gesture, as if by an invisible thread. 'Allons, voilà qui est bien' was the gentle formula which they all understood.

'Hers was a singular character difficult to portray because it was all in half-tones and nuances; though very decided, there were no salient traits. She was kind though not tender; beneficent but without the charms of benevolence; eager to succour the unfortunate, but without seeing them for fear of being upset; a steady, faithful and even zealous friend, but timid in the service of her beneficiaries for fear of impairing her credit or her repose. She was simple in her tastes, her clothes, her furniture, though it was a studied simplicity. She was modest in her demeanour and her manners, but with a decided touch of pride and even a little vainglory. Nothing flattered her so much as association with the great. On her rare visits to their houses she was ill at ease, but she attracted them to her own with an imperceptible flattery, and her natural manner, blending respect and familiarity, was a triumph of art. Always uninhibited, she never crossed the boundary of good taste to be on good terms with heaven; without breaking with her circle she practised a kind of clandestine piety, and went to mass. She disliked every sort of display, and took the greatest pains to make no noise. She ardently desired celebrity and consideration in the world, but of a discreet character.

'It was easier for her to open her purse than her mouth. It was one of her maxims that vigorous refutation of hostile criticism of her friends merely stung the critic into sharper attacks. What she most appreciated in a friend was a prudence which never led into trouble. With a certain friend, she remarked, one had no anxieties, for no one ever complained of him, and thus he never required defence. This was a warning for the more ebullient members of her circle like myself; if any of her friends was in danger or trouble,

I

whether he was in the right or the wrong, her first instinct was to blame them. One day I ventured to tell her that her friends ought to be infallible and always to have good luck. One of her foibles was to mix herself up in their affairs, to be their confidant, their adviser and their guide. In confiding to her one's secrets and allowing her to direct and sometimes to lecture one we could be sure of striking her most sensitive chord; but lack of docility, however respectful, at once produced a chill in the atmosphere, and she made one aware of her annoyance. It is true enough that in order to live according to the rules of prudence one could wish no better guide. *Savoir faire* was her master quality: on everything else her ideas were superficial and commonplace. But in the study of manners and customs, in knowledge of men and above all of women, she was profound and could teach valuable lessons. Thus if there was an element of *amour-propre* in this proffering of advice and guidance, there was also kindliness, the desire to be useful and sincere friendship. Her mind, though trained extensively in social contacts, was shrewd, just and penetrating. An instinctive taste and sense of fitness fashioned her talk. She wrote correctly and simply but like a woman who had been badly educated. Her real talent lay in description, and she used it to entertain her guests, though quite artlessly. To win her favour one had to steer a middle course between negligence and assiduity; empressement she detested. Even from the most amiable society she only cared to take what she needed, at her own time and convenience.'

Marmontel frankly explains why he never found his way to her heart. 'I kept in my place, neither too forward nor too timid, gay, natural, even a little free, generally liked. Though I lived in her house I was not one of her favourites: not that she disapproved the little tales and jokes with which I enlivened the company. But I was not sufficiently inclined to ask and follow her advice, and she was never quite sure as to my prudence. Though kind and considerate, she was always on her guard; and I, equally reserved with her, tried to please her but declined to be bossed.' Despite the lack of cordiality Marmontel was not only a guest at the Monday and Wednesday dinners but at the smaller and more informal and more intimate 'little suppers'; for when he was present the conversation never flagged. Even when he changed his lodgings they remained on friendly terms to the end. 'Yet I may as well be perfectly frank:

her society lacked one of the charms to which I attach supreme importance—liberty of discussion. With her gentle *Voilà qui est bien,* she tried to keep us on the lead; and I went elsewhere to be more at one's ease.' Though similar complaints were to be made a few years later by some of the *Philosophes* who thronged the salon of Mme Necker, there was never any lack of candidates for admission to these charmed circles either among those who were climbing the ladder of fame or those who had reached the top.

The brightest luminary and the most welcome of guests was d'Alembert. In 1760, at the age of forty-three, he analysed his own character in one of the elaborate portraits in the third person so much in vogue. 'M. d'Alembert is nothing remarkable to look at, either good or bad. His conversation is serious or gay according to his mood, often lacking in sequence but never wearisome or pedantic. One would never guess that he devotes most of his time to grave studies, for his talk is never too high-brow for the company, and thus everyone feels at ease with him. Sometimes he is like a child, and the contrast between this schoolboy gaiety and his scientific reputation, for what it is worth, makes him generally liked. He rarely strives to please and merely tries to entertain those he likes. He is not contentious and is never sharp, not because he lacks convictions but because he has no urge to convert people to his ideas. Moreover, except in the exact sciences, hardly anything seems to him clear enough to prevent differences of opinion. The principal characteristic of his mind is precision and objectivity. To the study of geometry he brought some talent and flair which made his name at an early age. This left him time to cultivate *belles-lettres* with some success.

'Immersed in work and solitude till the age of twenty-five he entered society very late, never cared much for it, never tried to learn its usages and idiom, and perhaps he is a little vain of despising it; but he is never impolite, because he is neither coarse nor rough. Compliments embarrass him because he cannot improvise suitable replies. His talk lacks gallantry and grace; when he says nice things it is only because he means them. Impatient and irascible, everything which wounds him produces a lively impression which he cannot control but which quickly evaporates. At bottom he is very gentle, very easy to get on with, fairly easy to lead, provided he does not suspect the intention; for his love of independence is a passion, and he has called himself the slave of his liberty. Some think him ill-natured because pretentious fools bore him, but he could not bear to hurt anyone, even those who have tried their best to harm him. Experience has taught him to distrust mankind in the mass but not individuals. Without family or ties, thrown on himself, accustomed from infancy to a narrow and obscure but free existence, and luckily with some talents and few passions, he found solace in study and in his natural gaiety. He despises names and titles and is more inclined to appreciate what is beneath than what is above him. No one is less jealous of talents and success, provided there seems to be no charlatanism nor presumption. Though he is not so vain as many think, he is very susceptible at the moment to praise or blame, but reflection soon steadies him and then he despises both. A man of letters should be very careful of what he writes, fairly careful what he does, and relatively careless of what he says. No one is more disinterested, but since he has neither needs nor fantasies, these virtues merit no praise. Since he really loves very few people and is not very affectionate even with them, those who do not know him well think him little capable of friendship. On the contrary, no one cares more about the joys and sorrows of his friends; he loses his sleep and peace of mind and is ready for any sacrifice. His sensitive soul loves to respond to all the gentle sentiments; that is why he is at once very gay and very prone to melancholy. After devoting his early years to study and reflection, he has learned that knowledge cannot satisfy his heart. His soul needs to be filled but not tormented. He desires only gentle emotions, for shocks wear him out.' The truth of the portrait is not in doubt, and it helps to explain why no *salonnière* felt her circle to be complete without including the most attractive and the most respected of the *Philosophes*.

During the third quarter of the century Anglomania was at its height in France. When Hume, equally celebrated as a philosopher and historian, took up his post as Secretary to the British Embassy in Paris in 1763 after the Seven Years War, he was amazed at the warmth of his reception. 'I have been three days at Paris and two at Fontainebleau,' he reported to his friend Adam Smith, 'and I have everywhere met with the most extraordinary honours which the most exorbitant vanity could desire. The compliments of Dukes and Marshals and Ambassadors go for nothing with me at present: I retain a relish for no kind of flattery but that which comes from the ladies. Even Mme Pompadour's civilities were, if possible, exceeded by those of the Duchesse de Choiseul, wife of the Favourite and Prime Minister. There is not a courtier in France who would not have been transported with joy to have half these obliging things said to him by either of these great ladies; but, what is more extraordinary, both of them, as far as I could conjecture, have read with some care all my writings that have been translated, that is almost all my writings.' A month later he reported in similar terms to another Scottish friend, William Robertson, the historian of the Emperor Charles V. 'Do you ask me about my course of life? I can only say that I eat nothing but ambrosia, drink nothing but nectar, breathe nothing but incense, and tread on nothing but flowers. Every man I meet, and still more every lady, would think they were wanting in the most indispensable duty if they did not make me a long and elaborate harangue in my praise.' The writers, he added, were very agreeable; all of them living in entire or almost entire harmony amongst themselves, and quite irreproachable in their morals. After a year at the Embassy he was more in love with Paris than ever. 'I am a citizen of the world; but if I were to adopt any country, it would be that in which I live at present and from which I am determined never to depart unless a war drives me into Switzerland or Italy.' Paris, he declared after two years, was the most agreeable city in Europe and suited him best. Like most other visitors, he found d'Alembert particularly to his taste. He had spent some years in France as a young man, and his French was good enough to pass muster though not so perfect as that of Gibbon. All that was necessary to unlock the doors of the salons was celebrity and a tolerable command of the language, for English was an almost unknown tongue.

Among the foreign visitors to Paris who were invited or invited themselves to receptions in 1753 was Count Poniatowski, accompanied by his son. When the old soldier returned to Poland he begged the kindly hostess to mother the handsome, pleasant and intelligent lad who had just come of age. She took her responsibilities seriously, and when his frivolities landed him in prison she bought him out. Thus began the most valued connection of her life, for Stanislas Poniatowski's gratitude for her kindness during his five months' stay ripened into a platonic friendship which lasted till her death. Their correspondence, published by the Comte de Mouy in 1875, revealed a new Mme Geoffrin and a relationship at once romantic and honourable to both. He addressed her as *Maman* and signed himself *votre fils*; she, though old enough to be his mother, wrote to him in terms of tenderness which she adopted neither with her daughter nor anyone else. The large volume is all the more valuable since, unlike Mme du Deffand, she had no love for writing letters, and with this significant exception almost all her correspondence is lost. The verdict of the best of her biographers, the Marquis de Ségur, 'kind rather than loving,' is surely inadequate. That with her 'son' she for once let herself go suggests an unsatisfied craving for a little warmth and love.

A few years after his visit to Paris the young aristocrat, whose mother was a Czartoryski, was appointed Polish Minister to St Petersburg at the age of twenty-five. He became the lover of the Grand Duchess Catherine and was rewarded by the throne of Poland when Augustus III died in 1763. Though there was nothing of the snob in Mme Geoffrin, it was natural that she should welcome the elevation of her *protégé* and dream of a visit to Warsaw. 'Mon fils, mon roi,' she wrote in ecstasy; 'I alone can say that.' 'Congratulations on the elevation of your son,' wrote Catherine, a friendly correspondent. 'How he became king I know not. Providence willed it, and his kingdom is to be congratulated. They could have no one more fitted to make them happy.'

For a woman who had never travelled more than a few miles from her home to contemplate a journey of 1,000 miles over atrocious roads seemed to her friends fantastic, but when the young sovereign welcomed the plan she determined to carry it out. 'I will die in your arms of joy, pleasure and love,' she wrote. At first he was unenthusiastic, but later he confessed 'Je vous désire passionnément'. The advice of Grimm, who described himself as 'le sous-doyen de vos amoureux', to take the Berlin route was rejected because she disapproved of Frederick, who in her eyes was neither great nor virtuous and disliked women. Starting off in a roomy carriage with two maids in May, 1766, she arrived eighteen days later at Vienna, where she was welcomed with almost royal honours by Maria Theresa, the Emperor Joseph and Kaunitz, the main architect of the Austro-French alliance and formerly Austrian

Ambassador at Paris. 'Je crois rêver', she wrote home. Her flattering reception at Vienna, where she spent four days, genuinely surprised her, made her journey the talk of Europe, and was enough to turn the head of a woman with less poise. At Schönbrunn she saw Marie Antoinette, a child of eleven, 'belle comme une ange', to whom she was informally presented a few years later in the Louvre.

Ten days more of execrable roads, filthy inns, ill-cooked food, and she had reached her goal. 'J'ai été très heureuse et très amusée à Vienne,' she wrote to her daughter, 'mais ici je suis dans les délices.' 'He is charming and is adored by all his entourage.' 'La reine-mère de Pologne,' as Mme du Deffand called her, was lodged in the Palace and saw or wrote to her host every day. Her letters home, which were widely circulated in Paris, described the warmth of her welcome and her pride in the endeavours of her 'son' to promote the welfare of his country. The visit lasted three months, but the radiant dawn was soon overcast, for reasons which the correspondence fails to reveal. She may have wounded his pride by comments on the misery of the peasantry, the selfishness of the nobility and the intolerance of the Church. 'If I have a complaint to make,' he wrote, 'it is your remark: It seems to me that I have stayed long enough. No, Maman, I swear it.' The wound was plastered over and the parting took place amid demonstrations of affection. Indeed it was only now that he addressed her as *tu*. 'It would have made me die of love and joy a few months ago,' she replies, 'but I have found such a great difference between words and actions that I regard this *tu* as an illusion of Satan. Yet all my discontents have not altered my old feelings, which nothing could destroy.' Though the glamour was gone the correspondence continued, and on her death-bed she wrote to him with trembling hands: 'Je vous aime de tout mon coeur.' She had always loved him much more than he loved her. The Tsarina, who expected her to extend her journey to St Petersburg, never forgave her for neglecting the opportunity, and before long ceased to write.

Friends wondered whether the woman who had been feted at Vienna and Warsaw would settle down to the old routine. 'La Princesse Geoffrinska arriva avant-hier, engraissée, embellie,' reported Mme du Deffand to Horace Walpole. 'Elle a trouvé la fontaine de jouvence. Toute la France est empressée à lui rendre hommage. Elle ne peut plus mourir que d'une réplétion de gloire.' Such apprehensions were needless, for she resumed her dinners and receptions as if there had been no break. She enjoyed her celebrity but never suffered from swelled head and never attempted to hide her years. It was her Indian Summer. She welcomed an unceasing flow of celebrities from foreign parts, among them Benjamin Franklin, and added new members to her circle, among them Condorcet and La Harpe. The youthful prodigy, Mozart, played to her. A delightful letter of thanks to Hume, whom she called 'mon gros drôle', for a sumptuously bound copy of the translation of his *History of England* chided him for making a revolution in her drab shelves. 'You must have a furious opinion of your works to clothe them in such beautiful garments.' Her gifts in money and kind were innumerable, and those most in need received an allowance for life. Burigny, her majordomo, served her with loyal devotion for forty years.

Her goodness of heart was illustrated by her ready welcome to Mlle de Lespinasse when she was evicted by Mme du Deffand, not merely because she was the friend of d'Alembert, but for her own sake. Though women were rarely to be seen in her salon, the newcomer proved a general favourite and expressed her gratitude by touching devotion. She and d'Alembert visited her every day, and sometimes twice a day. 'Remember your promise to me to dine with that excellent woman,' wrote Julie to Guibert. 'She is only kept alive by the pleasure she finds in giving and forgiving. I love her with all my heart, and I think that proves that I still cherish virtue. My friend, let us love her. She will add to your happiness and will sustain me in my troubles.' The high favour they enjoyed was resented by Mme Ferté, who suspected them of trying to persuade her mother to divert part of her fortune from herself. When the younger woman passed away at the age of forty-three, the broken-hearted d'Alembert found his chief comfort in the sympathy of their common friend.

Taking a lively interest in the fortunes of her circle, Mme Geoffrin occasionally volunteered unwelcome advice. Suard married a penniless girl despite the warnings of his hostess, and in the belief that his wife might not be welcomed he ceased to attend the salon. When, however, the hostess met the young bride at the house of a common friend she surrendered to her charm, expressed regret for having advised against the marriage, and took her to her heart. 'She dislikes the unhappy and even the sight of other people's misfortunes,' declared the Abbé Galiani, 'but there are good reasons. She has a sensitive heart, she is elderly, she wants to keep her health and peace of mind. When she learns I am happy she will love me.' The verdict was unjust. How numerous were her benefactions was realised only when her will and her papers were examined after her death. 'A certain celestial flame is lacking,' complains Sainte-Beuve; 'one never sees in the distance the blue sky nor the light of the stars.' 'Ce n'était que raison cette âme,' echo the de Goncourts. Such critics were unaware of the letters to King Stanislas. The illumination, it is true, was not of blinding intensity, but there was no flickering. Caprice was not in her, for good sense was wedded to a motherly heart. She did not like her circle or herself to be upset in any way, records Abbé Morellet, and was careful to avoid trouble with the Government; and only those who knew her well realised the store of kindliness half hidden by her austerity and reserve. The only worry of her closing years was the posthumous publication of the *Lettres Familières* of Montesquieu containing some discourteous remarks on his old hostess. The jealousy of Mme du Deffand, whom she dismissed as *une méchante bête*, caused her no distress.

In 1777, at the age of seventy-seven, Mme Geoffrin had a stroke, and the salon closed its doors. Though she lingered for a year she no longer ordered her own life, for her strong-willed daughter assumed control. When the faithful d'Alembert, who was often at her bedside, noticed a copy of *The Imitation of Christ* on the table, he tactlessly advised her to substitute fairy tales or the *Arabian Nights*. Mme Ferté wrote an angry letter telling him to behave himself lest she would have to forbid his visits, adding roughly, 'She has always loved God more than you and your like'. Soon most of her old friends were excluded from the room where the bedridden old lady, paralysed in arms and legs, lay waiting for the end. When she was induced to say that she would never see d'Alembert again, the daughter wrote 'Mon triomphe est complet'. Her intolerance shocked old friends, and Turgot lashed out at *la vilaine fille*. Among the few visitors admitted during the closing months was the Emperor Joseph, then on a visit to his sister Marie Antoinette.

Mme Geoffrin's friends had once extracted a promise that she would write her Memoirs, but nothing came of it beyond a single sentence: 'A happy life, sweet to recall.' She had fulfilled the dream of her youth. Her salon had been her profession and her pride. She had formed delightful friendships and left affectionate memories in many hearts. The *éloges* published after her death by d'Alembert, Morellet and Thomas breathed genuine gratitude and esteem. She had won a place in the history of her country as honourable as it was unique.

## II. *Mme du Deffand*

THE most formidable rival of Mme Geoffrin among Parisian *salonnières* during the middle decades of the eighteenth century was Mme du Deffand, though there was plenty of scope for them both. Between these remarkable women, who had no love for each other, the resemblances were as marked as the differences. Both were born at the close of the *Grand Siècle* and lived on till the distant thunder of the Revolution could be heard by sensitive ears. Both were assigned in early youth to husbands of whom they knew nothing and whom they found impossible to love. Both sought compensation in middle life in entertaining a circle of intellectuals on which they depended for their happiness. Both—to the amazement of their friends—experienced an Indian Summer in which their emotional needs, which had never been very strong, found expression through platonic attachments to foreigners young enough to be their sons. Their differences were no less marked. While the cool-blooded Mme Geoffrin was a model of propriety, Mme du Deffand sowed her wild oats in the most dissolute Court in Europe. The former was the Moderator rather than the Conductor of her salon, the latter a witty conversationalist who held her own with the cleverest of her guests. The one detested letter-writing, and only her autumnal romance with Stanislas Poniatowski forced a pen into her hand. The other, a born letter-writer, left in her voluminous correspondence with Horace Walpole, the Duchesse de Choiseul and Voltaire some of the choicest specimens of the epistolary art. The former we visualise mainly through the eyes of her friends, the latter, far more intimately, through the

unstudied outpourings of her heart. Mme du Deffand was by far
the more interesting and the more cultivated personality but also
the least satisfied. While Mme Geoffrin could look back on a
record of self-fulfilment, Mme du Deffand's career was a drama of
storm and stress, of inner loneliness, of partial failure. Nature had
denied her the priceless gift of full enjoyment. She was much too
critical of others and of herself ever to find settled happiness. Her
own worst enemy, she was never at peace with herself.

Marie, daughter of Gaspard de Vichy, Comte de Chamrond, a
member of an old Burgundian family, was born in 1696. Her
mother was sister of the Duchesse de Luynes. Girls of her rank
were usually sent to convent schools, but the Convent de la Made-
leine du Tresnel, one of the most fashionable in Paris, was anything but a model of piety or discipline. There were religious
ceremonies but there was nothing of a convent except the name,
for the inmates received company of both sexes and accepted
invitations. When the precocious girl professed herself a sceptic,
the Superior informed her pious aunt, the Duchess, who was
charged by her parents with looking after her welfare. Père
Massillon was called in to reason with her, but the intervention of
the most celebrated preacher of the age was in vain. Though she
disapproved open attacks on the Church and its creeds, she was,
and always remained, a daughter of the *Aufklärung*, and the most
enduring friendship of her life was with Voltaire.

On leaving school Marie de Vichy returned to her home in the
country, the utter emptiness of which directed her thoughts to the
only practical method of escape. The Marquis du Deffand, a
distant cousin, was selected by her parents, despite her crushing
verdict: 'Il est ennuyeux'. Since no prominent woman of her time
was so easily bored, there was little prospect of a happy partnership. Such *mariages de convenance* among the nobility were scarcely
more than a legal ceremony, especially when there were no children, and there was little surprise that the experiment lasted less
than four years. 'Nous nous ennuyons parfaitement', she reported
from their country home. The pretty, witty and vivacious young
Marquise, bored to distraction by her colourless husband, attracted the attention of the Regent Orleans and was invited to join
the Smart Set at the Palais Royal under the auspices of the Duchesse
de Berry, the profligate daughter of the dissolute *de facto* ruler of

France. That she was for a brief space one of his numerous mistresses was reported by Horace Walpole when he paid his first long visit to Paris in 1766 and collected the gossip of society. It may well have been true, for Mme du Deffand, like his other favoured beauties, obtained a pension. The friendship survived the passion and she continued to share in the glittering fêtes. His early death scattered the circle, but there were plenty of other tempters at hand. She became the acknowledged mistress of the Comte de Fargis, a crony of the Regent and a notorious *roué* whom she had met at a masked ball. This loveless *liaison* was also soon over, and the young wife reluctantly consented to rejoin her dull husband in Normandy. Once again she found it impossible to bear a man who lived for the chase, and when her grandmother, the Duchesse de Choiseul, left her money she returned to Paris. He followed her, but, as she complained to a friend, he bored her to death. Appeals from her long-suffering partner and her own family failed to overcome what she described as *une aversion outrée*. A legal separation was arranged, since in a Catholic country there could be no hope of a divorce.

When Mme du Deffand had had her fill of gallantry she resolved to rebuild her life on a firmer basis. 'Je m'ennuyais de toutes mes sottises.' Many doors were open to her, above all that of the Duchesse du Maine, grand-daughter of the Grand Condé and wife of the royal bastard who had been brought up by Mme de Maintenon and whom Louis XIV desired to hold the reins for his great-grandson Louis XV. When the Duke of Orleans, who had the better right, secured the coveted post, the colourless Duc du Maine and his autocratic wife left the Court and settled at Sceaux, where she consoled herself for the loss of political influence with literary lions and amateur theatricals. Her little kingdom is mirrored in the memoirs of her *dame d'honneur* and factotum, Mme de Staal-Delaunay. To pass from the glittering frivolities of the Palais Royal to the highbrow occupations of Sceaux was no sacrifice for Mme du Deffand, who for the first time could enjoy the intellectual society for which she craved, and before long she was more like an inmate than a visitor. The brightest stars were Voltaire, the aged Fontenelle and the Abbé Prévost, reinforced in later years by the leaders of the younger generation such as Marmontel and d'Alembert, Grimm and Helvétius. The fair sex was represented by the respected Duchesse de Luynes, *dame d'honneur* to the Queen, and the less reputable Mme de Châtelet, Mme de Tencin and Mme d'Epinay. The character of the *salonnière* herself was beyond challenge, but hostesses were rarely exacting about the moral record of their guests.

Among the minor luminaries at Sceaux was Hénault, a rich, easy-going, agreeable and cultivated lawyer, dramatist and poet, President of the First Chamber of the Paris Parlement, member of the Académie Française, author of the *Abrégé Chronologique de l'histoire de France*, the first widely read summary of the fortunes of the French people described by Voltaire as 'the most useful of books by the most amiable of men', and of lively Memoirs depicting the society he adorned. This well-known, respected and accomplished man seemed able to offer Mme du Deffand just what she needed. His past was no more spotless than hers, and he admits in his Memoirs that his conduct had been a little irregular, but he claimed that he had done no one any harm. Both had had enough of adventures. His aim was to make life pleasant for himself and his friends, and Grimm saluted him as one of the happiest men of his time. As a gourmet he provided excellent suppers in his spacious house in the Rue St. Honoré, and, like Mme du Deffand, he suffered the penalty of over-eating. The Duc de Luynes describes him as well informed, a good talker and a man of considerable charm. Though a welcome guest in the literary coteries of Paris, he was rather a light weight, and Mme du Deffand, whose eyes were as sharp as her tongue, had few illusions. There was no pretence of deep affection on either side. It was a *liaison de convenance* and was accepted as such by society, like that of Mme d'Epinay and Grimm, Mme d'Houdetot and Saint-Lambert, the Prince de Conti and Comtesse de Boufflers. In 1730, when it began after the death of his wife, he was forty-five and she was thirty-four. When her husband passed away there was no obstacle to a marriage, but neither had the slightest desire for a change. When they ceased to be lovers he remained a faithful and useful friend, secretly paying her a substantial annuity and securing a similar grant from the Treasury through his influence at Court. Most of the affection of which he was capable was claimed by another lady, Mme de Castelmoron, of whom he declared after her death that for forty years she had been the principal object of his life. It was the

misfortune of Mme du Deffand—and to a large extent her own
fault—that she never held the first place in any human heart.

Among the literary diversions at Sceaux was the practice among
the guests of composing estimates of each other's characters.
'Here he is in 1730,' wrote Mme du Deffand of the President at the
outset of their forty years' partnership. 'All his merits and even
his failings are an asset to society. His vanity inspires an extreme
desire to please, and his easy-going nature enables him to get on
with different types. Everything combines to make him the most
attractive of men. He is impetuous in all his actions, disputes,
approbations. He appears eagerly concerned with the objects he
sees and the subjects he discusses. Since, however, he passes so
suddenly from the greatest vehemence to the most perfect indifference, one realises that if he is easily moved he is rarely
stirred. This impetuosity, which would be a failing in anyone else,
is almost a merit in him, for it lends an air of sentiment and passion
to all he does, which greatly pleases the majority. Everyone thinks
that he inspires in him a very lively interest, and this has won him
as many friends as his truly estimable qualities. One may blame
him for being too proud of this sort of success, and wish he were
less indiscriminate in his desire to please. He is exempt from the
passions which chiefly affect our peace of mind: ambition, self-
seeking, envy are unknown to him. His passions are mild, his
humour gay and unruffled. To much intelligence he adds all the
grace, facility and tact imaginable. He is the best company in the
world. His wit is lively and does not wound. His conversation is
full of ingenious and agreeable traits which never lapse into puns
or spiteful epigrams.'

The portrait of Mme du Deffand in Hénault's Memoirs is less
flattering, since it was based on the experience of half a life time.
'The Court of Sceaux was very different from what it had been
under Louis XIV. Then the stock of the Duc du Maine stood
high, and the Duchess utilised it to enjoy herself. All the Court was
at her feet. She acted in comedies with as much intelligence as
grace. People talked of the *grandes nuits*, the music, the balls. Then the
times changed. I was only presented after the return from prison.[1]

---

[1] The Duke and Duchess were interned for several months for complicity in the
so-called Cellamare conspiracy against the authority of the Regent Orleans. Cellamare
was the Spanish Ambassador.

Though the Court was less brilliant, it was no less agreeable, for it was composed of respected and intelligent people.' Among them were the Duchesse de Luynes, Mme de Staal, and the Marquise du Deffand, the latter, who had no house of her own, passing almost the whole year at Sceaux till the death of the hosts. Then she began to form a circle of her own, moved into the Convent of St Joseph, and gave supper-parties every night. Her income, augmented by the death of her husband, amounted to about 20,000 francs. 'Never did a woman possess more friends nor so fully deserve them. Friendship with her was a passion. Soon the most brilliant company gathered round her and bowed to her sway. Her noble, upright and generous heart was always planning how to be of use, as many persons could testify. She had a just mind, an agreeable imagination, a gaiety which lifted years off her shoulders for her figure had been charming, a cultivated intellect. Who would believe that I am speaking of a woman who had lost her sight? This misfortune had no influence on her talk or her spirits—one would have said that sight was a superfluous sense. The sound of a voice called up a vision of the speaker, and she was as quick in the uptake as anyone with a pair of eyes. Yet to be more convincing I must add that age, without robbing her of her talents, renders her jealous and distrustful, with a little too much *bel esprit*; that her armchair was a tribunal from which she uttered verdicts rather than conversed; that her judgments of people were largely coloured by their attentions to herself; that she displayed little consideration for the feelings of her old friends; that it was dangerous to contradict her.'

The discreet association with a man occupying a lofty official position helped Mme du Deffand to live down her Bohemian past, and his prestige was enhanced when the injured and uncomplaining Queen Marie Leczinska admitted him to her intimate circle at Versailles. She had heard about him from her beloved *dame d'honneur* the Duchesse de Luynes before she met him at Metz on the occasion of the grave illness of the King. She took to him at first sight and appointed him her Superintendent with an apartment at Versailles. That the attraction was mutual we may read in his chatty Memoirs, for, though not a man of very profound emotions, he was a friendly and helpful soul. 'He is most attractive and accomplished in every way,' noted the Duc de Luynes in his

voluminous diary. 'He is gentle, clever and agreeable. The Queen
has taken to him. Every day after dinner she sends for him and
they talk for an hour or more. Her virtue and genuine piety place
her beyond the range of scandal. She likes conversation and clever
people. She has read widely and is well informed; evil is something
she cannot even imagine.' She allotted half her income to the
poor, and her Superintendent had to dissuade her from giving still
more. She painted, played, read a good deal in Polish, French,
German and Italian, and was glad to talk with him on literary subjects beyond the range of other members of her little circle. With
politics she never meddled. The dissolute King, who had perfect
confidence in his gentle wife, approved the friendship and allowed
her to see whom she liked. That she enjoyed the card-table like
everyone at Court and played for small stakes was natural enough.
Her only weakness was over-indulgence of her appetite at table.
'When one has no other pleasure', she remarked with a quiet smile,
'one may permit oneself that.' Though she dutifully visited the
King every day, he was frankly bored by her company and the
interview lasted only a few minutes.

The President's duties at Versailles diminished his attentions to
Mme du Deffand, and his heart, as she was well aware, was given
to another woman; yet the *liaison*, which resembled a morganatic
marriage, worked well enough. Neither of them was capable
of the deepest emotions. They never lived under the same
roof and he left her nothing in his will. The nearest approach to
warmth on her part is recorded in a letter during his absence at a
spa in 1742. 'I am accustomed to a letter every day, and two days
without one are a sore trial. You are more necessary than my
life. I could not do without you.' When he wrote happily of his
doings and amusements, but without the note of tenderness she
craved, she replied ironically 'I am sorry not to see you, but I bear
this misfortune with a fortitude of which you set the example.'
Now, for once, the limited liability lover played up. 'What I love
I love always, and it is you I love.' It proved difficult to live at
such emotional altitudes, and in their old age, when he was deaf
and she was blind, both were unashamedly bored. Though he was
never much more than a *pis aller* he was the more attractive because the less self-centred of the two. Meeting him when he was
nearly eighty Hume described him as decaying, but still retaining

the amiable character which once had made him the delight of all France.

The death of her husband in 1750 placed Mme du Deffand in comfortable circumstances, for he had retained part of her dowry; and the death of the Duchesse du Maine in 1753 deprived a number of literary men of a pleasant rendezvous. Terrified of solitude, she resolved to form a salon with the aid of the friends she had made at Sceaux, with the President and d'Alembert as the core. To become an *habitué* of a literary salon there was no need to be an intimate friend of the hostess. People came because they enjoyed good talk, and they were welcome if they could contribute to the entertainment. It was not for the quality of her suppers that Frenchmen and foreigners flocked to her drawing-room. Hénault complained of the 'terrible sauces', wryly observing that the only difference between her cook and the celebrated poisoner Brinvilliers lay in their intentions. Living in a suite attached to the Convent of St Joseph which had housed its foundress Mme de Montespan after her fall, she was at home every day after six unless she dined out. Hénault was usually the first to arrive, but his duties at Versailles rendered his visits irregular. An even older acquaintance from the Regency days was Pont de Veyle, ever good-tempered and gay, whose main ambition, like that of Hénault, was to seek pleasure for himself and to provide it for his friends.

There was always plenty of entertainment, for the vivacious sallies of the hostess and the intellectual distinction of the guests made admission to the circle a privilege. Unlike the masculine kingdom of Mme Geoffrin, women, with the Maréchale de Luxembourg and the Duchesse de Choiseul at their head, had their place in the sun. 'Young and pretty women are needed by society as sugar is required in coffee,' remarked Morellet, one of the *habitués*. From time to time Clairon would recite, and the latest sparkling letter from Voltaire would be read aloud. Here were to be found d'Alembert, the most brilliant of talkers; Montesquieu, the prince of publicists; Maupertuis, the *protégé* of Frederick the Great; Beaumarchais, d'Argenson, members of the diplomatic corps, and English celebrities, among them the beautiful Lady Hervey and George Selwyn, whose ghoulish hobby was to witness public executions. Other capitals struck observant travellers as

K

provincial in comparison with *la ville lumière* where conversation was cultivated as a fine art.

In the early fifties Mme du Deffand was as happy as her caustic temperament allowed her to be when a dark shadow fell across her path. 'You seem mortally sad,' wrote d'Alembert, 'but why? With your intelligence and your income can you lack agreeable acquaintances? I do not say friends, for you know how rare they are. With a good supper one can have what guests one desires, and you can always laugh at them when they are gone.' Tronchin, the fashionable Geneva physician, could suggest nothing for failing eyesight except residence in the country. As a long-term policy it was impracticable, for company and conversation were her meat and drink, but perhaps she might try the experiment for a time. Her salon, she feared, would have to close, for she could no longer see her guests. She had kept up with her younger brother, the Abbé Nicolas de Champrond, and to a lesser extent with her younger sister, Anne de Vichy, who had married a neighbour in the Lyonnais, the Marquis d'Albon. With her familiar world crumbling around her she was almost in despair. 'Quel néant que la vie,' she cried, 'mieux vaudrait n'être pas née.' To make matters worse she suffered from chronic insomnia. At this moment her elder brother, Gaspard de Vichy, suggested a visit, and her closest friends advised her to accept the invitation. The prospect of life in a fifteenth-century château in the depths of the country was not alluring. Brother and sister had not met for many years and had nothing in common, and his wife was equally lacking in intellectual interests; but there was no obligation to stay longer than she wished. When her carriage rolled into the courtyard of her birthplace in May, 1752, first impressions were encouraging. 'All I need is rest,' she reported to her sister. 'They cannot do enough for me, and they tell me to consider their house as my own. The quiet life does me a lot of good.' The charm of novelty soon wore off, and after four months she wrote that she could not possibly winter in the country. 'My health is not so good the last few days, and I greatly fear it will become as bad as ever.'

The visitor found an inmate of whom she had never heard but whose company was to make her sojourn unexpectedly enjoyable. Julie de Lespinasse, who was introduced as the governess of the

Vichy children, was a mystery child whose secret was recently discovered by the Marquis de Ségur in the family papers. Born in Lyons in 1732 in the house of a doctor and a midwife, she was registered as the legitimate daughter of Claude de Lespinasse, a citizen of Lyons, and Julie de Navarre, his wife, neither of whom had ever existed. The mother was Comtesse d'Albon, who had been married at the age of sixteen and whose husband had left her after the birth of four children. Subsequently she formed a *liaison* resulting in the birth of two more children, the elder of whom became a monk. The second, a daughter, was brought up with the legitimate children, till her mother's death, when Julie was fifteen, raised the problem of her future. Mme d'Albon could only settle an annuity of a few hundred francs on the child she adored, plus a considerable sum in cash which she handed over on her deathbed with the injunction to keep it for herself. The girl gave the money to her eldest half-brother, the head of the family and never saw it again. A temporary solution was provided by an invitation to look after the children of Comte Gaspard de Vichy, who had married one of her half-sisters. The girls had always been on friendly terms, and with the Vichy children it was a case of love at first sight.

The bright dawn was soon overcast, for the ill-tempered master of Champrond proved anything but a friend. The pretence of equality faded away, and the unpaid governess found herself treated as a drudge. In later years she was to speak of her employers, with some exaggeration so far as her half-sister was concerned, as barbarous persecutors compared to whom tigers were merciful. What was the reason for this shattering of her hopes? It seems almost certain that Comte Gaspard, who was as dissolute as most of the French nobility, had been the lover of Comtesse d'Albon, that he was Julie's father, and that he wished to hush up the guilty secret. In any case he visited his spleen on the defenceless girl. After four years she felt that she must escape, and, in the absence of any alternative, resolved to enter a cloister in Lyons.

Mme du Deffand arrived at the psychological moment and took to the girl without guessing that she was her niece. With her she could talk, for Julie loved the French classics, knew English and Italian, and listened wistfully to descriptions of the delights of

Paris.  Beautiful she was not, but her dark, expressive eyes suggested personality, and an air of mystery and melancholy increased the attraction.  'I noticed she was very sad,' reported the visitor, 'and there were often tears in her eyes.'  The disillusioned *Parisienne* was fascinated by her vibrating sensibility and the warmth of her response to comradeship and consideration.  When the girl, unable to bear her humiliation any longer, left to become a paying guest in a cheap Lyons convent, Mme du Deffand wrote to her, 'Vous avez beaucoup d'esprit.'  She had begun to dream of a new life for herself and her new friend, for with the onset of blindness she had come to a parting of the ways.  Vistas of infinite boredom rose before her active mind, and there was a void in her heart which neither Hénault nor d'Alembert could fill.  Why should she not invite the homeless girl to Paris as an equal and a friend?  She broached the subject before Julie's departure and followed it up in correspondence.

Soon after her visit to her brother, Mme du Deffand spent ten days at Lyons in consultation with the girl, who was as thrilled by the prospect as she was apprehensive of a plunge into an unknown world.  She finally decided only when her half-brother Count d'Albon refused to increase her meagre allowance.  Undeterred by the protests of the d'Albons and the Vichys, who feared that Julie might one day lay claim to an inheritance, the elder woman held to her course and warmth flowed into her withered heart.  Never before had she written to a friend or relative *Ma reine*.  Fully aware of the significance of the step she proposed to take, she placed her cards on the table in a carefully considered memorandum to her new friend, dated February 13, 1754.  'I am delighted, my queen, that you are pleased with my letters; but you must give the project of living with me the fullest consideration and feel sure you will not regret it.  Your last letter was most tender and flattering, but remember that two or three months ago your feelings were different.  You told me that you were afraid of the little worries for which I prepared you; that, accustomed to it though you were, it would be still more unbearable in the great world; that your discouragement would make you impossible and make me repent.  So think it over very carefully.  I have already described the life you would lead with me, and I will repeat it to prevent misunderstanding.  I shall not announce your arrival.  I shall tell people that you are a young lady from my birthplace who desires to enter a convent and whom I have invited to stay till you find what you want. I shall treat you not only with politeness but with all consideration in company. I shall only tell a very few friends my real intentions and even then only after three or four months. By that time we shall know how we suit, and then we can treat each other with less reserve. I shall never make a point of introducing you. My plan is to let you make your own way, and if you really know me you can have no apprehension as to how I shall study your *amour-propre*. But you must trust to my knowledge of society. If people at once assumed that you had settled down with me, they would not know how to behave to you. Some might think you were my daughter and others my companion, and they might make impertinent remarks. So they must learn first to know your merit and your attractions. This will be easy, aided by your efforts and those of my friends; but you must be ready to bear in patience the little worries of the opening phase.'

At this point Mme du Deffand inserted a solemn warning, the relevance of which was only to appear in later years. 'The slightest artifice in your conduct towards me I could not tolerate. I am instinctively mistrustful, and people in whom I seem to detect *finesse* arouse my suspicions and forfeit my confidence. I have two intimate friends, Formont and d'Alembert, whom I love passionately, less for their attractiveness and their friendship for me than for their extreme truthfulness. I might add Devereux [1] since real merit makes us all equal, and for that reason she is more to me than all the potentates. So, my queen, you must make up your mind to live with me in perfect sincerity. Never sacrifice one of the chief charms of youth—simplicity. You have plenty of intelligence, gaiety, sensibility; with all these qualities you will be charming so long as you remain yourself, without pretention and equivocation.'

The kindly old President had the first right to be informed. Realising the need of a refined and intelligent girl to help the blind hostess with her correspondence, read to her, and help with the salon, he raised no objection, though his long experience of her changing moods made him doubt the wisdom of a definitive engagement. Next in importance was her aunt, the universally

---

[1] Her devoted maid.

respected Duchesse de Luynes, whose approval was sought by letter. 'It is not, madame, to the person I most respect and on whom I chiefly depend but to the tenderest and most sincere of my woman friends that I speak with the most entire confidence, promising you the exact truth and perfect submission. I am blind. People praise my courage, but to despair would be no help. Yet I feel the whole bitterness of my situation, and it is natural that I should seek some relief. Nothing would be more helpful than to have with me someone who would keep me company and save me from the boredom of solitude, which I have always dreaded and which I now find intolerable. By chance I have met someone of intelligence and character who would just suit me; a girl of twenty-two, without relatives willing and under an obligation to avow relationship. That explains her condition. I found her at Champrond.'

After talking it over with the President, the Duchess replied in a more critical vein than had been expected. It was for her to decide, but an alternative arrangement seemed worth considering. 'If Mlle de Lespinasse were to live in a convent whence you would often send for her and whence she might sometimes emerge to spend a few days with you, you could increase or diminish your contacts just as you wished.' That it was excellent advice events were to show, but it was too late, for Mme du Deffand felt sure of her ground. She had taken the girl to her heart, and only her presence under the same roof could help her to carry the burden imposed by blindness and the torments of *ennui*. That the request for the approval of the Duchess was a mere formality was proved by her next letter to the new friend. 'This moment, my queen, I have received the reply of Mme de Luynes. It is absolutely what I hoped. I hope, my queen, that I shall never have to regret what I am doing for you. Adieu, my queen. Pack your boxes and come to be the happiness and consolation of my life. It will not be my fault if it is not reciprocated.' That is not the utterance of a woman without a heart. Mme du Deffand returned to Paris after a year's absence and in due course was joined by her young companion. The reunion was cordial, and warm sunshine streamed through the windows of the Convent of St Joseph. 'She is come to be my eyes and to keep me company in my eternal dungeon of blindness to which I am doomed.'

Julie lived on the floor above her employer and was fitted out

with suitable clothes. The routine in the salon established before
the hostess was stricken by blindness was resumed and continued
to the end. The great event of the day was supper, usually with
three or four guests; once a week there was a larger party. After a
visit to the opera or the *Comédie Française* she sometimes remarked
that it was too early to go to bed and would drive about the streets
till 2 a.m., for she dreaded the sleepless hours of the night. Julie
took her place in society without effort and the hostess congratulated herself on her luck. 'Every day I like her better,' she reported, and Julie's letters breathed equal satisfaction. She enjoyed
the social equality which had been denied her in the Vichy family,
and the two most important members of the salon took to her
from the first. According to La Harpe, the septuagenarian
Hénault thought of marrying her, and d'Alembert formed a
touching friendship which endured till her death. There seemed
no danger of losing the girl who had brought warmth into her life
and increased the amenities of her circle, for who would dream of
marrying an almost penniless companion whose parentage was a
mystery? Mme du Deffand had miscalculated. Though there
was nothing of the coquette in Julie, there were depths of feeling
of which her employer had no conception. Of the celebrated
Parisian *salonnières*, moreover, Julie was the only one who possessed real charm. She was as much appreciated by the women as
by the men friends of the hostess. The oldest and closest of them,
the Maréchale de Luxembourg, came almost daily, and when Mme
du Deffand visited her in her country home in summer she took
Julie with her. For the first year or two all went well.

Julie found no less favour with the old President than with the
hostess herself. 'Mademoiselle,' he wrote in one of the literary
portraits then in vogue, 'I will tell you what I think of you. Those
who regard you as only a Parisian do not know you: you are a
cosmopolitan at home in any environment. You like society but
you love solitude. You appreciate pleasures but you are not their
slave. You do not wear your heart on your sleeve. Your soul is
noble and elevated and you will never be lost in the crowd.
Though not a beauty you attract attention by your air of distinction. There is something piquant about you. One must await
your coming, not summon you to come. You possess two qualities rarely found together: you are both gentle and strong. Your

gaiety lights up your face and relaxes your over-sensitive nerves. You form your own opinions and allow others to do the same. You see things in broad perspective. You are extremely polite. You have guessed the riddle of society and you would take root anywhere—at Madrid, London, Constantinople. To sum up, you are unique and I like you very much.' Hénault's generous tribute to the newcomer was no mere literary exercise, for he was one of her earliest admirers and remained a helpful friend to the last.

The earliest sign of trouble arose when Taaffe, a young Irish nobleman on a visit to Paris, fell in love with her. The blind hostess sensed the situation and forbade him the house. Though Julie's heart was not very deeply engaged, she resented the veto and sought relief in opium. Scenes occurred, followed by tears and reconciliations. The growing consciousness of her companion's charms led the ageing hostess to wonder whether she had been wise in inviting such an attractive girl to share her home. Julie, for her part, while grateful for many kindnesses, soon began to complain. 'I am distressed to see how my days are taken up— nothing but complaints and frustrations.' Her employer, described by Marmontel as a woman of art, malice and moods, had a sharp tongue, and her young companion was as sensitive as an aspen leaf.

The most important factor in the growing estrangement was the discovery by the hostess that d'Alembert—'mon petit ami', 'mon chat sauvage'—the brightest ornament of her salon and an almost daily visitor, had transferred his devotion to the newcomer. 'He is my intimate friend, and I love him passionately,' Mme du Deffand had confided to Julie. Her love, though purely maternal, was sufficiently deep to render the thought of its loss a nightmare. At first she had been pleased that the two people who meant so much to her had taken to each other, but it was not long before the demon of jealousy crept in. For d'Alembert it was the beginning of a new and happier life; for Mme du Deffand it was to involve the loss both of her companion and her most valued guest. During d'Alembert's visit to Frederick the Great he sent greetings and asked for news through Julie instead of direct. 'No, sir,' replied the old lady, who was hurt by the growing coolness, 'I shall not trouble anyone to give you my news. Let us love each other as we used to do. I do not think we could do better. For you I am and always shall be the same.' The appeal came too late. On his return after a year's absence Julie was everything, the hostess nothing. 'More than ever I realise that the supreme misfortune is to have been born,' she confided to Voltaire. 'This is true not only of Job, Judas or myself but of you, Pompadour, everyone. My blindness and my old age are the least of my troubles.' 'Enjoy your food and take care of yourself,' replied the sage of Ferney cheerfully; 'you have the best company in Paris.'

Desiring more of Julie's company than the publicity of the salon allowed, d'Alembert formed the habit of mounting to her apartment an hour before the hostess was ready for her guests at six o'clock. Other friends were also welcomed to these informal gatherings, among them Turgot, Condorcet, Marmontel, La Harpe and Hénault himself. Leaving her bedroom one day an hour earlier than usual, Mme du Deffand heard voices upstairs, entered unannounced, and discovered the existence of a rival salon. The scene, which is described in Marmontel's Memoirs, ranks as the most celebrated quarrel in the literary history of eighteenth-century France. Bitter words were exchanged which could never be forgotten. Julie was charged with treachery to her benefactor and retorted with shrill complaints. During the last two years of the decade of partnership affection had melted into indifference. Now indifference turned in a flash to hatred on both sides, and a substantial legacy to her late companion was struck out of the older woman's will. When the angry hostess requested d'Alembert to choose between them, he walked out. A third blow was that most of the *habitués*—Hénault, Turgot, the Maréchale de Luxembourg and others—took the side of the rebel. The old President continued his visits, but he was never fully forgiven, and on his death she coldly observed that her grief was moderate. 'I had so many proofs of how little he cared for me that I merely feel I have lost an acquaintance.' Even Hume, the most amiable of men, lost her favour by his attempt at neutrality. The departure of 'la Lespinasse', as she was henceforth described, left the blind woman lonelier and unhappier than ever before. The best and most faithful of her few women friends, the Duchesse de Choiseul, declared that events outside her (*hors d'elle*) meant nothing to her. She loved nobody and she believed that nobody loved her. For the moment there was as little warmth in her heart as there was light in her eyes. 'Last night I had twelve at my table,' she reported to Voltaire, 'all of them bores.' Life had lost its savour. Everyone, she declared, was vain and egoistic. 'I esteem nobody, yet I cannot do without people I despise.'

A few days after the explosion Julie suggested a visit, but the reply indicated that the breach was irreparable. 'I cannot see you so soon, Mademoiselle; our last decisive conversation is too fresh in my memory. I cannot believe that your wish derives from sentiments of friendship. It is impossible to love people whom one detests and abhors, who have humiliated and destroyed their *amour propre*, etc. etc. Those are your own phrases and are the result of the impressions you have long received from those you call your real friends. Perhaps they are, and I hope with all my heart that they will procure for you all the advantages you anticipate: satisfaction, good luck, consideration, etc. What use could I be to you now? My company would not be agreeable, merely serving to recall the early days of our acquaintance and the years that followed. All that is best forgotten. However, if in due course you remember them with pleasure, and if the recollection causes you some remorse and regret, I do not profess a rigid austerity, I am not without feeling, and I recognise truth. A sincere change of heart might touch me and revive in me the liking and tenderness I used to feel. Till then, Mademoiselle, let us leave things as they are, and content yourself with my wishes for your happiness.'

Julie can hardly have expected or desired a different response, and they never met nor corresponded again. The wounds each had inflicted on the other were too deep to heal. Julie complained bitterly of her 'years of martyrdom and the absolute loss of my health.' 'If she wished to save me from the scaffold', snapped the old lady, 'I would not see her.' When Julie passed away four years later Mme du Deffand curtly observed: 'It ought to have happened fifteen years ago; then I should not have lost d'Alembert.' Though Julie never discussed her late employer in public, she poured out the bitterness of her heart in one of the most elaborate of the pen portraits so popular in eighteenth-century France. The document was discovered among the papers of d'Alembert and published in 1893. Though it bears no date, it must have been written while the smart of the encounter burned like a flame.

'She was absolutely natural. She could not bear affectation of any kind and she had a keen sense of the ridiculous. Consequently she disliked what is called eloquence and sentimentality, and here she was often right; but her aversion often led her to regard as affectations all the feelings she had never experienced and all the ideas she had never entertained. Though a creature of moods she is—or rather she was—naturally gay and pleasant, and some of her *bon mots* have become current coin. I say she used to be gay and pleasant because such moments are now extremely rare. Her bad health, her loss of sight, the real or imaginary causes of complaint of her friends, have produced a fund of sadness and caprice which render her discontented with everything she sees and reads and almost everything she hears. She is convinced she is always fair, for she prides herself on her taste and judgment. These qualities she displays when she reasons coolly, but unfortunately that is rare. There is an element of passion in most of her verdicts. One sees her first praising to the skies and then violently denouncing the same works or the same persons, tearing to pieces what she exalted a few days earlier and praising what she had recently denounced. All this is done solely to satisfy the feelings of the moment. The present alone concerns her, for she thinks little about the past and never about the future.

'Her aversion to what is known as modern philosophy has several causes. Some of its teachers proclaim, with perhaps excessive ostentation, the virtues which she does not know and contempt for the great whom she adores while persuading herself of her indifference. Some of them, moreover, have displeased her by declining total submission to her desires and opinions. Finally this philosophy and its champions have the misfortune to be esteemed by a woman whom she regards and treats as her rival, and whom for this reason she pursues with implacable hatred and delights in running down at every opportunity. If she is ever fair it is only with her domestics, for she is generous as well as economical. This generosity, however, does not derive from a nobility of soul, for hers is possessive and cringing: it comes from her need of her entourage. She only tries to make people like her because she cannot make them her slaves. She has often expressed regret that slavery has been abolished, for she is a great enemy of natural equality, and that is one of her objections to the new philosophy. Moreover she is hard on those who are of no use to her.

She lacks humanity, charity, compassion, having no idea of them herself and ridiculing them in others. In her dislike of equality she grovels before the personages of the Court, particularly if they are in favour, and demeans herself in the most humiliating manner. She is amazed that hardly anyone shows her friendship or confidence; for she cherishes the delusion that she deserves friends, though her nature prevents it. Inconsiderate, indiscreet, egoistic and jealous: such is her character in four words.'

This summary indictment is elaborated in a series of paragraphs.

'*Inconsiderate.* She is brusque and disdainful in conversation, scarcely attempting to hide her indifference to those whom she despises. She answers them with a shrug of her shoulders. In their presence she says in audible whispers what she dislikes in their person and their talk, and is astonished after that not to find everyone at her feet. Convinced that her lack of consideration is only praiseworthy frankness, for frankness is one of the virtues to which she lays claim, she only adopts it with people from whom she has nothing to fear. Noble independence—a virtue unknown to her—she calls impertinence.

'*Indiscreet.* She is utterly incapable of holding her tongue. All that she knows, guesses, suspects, believes, she communicates to the first comer without a thought for those whom it may damage, though not with a desire to do so, for she is much more thoughtless than malicious. She is without friendship or confidence for those to whom she entrusts her secret, and she does so solely from the urge to talk about it unless she has some vendetta to pursue; for then she pushes indiscretion to denigration and perfidy, betraying the secrets confided to her in order to ruin, if she can, the honour and reputation of those who unwisely spoke to her about their private affairs.

'*Egoistic.* Without consideration and delicacy, she never troubles to show herself better than she is, whereas most people, however self-centred, wish at any rate to appear a little interested in others. This social obligation she ignores. She demands everything and gives nothing, though she persuades herself that she is not exigent. Since she refers everything to herself, she seems to say to all her acquaintance like Christ to his disciples: Sell all thou hast and follow me. It is harder to win her favour than that of God. A venial offence cancels in a moment the services of many years. She repays a compliment by praise which she retracts next day at the first trifling occasion of disapproval, and swings over to satire and libels. With the character I have described it is not surprising that she is inquisitive and distrustful to excess. She is inquisitive merely to know what people are saying and doing, above all what they say about herself. She is distrustful because she judges the souls of others by her own, and because, exclusively interested in herself, she always suspects that people are setting traps for her even when they are not thinking of her at all. Such is Mme du Deffand. Her wit should make people desire her acquaintance, and to that alone she owes the consideration she enjoys. Knowledge of her character results in their withdrawal and should prevent any attachment. Subservient to her superiors, fair enough to her inferiors, she is unbearable and tyrannical with her equals. Unable to boast of a single friend among the large number of her acquaintances, she is full of wit, prejudices, caprice and injustice. In a word she is a naughty child who has not been spoiled, for she is her own worst enemy.'

Such blistering broadsides discharged in a paroxysm of fury are far less damaging than a few well-directed arrows at vital points. Mme du Deffand was too self-centred to possess many real friends, but had she been such a cold-blooded monster she would have had none at all. Yet the larger share of the blame for the catastrophe falls to her, since she was responsible for an experiment which was more likely to fail than to succeed. How could she expect an exceptionally gifted, cultivated, attractive, temperamental young woman to play second fiddle for the rest of her life? And was it likely that the *habitués* of the salon, particularly the younger members, would be indifferent to the subtle charm of the newcomer quivering with sensibility and possessing qualities which were lacking in the desiccated soul of the ageing *salonnière*? The parting was to prove a blessing for both. At last the younger woman, released from her gilded cage, could spread her luminous wings. And at last the elder, shaken to the depths by the blast of the tempest, was to discover depths of feeling in herself of which she had been unaware and to taste the delights of enduring friendship for the first time. That she was her own worst enemy was obvious to friend and foe. Yet had Julie been able to read the affectionate outpourings of her late employer to Horace Walpole she would have recognised that her darkly tinted portrait, true though it may have been in certain features, was very far from the whole truth.

### III. *Julie de Lespinasse*

At the age of thirty-two Julie left the Convent of St Joseph with mingled feelings. The dominant sentiment was one of heartfelt relief at her escape from a position which had become intolerable. She had experienced a similar spiritual liberation when she fled from the Vichy household ten years earlier. At that time the offer of a post in Paris removed all material anxieties; now she was confronted with the problem how she was to live, for she only possessed the annuity of 100 crowns from her mother. That her friends rallied round her is a tribute not merely to their generosity but also to the affection she inspired. She rented a small apartment in the Rue Dominique, only 100 yards away from her old address, which Hénault, Turgot and the Maréchale de Luxembourg helped her to furnish, and Choiseul obtained a small pension from the King. But the guardian angel was Mme Geoffrin. They had never met, but the quarrel was the talk of Paris, and d'Alembert doubtless pleaded her cause. The kindly old hostess sold three pictures by Van Loo to Catherine the Great and gave most of the proceeds to Julie. The rebel settled in with three maids and a valet, and gathered round her a circle which competed in distinction though not in hospitality with that of the Convent of St Joseph. Since she had never kept accounts and possessed no sense of money, she needed guidance, and found it in the quarter to which she had the best right to look.

D'Alembert's position in the social and intellectual life of Paris was unique. Since Voltaire felt impelled to leave his country no one was so generally in demand as the celebrated mathematician, Assistant Editor of the *Encyclopédie*, Perpetual Secretary of the Academy of Sciences, Member of the Académie Française. His unblemished character inspired no less respect than his splendid intellect. Caring nothing for money, the honoured guest of princes continued to live in a dark and unhealthy room at the home of the working-class foster-parents who had brought him up. In the salon of Mme du Deffand he and Julie had taken to each other, and the catastrophe brought them even closer together. When shortly after settling into her new home she was struck down by smallpox, the faithful friend paid her daily visits despite the risk of infection. Soon afterwards, when he in turn fell dangerously ill, she nursed him back to life and persuaded him to move into a vacant room in the large apartment house where she lived. Sharing their meals and their interests and invited out together, the two gifted illegitimates entered on the happiest period of their lives.

Those who did not know them not unnaturally believed that they were lovers. 'I have seen Mlle de Lespinasse, the mistress of d'Alembert, one of the most intelligent women in Paris,' reported Hume, at that time on the staff of the British Embassy. He was mistaken, as any of their intimate circle could have told him. Mathematics, declared d'Alembert at the close of his life, had been his mistress. Why, then, did they not marry? The answer was supplied in a letter to Voltaire. 'What should I do with a wife and children? The person I am expected to marry is made to render a husband happy, but she deserves a better establishment than I can give her. There is no question of marriage or love but of mutual esteem and all the sweetness of friendship,' The man who had been like a son to Mme Geoffrin and Mme du Deffand was like a brother to Julie de Lespinasse. Such a platonic partnership in eighteenth-century Paris seemed almost a miracle, but it was all that d'Alembert required. Though his appointment as Perpetual Secretary to the Academy of Sciences entitled him to apartments in the Louvre, he preferred to remain where he found companionship and peace. Julie, on the other hand, deeply grateful though she was, required something more. She had surprised Mme du Deffand by her reaction when the Irish nobleman crossed her path, and before long she was to surprise d'Alembert.

His first task was to introduce his friend to Mme Geoffrin, who loved her from the start. Recognising her outstanding social and intellectual qualities, the hostess treated her as a daughter and admitted her—the only woman guest—to her Wednesday dinners. Her daughter resented such marked favours and complained that the newcomer was usurping her place. Had she spared a little more love for her mother, there would have been no vacuum to fill. Julie's popularity in Mme Geoffrin's wide circle encouraged her to start a salon of her own. It was small, not owing to lack of space, but because she deliberately resolved to keep it select. She possessed the gift of intimacy in a degree unapproached by any French *salonnière*. 'Mme Geoffrin was feared, Mme du Deffand admired, Mme Necker respected, Julie loved,' declares the Marquis de Ségur, the best of her biographers. That she was a gifted talker and a lover of good literature was well known to the *habitués* of her late employer's salon, and now she had no longer to play second fiddle. The little drawing-room was adorned by busts of d'Alembert and Voltaire and a portrait of Turgot. Grimm describes her as 'l'âme et le charme' of the group. 'After the first fortnight', echoes La Harpe, 'everyone wanted to tell her the story of their lives. No one had ever possessed so many friends, yet each was loved as if he or she were the only one.'

Next to d'Alembert, Turgot, to whom France looked for a fleeting moment for financial salvation, and Condorcet were the chief ornaments. 'I know only one pleasure, one interest—friendship,' she declared; 'I exist only to love and cherish my friends.' No other *salonnière* before or after her time could have written such words without a touch of insincerity. Though women were admitted, with none of them was she very intimate. Anything but 'a man's woman', she appealed to Intellectuals precisely because she was so intensely feminine. The routine of the salon was much the same as that of Mme du Deffand, though she could not afford suppers or wine. Except when she and d'Alembert dined with Mme Geoffrin she was at home every evening. There was less formality than with Mme Geoffrin and a warmer atmosphere than at the Convent of St Joseph. The undying resentment of her late employer kept a few English visitors away, as we learn from a letter of Horace Walpole to his cousin Henry Conway on the eve of a journey to Paris in 1774. The young hostess is described as 'a pretended *bel esprit* who was formerly a humble companion of Mme du Deffand and betrayed her and used her very ill. I beg you not let anyone carry you thither. It would disoblige my friend of all things in the world. She has done everything on earth to please and serve me. I dwell upon it because she has some enemies so spiteful that they try to carry all English to Mlle de Lespinasse.' But there were plenty of others only too eager to be enrolled among her guests.

'Except for some friends of d'Alembert,' testifies Marmontel, our best guide to the salons, 'her circle was composed of people bound by no common tie. She had picked them here and there, but they were so well matched that in her company they were all entirely *en rapport*, like chords of an instrument controlled by a single hand. On this she played with a virtuosity approaching genius, for she seemed to feel instinctively what sound every chord she touched would produce. Our minds and characters were so completely known to her that to set them in motion a single word sufficed. Nowhere was the conversation more brilliant nor better supervised. This atmosphere of tempered and steady warmth which she managed to maintain, moderating or animating in turn, was a rare experience. Her ceaseless activity of soul awoke response in us, though it was always kept within bounds; her imagination was the mainspring, her reason the regulator. Moreover, her guests had minds of their own, while d'Alembert was at her side like a docile child. She could toss out an idea for debate, make her own contribution with clarity and sometimes with eloquence, and direct the conversation with the skill of a fairy who, with a touch of her wand, transforms the scene of her enchantments at will. This gift was that of no ordinary woman. It was not with the trifles and vanities of the day that she maintained the interest of such Intellectuals without flagging for four hours every day. One of her charms was the natural fire of her talk, though often, very often, there were lighter moments. D'Alembert called the tune, and no one knew better how to mingle grave and gay.' That Marmontel was difficult to please we know from his other full-length and much more critical portraits.

Marmontel's testimony is confirmed by other witnesses. She made the best of the minds of others, records Grimm, stirring them to action without any sign of effort. 'She could unite the different types, even the most antagonistic, sustaining the conversation by a well-aimed phrase, animating and guiding it at will. She allotted to everyone his place, and everyone was content. Politics, religion, philosophy, news: nothing was excluded. Her circle met daily from five till nine. There one found men of all ranks in the State, the Church and the Court, soldiers and foreigners, and the leading writers of the day. She rarely went to the theatre or the country, and then all Paris was informed in advance.' It was

L

the least unhappy phase of her short and agitated life. She welcomed diplomatists and visitors from many lands. Creutz, the gifted Swedish Ambassador, was as happy in Parisian drawingrooms as at the Court of Versailles. Abbé Galiani, the little Neapolitan, gave rein to his droll fancies more freely than in the stiffer circles of Mme Geoffrin or Mme du Deffand.

Since Anglomania was at its height, British aristocrats and Intellectuals were lionised in all the salons. Translations of *Tristram Shandy*, *Clarissa* and Hume's *History of England* were eagerly read. None of the leading *salonnières* showed so much interest in British politics, for Julie believed in limited monarchy. Her interest increased when Lord Shelburne spent several months in Paris in 1774 and visited her almost every day. Her first experience of a leading statesman from a free country confirmed her instinctive dislike of autocracy. 'A man of energy, elevation and genius in France,' she declared, 'is like a chained lion in a menagerie. The consciousness of his powers tortures him.' She never shared the admiration for Catherine the Great expressed by Voltaire and Diderot, d'Alembert and Grimm, none of whom cared much about free institutions. Her admiration, like that of Montesquieu, was reserved for England, and she wished something on the model of the British Constitution to be tried in France. 'I would rather be the least member in the House of Commons than the King of Prussia,' she declared; 'only the glory of Voltaire consoles me for not being born English.' Though sharing the general rejoicing at the death of Louis XV, she had no sanguine hopes from a change of ruler. 'Mon cher Abbé,' she remarked to Morellet, 'nous allons avoir pis.' The appointment of her friend Turgot was a hopeful symptom. 'If he can keep his post', she commented, 'he will become the idol of the nation. He is a fanatic for the public good.' His virtues were to prove his undoing. He continued his visits and discussed his plans; but his was a hopeless task, for vested interests were too strongly entrenched. 'So we are to be governed by *Philosophes*,' sneered Mme du Deffand. 'A pity I have not secured their protection! For that one must have recourse to Mlle de Lespinasse.'

In 1771, before Guibert crashed into her life, d'Alembert composed an elaborate portrait of the hostess. The picture reveals almost as much of the artist as of the only woman he ever loved.

She begged him not to omit her faults, nor, if he found any, her vices. Vices he had not discovered, but faults there were from the point of view of those who loved her. 'I can only whisper it in your ear: you have no passion. Of your figure I shall not speak: you attach no importance to it, and in any case it does not interest an old and sad philosopher like me. But I will say that you have plenty of breeding and grace and, what is greatly preferable to cold beauty, a wealth of expression and sensibility in every glance. You attract people by your mind and character, your tone, your taste, your art in saying the right thing. Coming from the provinces, you were from the start as much at home in Paris as if you had passed your life in this brilliant and exacting society. You sensed its ways before you knew them, and improvised the language of what is called good company. The only thing in which you sometimes carry delicacy to the point of severity—and here I am pleading for myself—is your excessive attention to *bon ton* in manners and conversation. Lack of this quality is scarcely compensated in your eyes by the tenderest sentiments towards you. There are some people in whom this quality of *bon ton* covers everything, whom, selfish, pretentious and superficial, but amiable and well-mannered, you are much inclined to prefer to your most faithful friends.'

Passing to literature, which formed the main topic of conversation, d'Alembert notes a tendency to adopt the opinions of others, though they were not infallible and were less valid than her own. 'Sometimes you are carried away by enthusiasm, but in the realm of sentiment, which may be called your domain, you are never at fault. Your chief trait in society is that you adapt your words to each in turn, never talking of yourself but much of them—an unfailing method of pleasing. Neither pretentious nor careless, you are entirely natural but in no way naïve. Prudent and reserved, you can control yourself without effort and conceal your feelings without guile. Truthful and frank with those you esteem, experience has put you on your guard with the rest; but since you are frank by nature and discreet merely by reflection, nature occasionally asserts itself. You are both gay and melancholy—gay by nature, melancholy by reflection. The phases of melancholy derive from your unhappy experiences and you dislike attempts to restore your spirits. Though not always depressed you are penetrated by

something still worse: so rarely do you lose your distaste for life
that you would accept death without regret even in a cheerful
moment.

'Your character, no less than your attractions and your mind,
wins you friends. You abhor malevolence and satire. You hate
nobody except perhaps one woman who has given you cause;
yet you do not take up arms as she does to a degree which affects
her happiness. You have another quality which is rare, particularly in a woman: you are without envy. You do justice to all the
qualities of all the women of your acquaintance, and even to your
one enemy for what is good in her. But that is due to your feeling
that all human beings are equally to be pitied and that you would
not care to exchange with anyone. This absence of malevolence
and envy denotes a noble soul. Though you would be glad of
money and need it, you make no effort to obtain it. Your soul is
not only very lofty but very sensitive, and this sensitivity is rather
a torment than a pleasure. You feel one can only be happy through
the passions, and you know their dangers too well to give way
to them. So you ration your love. You give to your friends from
your superabundant sensibility all you can, but there is so much left
over that you lavish it on all comers. This makes you sympathise
with the unfortunate, even those you do not know, and you will
do anything to help. You stick up for your friends, be they right
or wrong. The unceasing travail of your soul renders it less harmonious than it appears. You are often capricious and sharp, but
you let no one see it except the author of this portrait. You recognise his friendship by showing yourself to him as you are, and this
qualifies him to tell you that your sharpness of tone and caprice are
unworthy of you. Keep them for occasions when your friends
deserve it, which will not be frequent in view of their devotion.
You admit this accursed sharpness: try to correct it. You were
born with a tender, gentle and sensitive soul, and its experiences
have been cruel. So this disagreeable fault is not due to nature.
Having been thwarted and wounded in your feelings and your
tastes, you have repressed sentiments which would have caused
you unhappiness and thereby dulled those which might have
brought sweetness into your soul. They lie as if asleep and
motionless at the bottom of your heart. You regret the pain
caused by your sharpness when you see how deeply it is felt, and

then a word, a moment, puts everything right. You try to give pleasure to everyone, and I know no one who is so generally liked. Sure of keeping your old friends, you think chiefly of making new ones and are not always too careful in your choice. You care nothing for ranks and titles: you see the great as they should be seen, without servility or disdain. Your courage is greater than your strength; poverty, ill-health, misfortunes of every kind, try your patience without destroying it. Your sufferings have made you friends whose attachment and esteem have brought a certain consolation.'

The only error in d'Alembert's subtle analysis, which reveals a delightful intimacy, is the assertion that she lacked passion, and before long the discovery of his mistake was almost to break his heart. Julie was justly proud of her salon, but she needed something more. Neither the most brilliant conversation of her guests nor the unselfish companionship of d'Alembert could satisfy that ardent soul. Living in the dawning romantic age of *La Nouvelle Héloise* and *Clarissa*, *Werther* and *Paul et Virginie*, she too could qualify as a *grande amoureuse*; yet most of her circle knew her merely as a gracious hostess. D'Alembert, who was never in love and was believed by some people to be impotent, spent hours in her company every day without fathoming her quivering sensibility. When, however, the Spanish Marquis de Mora appeared on the horizon, her infatuation became the talk of the town. Married at twelve to an heiress of eleven still playing with her dolls, the rich, handsome and cultivated grandee had *liaisons* but never a *grande passion* till he visited his father, Count Fuentes, the Spanish Ambassador in Paris, at the age of twenty-two. When his girl-wife died in childbirth, he became a highly eligible *parti* and was welcomed both at Court and in the salons. Sharing the advanced views of his father-in-law, Aranda, the leading reformer of eighteenth-century Spain, he fitted easily into the intellectual society of the French capital, which was completely dominated by the *Philosophes*. Julie, now thirty-four, fell in love with him at first sight. 'Un coeur, oh quel coeur! Cet homme remplit l'idée que j'ai de la perfection.' Her passion was reciprocated, but in January 1767 he was sent back to Spain on grounds of health. He returned in October 1768, saddened by the loss of his three-year-old son and depressed by the knowledge that he was a doomed

man. There was talk of marriage, but the air of Paris was bad for
him and he could not stay long. There was no thought of a
*liaison*, but their passion was reflected in Julie's health and spirits.
Having lost his wife and son, he felt lonely and was grateful for
her sympathy. When he visited the Court at Fontainebleau he
wrote to her twice a day. It was too good to last, for at this moment his father resigned the Embassy, partly to save his son from
a *mésalliance*. Mora had to tear himself away, and they never met
again. The correspondence continued, but on her side with
diminishing ardour. For him, slowly dying of consumption, she
was still the only woman in the world: for her the vacuum left
by his departure was quickly filled by a new and fiercer flame.
During the brief remainder of her life her heart was torn by the
loving letters she continued to receive from Spain while she tried
to conceal the fact that he had lost his chance.

The final chapter of Julie's life opened on June 21, 1772, when
she met Comte de Guibert at the house of a friend. Three days
later she wrote to Condorcet: 'I have met M. de Guibert and like
him much; he is unlike anyone else.' She ordered his *Essai
Général de Tactique*, which had recently won fame for the young
colonel, and she wrote to say how much she had enjoyed it. As
one of the classics of military literature, ranking with the *Rêveries*
of Marshal Saxe, it was praised by Frederick the Great, hailed by
Voltaire as a work of genius, and annotated by Napoleon. This
manual for commanders contained a Preliminary Discourse which
attacked absolutism and anticipated the ideas of 1789. It was for
this wider interest that it found its way into the Paris salons, in one
of which, according to La Harpe, the ladies spent an evening dis-
cussing which was most desirable—to be his mother, his sister or
his mistress. He was also a brilliant talker and a dramatist, and
could boast of conquests in addition to his *maîtresse en titre*, Mme
de Montsauge, a quiet, tolerant wife and mother who never made
scenes. A few days after the first meeting he called on Julie and
reported to Condorcet that he continued to like her very much.
She was soon madly in love with him and bared her heart in letters
which Sainte-Beuve justly ranks with the outpourings of Éloise
and the Portuguese Nun. The passion mounted to an ecstasy
which exhausted her in body and soul till it burned her to death
after three years, as a moth is extinguished by the scorching flame.

At Julie's reiterated demand Guibert returned her letters lest they should fall into careless hands and start rumours of a *liaison*. They were handed back to him after her death by d'Alembert, her literary executor. Most of them were published by his widow in 1809, and the complete correspondence, including a few letters from Guibert, was edited by his great-grandson, Comte de Villeneuve-Guibert, in 1906.

The earliest surviving letter dates from May, 1773, almost a year after their first acquaintance, when the young officer was about to embark on a prolonged visit to Central Europe. It sounds the two notes which echo through the 500 pages of the correspondence—her passion for him and her qualms of conscience for disloyalty to Mora. 'You are an amiable and excellent creature. Why do you combine everything that can please and attract, and above all why do you offer me a gift which I have not deserved? No, no, I do not want your friendship; it would console me but also exasperate me, and I need repose and to forget you for a time. I want to be frank with you and with myself. I have this moment received a letter from him (Mora) so full of confidence in my feelings. He speaks of me, my thoughts, my soul, with the intimacy and confidence one reveals when we feel strongly. Mon Dieu, by what charm or what fatality did you come in to cause distraction? Why did I not die last September? Then I should have had no cause to reproach myself. Even now I would die for him, sacrifice everything for him. I should not love him more but better. But he will forgive me, I have suffered so much. My soul and body were worn out by prolonged grief. It was then that I saw you, and you revived my soul and filled it with pleasure. But tell me, is that the tone of friendship and confidence? What is it that carries me away? Help me to know myself, to regain control, for my soul is in turmoil. Is that from remorse? Is it my fault? Is it you? Is it your journey? What is it that persecutes me? My strength is at an end. At this moment my confidence in you has no limits, and perhaps I may not speak to you of my life again. Adieu! I shall see you tomorrow, or perhaps I shall feel embarrassment at what I have written today. Remember your promise to burn my letters at once. I wish to heaven that you had been my friend or that I had never known you. Do you believe that you will be my friend? Think it over, just once. Is that too much to ask?' It was not the letter of a happy woman, and a further element of bitterness in her cup was her knowledge that the traveller would receive letters from another woman. Though she never met Mme de Montsauge, the rival hovered like a dark shadow over her thoughts. She was too tactful to demand a choice, but she never understood how a man who was all the world to her could love—or pretend to love—two women at the same time.

Julie was far too highly strung for quiet happiness. 'I thought I should die on Friday when a letter (from Mora) was brought to me by special courier,' she reported; 'I felt sure it would bring fatal news. I had not the strength to open it. For a quarter of an hour I sat motionless; my soul was frozen. Then I found that, though I am spared the worst, I have still much suffering to endure. How I am crushed under life's burdens! The duration of my sufferings makes them unbearable. Consider if I ought to love you and cherish your presence. You have contrived to cause a diversion in my acute and deep-seated malady. I await and desire your letters. Believe me, only the unhappy deserve to have friends. You will see that I know how to love. That is all I can do, but even with feeble resources one can effect a good deal by concentrating on a single aim. I have only one thought, which fills my soul and the whole of my life.' Writing to him at Berlin she complained of insomnia and reported that she had taken opium to calm her pain. She judged everyone by their ability to love, and few could pass her exacting test with full marks. Diderot, she wrote, was an extraordinary man. 'I like him very much, but he never goes beyond emotion. Nothing half and half, undecided, on the small scale, appeals to me. I do not understand the language of society people; they amuse themselves and yawn, have friends and love nothing. It all seems to me deplorable. Yes, I prefer the torment that consumes me to the pleasure in which they are benumbed. My type is not agreeable, but one is loved, and that is worth a thousand times more than giving pleasure.'

If love-letters are to qualify as literature the writers must let themselves go. Julie's side of the correspondence is one long cry of distress. 'Your absence weighs on me,' she wrote to Guibert at Berlin, 'but I am sure that your presence would do me good. Mon Dieu, what a horrible predicament in which pleasure, consolation, friendship, everything, turns to poison! Tell me what to do, how to recover my balance. How often one dies before death! Everything afflicts and hurts me, and I cannot cast off the crushing burden. To love, to be loved, is not an advantage. My sufferings are innumerable, and I have to reproach myself with troubling the repose and bringing unhappiness to the object of my love. My soul is worn out by distress, the machine is destroyed, yet I live and must live. Why do you wish it? What is my life to you? What value do you put on it? What am I to you? Your soul is so occupied, your life so full. How can you find time to pity my sufferings, and how can you conjure up sufficient sensibility to respond to my friendship? Yes, you are too kind; you seem to feel interest, though I think I should not inspire it. You need my letters: can that be true? Yes, since you say so. But why have you not written for so long? How comes it that she (Mme de Montsauge) does not love you madly, as you would wish and as you deserve? She has no taste, no sensibility, I am sure. She ought to love you, if only for vanity. But why do I interfere? You are satisfied, or, if not, you like the injury she inflicts. So why should I pity you? But this other unhappy person, it is she who excites my interest. Have you written to her?' Their friendship, she added, was quite unlike that of Montaigne and La Boétie. 'While they were tranquil, we are two sick people, but with the difference that you are full of strength and reason, always in excellent health, while I am stricken by a mortal malady in which all the alleviations I have tried turn into poison and intensify my maladies. They have deranged my reason and my judgment, for I do not want to get well but only to die.'

Every letter from Guibert was opened with trembling hands, for she knew that she meant infinitely less to him than he to her, and that the thought of marriage never entered his head. 'I love you too much to put on the brake on myself,' she wrote on August 1. 'I would rather have to ask your pardon than avoid mistakes. With you I have no *amour-propre*, and I do not understand all those rules of conduct which make one always pleased with oneself and so cold with those we love. I hate prudence. Forgive me for saying that I hate even the duties of friendship which substitute discretion for interest and tact for sensibility. I love *abandon*. I respond to the instinct of the moment, and I long for others to do the same with me. Mon Dieu, how different from you! I possess no virtues and with my friends I recognise no duties. I am close to the state of nature. The savages do not love with more sensibility or less pretence. Neither society, nor unhappiness, nor anything else has been able to corrupt my heart. With you I shall never be on my guard, and I shall never suspect you. You tell me you are my friend, and you are virtuous, so what have I to fear?'

Guibert returned from his journey with enhanced prestige. He had been welcomed by Frederick at Potsdam and by Voltaire at Ferney. Julie's passion had grown into a devouring flame and for the first time he seemed inclined to respond. He even promised to break with Mme de Montsauge, though the plan was never fulfilled. There was still a marked difference between them. While he was busy with other things, constantly dining out and writing successful plays, she lived for him alone. She coughed, spat blood, hardly slept, and bombarded him with letters. 'Je vous aime comme il faut aimer, avec excès, avec folie, transport et désespoir.' The correspondence slows down, for they met in Mme Geoffrin's salon and elsewhere, but the fever continued to rage. 'What afflicts me,' she wrote in the last letter of 1773, 'is the number of days which pass without seeing you. Mon Dieu, if you knew what they are, what life is, without the interest and the pleasure of seeing you. Mon ami, dissipation, occupation, movement are enough for you, but my happiness is you, only you. I should not care to live if I could not see you and love you every moment of my life.'

The parallel correspondence with Mora, once a delight, had become a penance, for in playing a double game Julie forfeited her self-respect. 'Come to Paris for treatment,' she wrote; 'Madrid will kill you.' Though the dying man had sensed the cooling of her love, his tender letters continued and he determined to reconquer her heart after an absence of three years, but when he reached Bordeaux a new haemorrhage ended his sufferings. His last letter written on the day of his death cut her to the heart. 'J'allais vous revoir. Il faut mourir. Quelle affreuse destinée! Je meure pour vous.' Back came her ring with a lock of her hair inside. 'I killed him,' she exclaimed. She and the faithful d'Alembert wept together, and her letters to Guibert were full of the shattering news. The shock completed the ruin of her health; headaches, giddiness, insomnia, spasms, were her daily companions, which ever-increas-

ing doses of opium failed to mitigate. For such a bundle of nerves
the only cure was death. D'Alembert, distressed by her sufferings,
did his best, but of the depth of her passion for Guibert he had
little idea. Her letters blend transports of devotion with jealous
rebukes. Hungering for his visits, she was disappointed when he
came. Sometimes he missed an engagement or neglected to write;
sometimes his thoughts seemed far away. Her behaviour, on the
contrary, was explained in three words: 'Je vous aime.'

The climax was reached on February 10, 1774, when they sat
together in a box at the Opera lent by a friend. Intoxicated by the
music, their lips touched, and, to quote the editor's terse note,
'their love ceased to be platonic'. For Guibert it was a familiar
experience, for Julie the opening of the gates of Paradise. Weeks
of almost delirious rapture ensued. 'My friend, I am perfect since I
love you to perfection.' It was too hot to last, and in retrospect the
evening at the Opera seemed more of a nightmare than a moment
of bliss. On the first anniversary she poured out her heart. 'Midnight strikes, mon ami. I have just recalled a memory which
freezes my blood—the tenth of February last year when I was intoxicated by a poison the effect of which still endures. In that
instant it stopped the circulation of my blood, carries it to the
heart with greater violence, recalls searing regrets. What a fatality that the liveliest and sweetest sentiment of pleasure should be
allied to the most crushing misery! What a terrible mixture! At
the same hour M. de Mora was struck down by a mortal blow.
And I, three hundred leagues away, was more cruel and more cul-
pable than the ignorant barbarians who have killed him. I die of
regrets—my eyes and my heart are full of tears. Adieu, mon ami,
I ought not to have loved you.'

Julie's first letters after the Opera incident blend ecstasy and
grief. One dated 'De tous les instants de ma vie' contains only a
single sentence: 'Mon ami, je souffre, je vous aime, et je vous
attends.' Her pain was intensified by the thought that at the moment Guibert was reading her letter he had just read another from
Mme de Montsauge. 'Mon Dieu, believe me when I say: Restore
her peace of mind and be happy. That is the wish of the unfortunate creature who always recalls Dante's line on the gates of hell:
Abandon hope, all ye who enter here. I have none and ask for
none. You lead me astray and cannot console me.' On May 12 she

launched the sharpest arrow in her quiver which hurt her more to write than him to read. 'Vous n'avez pas besoin d'être aimé.'

The distracted woman now lost interest in her salon and her friends. 'How I hate and despise them, and how horrible it would be to resume the life I have lived for ten years! I should prefer utter solitude to their horrible society.' Even the faithful d'Alembert got on her nerves. 'I feel unworthy of him and shall be glad when he goes away.' Her books lost their charm. 'You alone and my grief are all I have left in the world. I have no more interest, no more possessions, no more friends, and I do not need them. To love you and see you or die: that is the last and only wish of my soul. Yours does not respond, I know, but I do not complain. I feel I am no longer *myself*, I am *you*.' She was too sick at heart to reflect that these despairing cries might produce a feeling of satiety, almost of nausea, for she was rapidly becoming a liability, almost a bore. His efforts to comfort her were of no avail. 'Don't talk to me of what I find in society. It has become an intolerable constraint. Everyone would like to penetrate into my soul. I am surrounded by so much kindness, but I remain unhappy. You alone, my friend, can make me experience not happiness but pleasure, and what deadly poison that is!'

In July, 1774, six months after the night at the Opera, Guibert became engaged. He had been courting for a year without her guessing that anything was amiss. Desiring to cool off but without explaining the reason, he informed her that he no longer needed her love. His letter is lost, but her reply tells its own tale. 'Think me mad or unjust if you will,' she replied, 'but I must say that I never had such a blow. I feel so humiliated, crushed by having given anyone the horrible right to say what you have told me. My heart, my pride, everything in me, is revolted, wounded, offended for ever. You have taught me that you can no longer make me unhappy.' Stung by her reproaches, he begged and obtained her forgiveness, for she hungered for his love.

Guibert's earliest surviving letters, which date from the summer of 1774, are affectionate enough but are far removed from the passionate terms which Julie habitually employed. On the eve of a long visit to his parents in the country he assured her that he would need her letters and would often report. 'But this will not compensate for the *ton* of your society, your conversation, for the

sweet habit of seeing you almost every day. You have given me
thoughts of repose, glory, happiness, very different from those I
had. Nothing could take your place. My existence has never been
more strongly attached to another person. I have had sentiments
more lively, more tumultuous, but never so sweet or on which I
could build my happiness.' To her reiterated reproaches for his
association with Mme de Montsauge he calmly rejoined that it was
hardly for her to condemn him for not breaking entirely with
someone who had once been loved. 'I enjoy seeing her. Has not
your heart room for two sentiments? Am I to do you the injustice
of believing that you do not love me because you have other affections? Do I try to root out from your heart everything not related to
myself? My feeling for Mme de M. does not injure you, deceive you,
betray you. It is different from my feeling for you. It is neither
love nor friendship, but attraction and habit. Why do you torment me? I love you. Is not that enough?'

Julie demanded all or nothing and told him so in the plainest
terms. 'Your letter', he replied, 'surprises and confounds me. You
treat me with unexampled harshness. You speak of hatred, and
your letter breathes it.' He would keep her letter, but not to show
it to Mme de Montsauge, as she angrily assumed. 'No doubt it will
be your last, and it would be better to drop me altogether than to
say you hate me. I shall ask your friends for news of your health.'
She realised, replied Julie, that in asking for his love she had asked
the impossible. With M. de Mora it had been very different. 'By
unheard-of good fortune the tenderest, most perfect, most charming being who ever existed had given me his heart, his thoughts,
his whole existence. Unworthy though I was I was in transports
of delight. When I spoke of the immense distance between us,
he persuaded me that we were equals because I loved him. I
thought you too might love me and that crazy idea dragged me
into the abyss. It is very late to cure myself of this error, which I
detest. In despising myself, I ought to hate you, and indeed you
have stirred in me a horrible feeling. My friendship and interest in
your welfare will never cease, but it will be a more moderate sentiment which, if you respond, can still provide me with some sweet
moments without torturing my soul, which remains sensitive but
without passion. I no longer feel hatred nor passion nor. . . .
Mon Dieu, what word was I about to use?'

The best solution of the problem which generated such unceasing friction was for Guibert to find a wife. On October 22, 1774,
he wrote: 'I must marry, bon Dieu, I must. My father has a plan
for me. I will tell you everything and you will give me advice.
This would not separate you from me. Happiness is far away and I
see no prospect of bringing it within my reach. Mon amie, que vous
êtes bonne, que vous êtes aimable, que vous avez d'âme!' Despite
Julie's recent assertion that she had regained her balance the flames
shot up as fiercely as ever. 'Mon ami, je vous aime à la folie. I give
you more than you want. You have no need to be so loved, and I
need rest, by which I mean death. I am possessed by the desire for
deliverance from searing regrets. Mon Dieu, why do you keep me
suspended between life and death? Let me die or let my soul be so
filled by you that I do not feel the vacuum he (Mora) left.' Three
kinds of people, she added, had a right to pity and indulgence—
the mad, the sick and the unhappy. She could not sleep, took
opium, and thought of death twenty times a day. 'Regain your
freedom, leave me to my grief, let me occupy myself without
distraction with the only object I have adored and whose memory
is for me the dearest thing on earth. I ought not to bewail him for
I ought to have followed him. It is you who keep me alive and
are the torment of a creature consumed by grief and who spends
what little strength is left to her in asking for death. I pardon you
and I do not hate you, not from generosity or good nature but
because my soul is perishing of fatigue. Cease telling me you love
me. That balm turns to poison: you calm me and distract me in
turn. Stop persecuting me. I have only one wish—not to see you
alone. I beg you for the last time not to visit me except between
five and nine.' Despite such spasmodic efforts to ration their
intercourse her heart was to cry out for him till the day of her
death.

Though she had long been prepared for the news of Guibert's
marriage, Julie was crushed by the formal announcement of his
engagement in March, 1775. 'I felt in the depths of my heart that
our love must cease and reacted with all my remaining strength. I
cannot live. Mon ami, what I suffer, what I feel, is insupportable.
It seems impossible not to succumb, and I must merely let myself
die.' When three hours in her bath had calmed her nerves she
added: 'Your care and your anxiety persuade me that, whatever

you may say, we can still love one another.' She even expressed a
wish to meet Mlle de Courcelles, the pretty girl whose portrait
was painted by Greuze, and she was enchanted by her visitor. 'A
thousand times I was tempted to fall at your knees,' wrote Guibert
in gratitude; but her melting mood quickly passed. 'Then you
wrote me a cruel letter. What do you want? Your picture of my
conduct horrifies me, ranking me with Lovelace and all the rascals
of fiction. You say I have turned and twisted the poignard in your
wounds, that I enjoy your tears and convulsions, that I am your
executioner. That is enough to make me angry, but I love and forgive. I would still give my blood for you. Reread my letters, and
see if I am a criminal. Mon amie, calm yourself, I beg you.' Once
again he was forgiven, and Julie congratulated him on his choice.
'I found her charming and fully worthy of the interest she inspires
in you. Yes, you will be happy.' Thus the pendulum swung back-
wards and forwards between resignation and despair.

Guibert's marriage on June 1, 1775, unleashed a fresh tornado.
'Twenty times I desired a break and an end of my sufferings. I
could not cure myself, but now you have supplied the means.
Your marriage, in revealing your whole soul, has repulsed and
closed mine forever.' These moods never lasted long, and her
next letter sounded a softer note. 'My friend, yes my dearest
friend, do let us keep on good terms and forgive each other. There
are still reasons for mutual indulgence. Remember I am very ill
and very unhappy. If you wish me to live, help me, support me,
make up for all the harm you have done me.' At times death
seemed to be very near. 'This morning I was in an access of despair,' she reported on July 15. 'M. d'Alembert was alarmed, and I
lacked the presence of mind to calm him. His interest tore my
heart strings, relieved my soul, and made me burst into tears. I
could not speak and in my frenzy he tells me I cried twice over: I
shall die, leave me. These words moved him to tears. He wanted
to summon my friends and said to me: If only M. de Guibert were
here! He alone could help you. Your name recalled me to my
senses. I felt I must calm myself for the sake of the peace of mind
of this excellent man. I told him it was a *crise de nerfs*, and indeed
one arm and one hand were taut. I took a sedative and he sent for
a doctor. I shut myself up in my room and waited for the post. It
brought two letters from you, but my hands trembled so violently

that I could not open them. Happily the first word I saw was *Mon amie*. My soul and my lips were glued to the paper. I could not read further but only made out occasional words. I read: You restore me to life. I breathe again. My friend, it is you who restore me to life. I should die if you did not love me. Never, no never, have I experienced a feeling so tender and so passionate. I have read and reread ten times, twenty times, these words which brought consolation to my heart. We will keep straight, I swear to you. Your happiness, your duty, shall be sacred to me. I should be horrified by any feelings which could disturb them. If you are happy I will not mention my unhappiness. You know what passion is, the strength it brings to a soul of which it has taken possession. To this strength I promise you to join that which derives from the love of virtue and contempt of death, in order never to disturb your peace of mind and your duties. If you love me I shall possess a martyr's strength. If I doubt you, nothing will remain but deliverance from an intolerable burden. Do you think there is no degree of passion beyond what I have displayed? If so, you do not know everything. No words can express the force of a passion which feeds on tears and remorse and faces the stark alternative of love or death. That you will not find in the books. I have spent an evening with you which would seem exaggerated if one read it in Prévost, the greatest authority on the sweetness and terror of this passion.'

Morellet pictures the frail hostess at this period as intermittently vivacious in her little drawing-room, where a few intimates still gathered round her, but they gave her scanty pleasure. She was surrounded by people, she complained, but she could not have felt more lonely in the desert. Guibert was now the only ray of light in a darkening world. Letters and visits, reproaches and reconciliations, continued. When her health was visibly failing, he became more gentle and patient. Her last brief message began with the familiar assurance, 'My friend, I love you,' and ended: 'Je m'étiens, adieu.'

When she took to her bed her half-brother, the Marquis de Vichy, was summoned. Her persuaded her to receive the sacraments and was present at her death. Guibert sat upstairs with d'Alembert, who inquired every half-hour for news. While d'Alembert and Condorcet conducted the funeral service, Guibert stood in the crowd. Her will left him 'all my English books, all my quarto volumes of French literature, and other fine editions'. Her writing-table went to Suard, the busts of d'Alembert and Voltaire to Condorcet. 'To Mme Geoffrin, who has overwhelmed me with kindness and whom I love so tenderly, my little marble bird on its ormulu stand'; to d'Alembert, 'as a mark of my tender friendship', some furniture. No hostess of her time—perhaps of any time—gave or received so much love as Julie de Lespinasse. None of them sounded the heights or plumbed the depths of life in the same overflowing measure. 'Mon âme à la fièvre continue', she confessed, and the disease was mortal. Born to love and to suffer, she owes her fame, not to the novelty of her experiences, but to her unrivalled capacity to describe the tumults and the torments of a woman's soul. Of all the celebrated *salonnières* during three centuries of French history, she is the woman whom we know best. None of them combined in equal degree the shining qualities of mind and heart which result in the flowering of personality.

When she was gone the two men who had stood nearest to her painted her portrait and bewailed their loss. Guibert's celebrated *Éloge d'Élise* reveals that she had been much more to him than a mere plaything, though he had never given her his whole heart. She was far from beautiful and her face was disfigured by smallpox, but her plain looks were forgotten when she spoke: never had he known such variety of expression in a face. Wanting nothing for herself, she emitted a spiritual radiance which cast its spell even over dull minds and torpid hearts. 'Élise, I said to her, you can make marble feel and matter think.' She was the soul of every conversation, but she preferred striking sparks from the minds of others to exhibiting her own. She was well-informed, knowing English and Italian and studying the literature of other lands in translations. Though she loved the French classics of the seventeenth century, she enjoyed Rousseau and the Abbé Prévost even more, Sterne and Richardson most of all. She also delighted in Tacitus and Montesquieu, Montaigne and Locke. Paintings, sculpture and music appealed to her no less than books. She wrote nothing for publication, but her letters surpassed those of Mme de Sévigné or Mme de Maintenon. Yet what was her mind in comparison to her soul? All that was vile and base aroused her

M

contempt and indignation. She pitied and helped the poor and unfortunate because she had suffered herself.

Guibert's sorrow was sincere enough, but it was nothing to the agony of d'Alembert, who received condolences from Frederick the Great and other friends. 'He buried himself in his apartment at the Louvre,' records Marmontel, 'and often complained of his loneliness. In vain did I remind him of what he had often told me—that his friend had changed. Yes, he rejoined, but I had not. She had ceased to live for me, but I continued to live for her. Now she is gone, I have no motive to live.' Two months after her death her literary executor poured out his heart in a paroxysm of grief on discovering from her papers that she had loved him far less than he had believed. 'Why did you assure me, ten months before your death, that I was always what you treasured most, when you were about so cruelly to prove the contrary? Why did that feeling suddenly change to estrangement and aversion? What had I done to displease you? Why did you not tell me if there was any reason for complaint? My heart has never ceased to belong to you even when it was so roughly repulsed. Twenty times have I longed to throw myself into your arms and beg you to tell me what was my crime, but I feared a rebuff. Your face, your words, even your silence, held me back, and you were too ill to bear my tender reproaches. The only time I could have bared my heart was that dreadful moment a few hours before your death when you asked my pardon, but then you were too weak to talk or to listen. Among your vast correspondence I found that you had not kept a single letter of mine. You so often told me that of all the sentiments you had inspired our love alone had not made you unhappy. Why was not that enough? You have taught me that the greatest pain is not to mourn those we love but those who have ceased to love us. Without relatives, exposed since birth to neglect, misfortune and injustice, we seem to have been created for each other, like two reeds buffeted by the wind which cling together. Why did you seek for other supports? They soon failed you, and you died in the belief that you were alone in the world when you merely needed to stretch out your hand to take what was so near but what you would not see. If you had lived longer, perhaps Nature, which had made us for one another, would have united us, never to part again.' Who can think of this suffering woman without sparing a thought for the most distinguished, the most devoted, and the most unselfish of her friends?

## IV. *Mme du Deffand and Horace Walpole*

THE quarrel between Mme du Deffand and Julie de Lespinasse left a deep furrow in the lives of both women. The younger set forth to win literary renown by her love affairs and to die of a broken heart at the age of forty-two. The affection of the elder for her old partner Hénault revived for a while, and she wrote to Voltaire: 'le Président fait toute la consolation de ma vie'. But in her later years he had become deaf, dull and somnolent, and the exacting hostess was at all times inclined to assess the value of her friends by the contribution they could make to the gaiety of her circle. The vacuum created by the departure of d'Alembert and other *habitués* was soon to be filled in a manner which neither she nor they could predict. Within a year she found a deeper happiness than she had ever known in a quasi-maternal friendship with a middle-aged Englishman whose face she never saw. The embittered old lady, now nearing seventy, entered on her Indian Summer, the romantic story of which is enshrined in a correspondence even more celebrated than that between Julie and Guibert. In both cases the association meant infinitely more to the woman than to the man, and the inequality of response constitutes the pathos of the partnership.

Horace Walpole was born with intellectual powers and social gifts which would have brought him to the front even if he had not been the son of an all-powerful Prime Minister. Possessing a talent for friendship, delighting in art and literature, well furnished with the means to travel and entertain, to build and to collect, he played a prominent part in the life of his country for half a century, leaving behind him a pile of correspondence which ranks him with Cicero and Erasmus, Mme de Sévigné and Voltaire, among the consummate letter-writers of all time. In the course of the Grand Tour—almost *de rigueur* for wealthy young aristocrats—he visited Paris in 1737 at the age of twenty on his way to Italy. For the next two decades he sat in Parliament, taking little part in debate, but through his family connections always close to the heart of affairs. Macaulay's portrait of an elegant trifler, judging everything that was great to be little and everything little to be great, does him less than justice.

Furnished with introductions to Mme Geoffrin from Lady Hervey and to Mme du Deffand from George Selwyn, Walpole found all doors open when at the age of forty-eight he revisited Paris in September 1765. Though his French was imperfect, his personal distinction, vivacity and wit made him a welcome guest. He was run after, he reported, as if he were an African prince or a tame canary. Though Mme Geoffrin won his respect by her solid good sense, he found her *Philosophes* rather a trial and preferred the more aristocratic salon, of which he quickly became the brightest luminary. Soon he was writing of 'that delightful, old, blind Mme du Deffand'. He was as anxious to learn about past times as she was longing to talk. 'I was in your debt', he wrote to George Selwyn, 'for making over Mme du Deffand to me, who is delicious —that is as often as I can get her fifty years back. But she is as eager about what happens every day as I am about the last century. I sup there twice a week and bear all her company for the sake of the Regent.'

The first full-length portrait was painted in a letter to the poet Gray. 'Mme du Deffand was for a short period mistress of the Regent. She is very old and stone blind, but retains all her vivacity, wit, judgment, memory, passion and agreeableness. She goes to operas, plays, suppers and Versailles, gives suppers twice a week, has everything new read to her, makes new songs and epigrams admirably, and remembers every one that has been made these four-score years. She corresponds with Voltaire, dictates charming letters to him, contradicts him, is no bigot to him or anybody, and laughs both at the clergy and the *Philosophes*. In a dispute into which she easily falls she is very warm and yet convincing, even when she is in the wrong. Her judgment on every subject is as just as possible, on every point of conduct as wrong as possible, for she is in all love and hatred; passionate for her friends to enthusiasm; still anxious to be loved—I don't mean by lovers; and a vehement enemy, but openly.' Soon he was visiting the wittiest woman in France every day, and the sojourn proved so enjoyable that it lasted seven months. The foundations of an historic friendship had been well and truly laid, and his recently published Paris journal reveals acquaintance with the cream of French society.

The correspondence began on the eve of his departure in April, 1766. Copious selections from her letters were published in 1810 by Agnes Berry, the closest friend of Walpole's closing years and his literary executor, and extracts from his letters were quoted in her notes. The interest of the exchange was widely recognised, and Napoleon took the volumes in his carriage on the long road to Russia. An almost complete collection was edited by Mrs. Paget Toynbee in three stout volumes a century later, and the definitive text fills five massive volumes in the sumptuous American edition of W. S. Lewis. Even now the collection remains incomplete, for only about 1,000 of the estimated 1,700 writen or dictated by Mme du Deffand survive. Of Walpole's contribution, estimated at about 700, only about 100, mostly brief fragments, are available, some taken from Miss Berry's footnotes, fourteen from copies made by the French Secret Police and discovered in the Police Archives in Paris. Some may have been destroyed by Mme du Deffand herself in response to his instructions, for he dreaded unfriendly comments in Parisian drawing-rooms on his friendship and his French. Most of them were doubtless burned by Miss Berry at the writer's request.

The first surviving letter of Mme du Deffand, written on the eve of Walpole's departure, reveals how close they had come to one another. 'You are wrong to leave us; I am sure you would find plenty to please you here. Your letter went to my heart and increased in me that word you have forbidden me to use. Come what may I shall be your friend in spite of you and despite common sense.' A missing letter from Chantilly on his way home mingling affection and rebuke provoked a lengthy apologia. 'Your letter was a great surprise but I see one may expect anything from you. I begin by assuring you of my prudence and I do not resent your advice. No one will see our correspondence, and I will faithfully obey your instructions. You are the best of men and full of such good intentions that none of your actions or words can ever be suspect. If you had told me earlier what you think of me I should have been calmer and more reserved. Since no one is listening I wish to tell you that no one can love more tenderly than I love you. I believe one gets what one deserves, and as I claim to possess a tender and sincere heart I am reaping my reward at the close of life. I will not allow myself to say all I think. In the pleasure you give me there is an element of sadness since you will be away for a long time, but I will not turn this letter into an elegy. I only ask you to keep your promise to write to me in full confidence and to believe that I belong more to you than to myself.'

Her next letter was a spirited rejoinder to a scolding (not preserved) from Amiens. 'If you were French I should think you a big coxcomb; as you are English you are only cracked. Where, I may ask, have I given way to indiscretions et emportements romanesques? Indiscretions, perhaps, but "emportements romanesques" makes me furious, and I should like to tear out your pretty eyes, though you cannot well suspect them of turning my head. I am the sworn enemy of that sort of thing. Please understand that I love you no more than I should. Come back and you will see how I shall behave. I want you to judge for yourself of the success of your admonitions and the effects of my wrath. Since you left my entourage seems to have become even more stupid, and I anticipate insufferable ennui. When we were together I guessed what you were thinking, you knew what I was thinking, and we always told each other. That time is over and God knows when it will return. Be an Abelard if you will, but do not expect Héloise. Did I never tell you how I detested those letters—false, exaggerated, disgusting? Adieu, my dear tutor. I choose that title only while waiting for another to occur to me. I am happy to be *votre chère petite*.' Since this charming endearment was his own invention, she could use it with impunity.

When Walpole suggested that she should paint his portrait she dispatched a singularly penetrating analysis. 'I know you are very intelligent and a very good sort. You have principles and courage. Your heart is good and your friendships reliable, though neither tender nor easy. I do not know if you have any sentiment; if so you resist it as a weakness. You have one failing, which is unpardonable, to which you sacrifice your feelings and by which you regulate your conduct—the fear of ridicule. You do good without ostentation or hope of reward. Finally your soul is both good and beautiful.' Had she re-read these sentences a decade later she would not have desired to alter a word. The fear of ridicule, he confessed to her, was nothing new. 'From the minute I ceased to be young I have had a horrible fear of being a ridiculous old man.'

Mme du Deffand consoled herself with the dream of a second visit. 'All my circle misses you, wants you, is charmed by you,' she wrote on May 5, 1766. 'You can guess how happy it makes me. Hurry up your business and return. You will have a thousand delights in this country; that I can guarantee. There is another reason: you are the best man in the world. It must be a delight for you to bring real happiness to someone who has never had it. You make me believe in Providence, you compensate for all the injustices I have experienced, and I shall no longer fear my enemies. I will do nothing without consulting you. I always want to be *votre chère petite*. I forget my long life and want to be only thirteen. If you do not change, and if you come back to me, my life would have been very happy. You will blot out the past and I shall start reckoning from the day we met. I don't know what effect absence will have on you. Perhaps your friendship was a straw fire. But no, I do not believe it. Whatever you have said to me, I never felt you were insensitive. Don't tell me I am romancing, which I detest. Anything like love (*amour*) is odious to me. I am rather glad to be old and hideous and entirely glad to be blind so that I can be certain that I have no feelings except pure and holy friendship. But friendship I do love madly. My heart was made for that alone.' Never had she used such glowing phrases to any other man. She had waited all her life for a miracle to happen and in her seventieth year it had come.

The first surviving letter from Walpole, a month after his return to England, began with expressions of disgust at the barbarous public execution of Lally for his record in India. 'Ah, Madame, what horrors you tell me! Let no one ever say the English are hard and fierce—truly it is the French. Yes, you are savages, Iroquois. I am thankful to have left Paris before this horrible scene.' The denunciation of her country was followed by an equally sharp rebuke to herself. 'Your letter upsets me very much. Will your lamentations, Madame, never end? Why did I avow my friendship? I wanted to please you, not to add to your worries, suspicions, perpetual disquietude! Really, if friendship has all the drawbacks of love without its pleasures it is not inviting. You reveal it in its worst aspect, not its best. I renounce it if it only breeds bitterness. You mock at the letters of Héloïse, but you are far more lachrymose. If you desire our contacts to continue, strike a less tragic note. Am I cut out for the hero of an epistolary romance? How can you, Madame, clever as you are, adopt a style which revolts your Pylades? Talk to me like a reasonable woman, else I will copy the replies to the *Lettres Portugaises*.' Though she complained that the Walpole of England was not the Walpole of Paris, their friendship was too firmly based for anything to break. 'Je serais votre mère,' she wrote on May 21, and in her heart she never ceased to regard him, cantankerous though he was, as her devoted son. When Walpole reported a bad attack of gout and a forthcoming cure at Bath her alarm revealed how precious the friendship had become. 'I am so worried about you,' she wrote, 'that you cannot in fairness decline to report twice a week. Not a word in your own hand, but I must ask you to dictate a detailed and truthful bulletin in English.[1] Naturally my tutor is not so occupied with his pupil as is this pupil with her tutor. Alas! perhaps at the very moment I am writing, perhaps at the moment you receive this letter, you will be in great pain and dangerously ill. I cannot think of anything else. I fear your doctors are detestable, worse, I imagine, than ours. Both may be poisoners, but they employ different drugs. Ours are slow, yours prompt and violent. Tell me frankly if my letters bore or tire you. Nothing can displease or upset me except your illness.' The faithful Wiart, who knew all her secrets, enclosed a letter of his own begging for a bulletin twice a week. 'I cannot describe how she is worrying. She talks of ceasing to write for fear that an answer would tire you. Every moment she tells me I ought to go to England and that I might be of some service to you. I should be very happy, sir, if I could help and I would not hesitate for a moment to come. I really mean it. I assure you, sir, that if real friends exist, you can boast of having found one in Madame. Deliver her from her anxiety as often as possible. If you could see her state you would pity her. She cannot sleep. I beg a thousand pardons, sir, for taking such a liberty, but I felt it my duty to tell you of Madame's anxiety.'

As 1766 drew to its close her thoughts turned increasingly to the visit promised for February. 'What can attract you here?' she

---

[1] Wiart, her devoted secretary, reader and factotum, was taking English lessons at her wish.

asked on November 14. 'You say it is me, and I think it is true. No one here is worthy of you except myself. Not that I claim any superior merit or attraction except that I have a true friendship for you. You know it. Although you have often been annoyed and have done everything possible to destroy it, I am convinced that you do not resent its existence. You are less weak than other men but also, I think, more sensitive; so you are flattered to be understood and you are touched at being greatly loved. I forgive you the grief your letters have caused me.' When February 1767 came and went her letters tempered assurances of devotion with a fear of seeming importunate. 'If you meant it when you said that I was the only attraction to Paris, and that without me you would be bored, you should not come. My friendship must not become a burden. You owe me nothing. I followed my bent. I found you very different from anything I had ever seen. You seemed to embody my idea of an absolutely upright man. You showed me esteem and for some time you seemed to like my company. But during a year's absence I have noticed a decline in your affection. I was wrong to complain, and I recognise how many reasons I have to be content, for no one could be so considerate as you, with your regular letters and your plan for a visit. I must not abuse it, my tutor, and I free you from your promises. I confess a visit would give me great pleasure, but I have the courage to make the sacrifice.'

The journey, as she expected, was postponed from month to month, and even the kindest letters failed to dispel her gloom. 'You wish me to live till ninety,' she wrote in May. 'Good God, what an accursed hope! Don't you know that I detest life, that I am inconsolable for having been born? I am not made for this world, and I know not if there is another. If there is, and whatever it may be, I am afraid of it.' She had shed her religious beliefs in her schooldays and had found no substitute in the cult of reason which satisfied the *Philosophes*. Walpole's outlook was more optimistic. 'I believe in a future life. God has created so much that is good and beautiful that we can trust Him for the rest.' Lacking belief both in God and man, she clung the more closely to her new friend. 'If there is no news by Wednesday I shall be a little alarmed,' she wrote in June. 'Philosophy is a fine thing, but in sentiment it finds no place.' Nothing could check her outpourings of affection. 'Adieu, my tutor. I should prefer to call you my son,' she wrote in July. 'I know why I am attached to you. Neither time nor your absence nor your moods will ever change my attitude. You are sincere and good, variable but constant, hard but sensitive, yes, very sensitive, whatever you may say; noble, proud, generous, human. Possessing such qualities you can afford to be fantastic, odd and sometimes a little mad.' For the preservation of such a precious friendship she was ready to bear the most undeserved rebukes. Fate, she confided to him, had ordained that she should never be perfectly happy; and, hungering for love, she was grateful for every crumb which fell from his table.

After an absence of sixteen months Walpole returned to Paris in August, 1767, and all the trumpets sounded. 'I can scarcely believe that a man of your importance, who has his hands on the levers of a great State and therefore of all Europe, resolved to quit everything to visit an old sibyl. Of course it is ridiculous, but I confess I am delighted.' Every cloud melted away. The day after his departure she excused herself for the display of her feelings. 'What cowardice, weakness and folly you witnessed! My intentions were quite different, but . . . but . . . . Let us forget it. Forgive me, my tutor, and only think of your little one to say to yourself that she is reasonable, obedient and above all grateful; that her respect, her filial fear, her tender but serious attachment will be the happiness of her life till her last breath. What matters it if one is old and blind, or where one lives, or what one's entourage is like? When the soul is deeply engaged nothing is lacking save the object, and when that object responds to one's feelings there is nothing more to desire.' Walpole's reply, from Chantilly, the first stage on the journey home, is lost, but she declared herself very pleased. 'Never, never will I write a word which could make you hurt me by your reply. I would rather suppress all my thoughts than that. If you could communicate to your letters the sound of your voice, your pronunciation, I should be as happy once a week as I am every day when you are here.' Living in the memory of his presence, she felt that her salon had lost its savour. 'Yesterday I had a dozen people. We were all quite stupid, each in his or her own way, but all alike in their lack of intelligence, all very boring. They all left at one o'clock and all without regret.' Her chief delight was to read and re-read his affectionate letters; the scoldings, she confessed, she would like to burn. 'You will make my sunset far more beautiful and happy than my noontide or my dawn. Your pupil, who is as submissive as a child, only wishes to obey you.'

Once again Walpole in England proved a different person from Walpole in France. As she never changed, she had a right to complain that since Proteus no one varied from day to day like him. Within a month of their tender leave-taking he sent the terrible news 'Je suis refroidi'. It would be kinder to kill her than to use such words, she rejoined; she would rather he told that he hated her. 'If I have loved tenderness too much, you have loved corrections, conditions and suspicions. It is useless to try to understand you. I really believe you are mad.' Yet in February, 1768, Proteus was his old affectionate self again. 'I am the happiest of men. I have just received your portrait. I tore off the wrappings and at last I have you again. Yes, yes, yourself. Here you are in person. I am speaking to you and only your impatience to reply is lacking. Your dog, your *tonneau*, your furniture, your room— everything is there.' Carmontelle's celebrated picture of the blind septuagenarian in her armchair with her refined features and her delicate hands outstretched in eager talk is a masterpiece. Walpole's grumblings were rendered bearable by the expectation and memory of such occasional flashes of tenderness. The author of the aphorism, 'Life is a comedy to those who think, a tragedy to those who feel', detested emotion, not because he was unfeeling but because he was too highly strung.

Three years later, in the summer of 1771, her 'tutor' paid his third happy visit to Paris. He found her in excellent health and spirits; when asked her age she replied, 'J'ai soixante et mille ans'. But for her blindness, he believed, nothing would prevent her from crossing the Channel. 'Affectionate as Mme de Sévigné, she has none of her prejudices and more universal taste. With the most delicate frame she hurries me through a life of fatigue which would kill me if I was to remain here. I sigh to be in my quiet castle, but it costs me a pang when I reflect that I shall probably never have the resolution to make another journey to see this best and sincerest of friends who loves me as much as my mother did.' He could pay no higher tribute, for Lady Walpole had adored her youngest son. A letter on the way home pleased her 'beyond my powers of expression. Be assured that I will never let myself go.

I am in your hands and submit to you all my thoughts and desires.
. . . If only I could have been your grandmother! There, I have
said it! Are you angry?' When she lost her pension he chivalrously begged permission to make it up. 'Would you take it
from Royalty and not from me? . . . Ma petite, permit me to put
you at your ease, and let this joy be a profound secret between you
and me.' She gratefully replied that it would be a glory to her, but
she did not need it. It is lucky for Walpole's reputation that one
of his few surviving letters shows him at his best.

Neither sunshine nor storms ever lasted long, and violent attacks of gout often soured his temper. Soon after this touching
offer he wrote her a letter about some trifle which she described as
so offensive that she felt inclined to burn and ignore it. 'If such
is your wish,' she replied, 'you must end this association which
you think so exacting and of which you are so much ashamed.' He
desired no such thing, but stipulated that she should not speak of
friendship. 'Never were reproaches so little merited,' she replied
with quiet dignity. 'I hope you will not refuse to send me news
of yourself. Adieu, my dear Monsieur Walpole.' A further unmerited rebuke brought, not rebellion, but an almost abject appeal. 'My friend—my only friend! In God's name, let us make
peace. Give me back your friendship.' A gentle reply evoked the
usual grateful response. 'I am as glad as a man condemned to be
hanged for his reprieve, but the rope has hurt my throat. Let us
forget the past. I would rather be thought wrong than risk another quarrel. I am at peace with the world.'

A fiercer hurricane blew up in 1772 when, rejecting his advice,
she paid a long and happy visit to her distant relatives the Choi-
seuls. His fear that it might be too much for her was genuine, but
there was not the slightest excuse for his tantrums. 'Rien n'égale
votre sévérité,' she wrote from Chanteloup; 'avec vous les puni-
tions surpassent beaucoup les crimes.' If she were not convinced
of his sincerity and his friendship, she would think that he was
seeking a pretext for a break. Whatever she did was wrong. She
trembled when she opened his letters. Her journey had done her
no harm, and the visit had surpassed her expectations. 'Tout le
monde a été content de moi, et je suis contente de tout le monde.'
On returning to Paris a new shock awaited her. 'Votre plume est
de fer trempé dans le fiel. Bon Dieu! quelle lettre! Jamais il n'y

eut de plus piquante, de plus sèche et de plus rude.' She was quite ready to drop the correspondence, which she could only enjoy if it were founded on friendship and esteem. 'I leave you to your remorse for treating so unworthily some one who deserved from you, more than from anyone, consideration, esteem, and, if I may say so, a little friendship.' After a further artillery battle at long range there was silence for several weeks, and it was the injured party who held out an olive branch. 'Am I to have no more news? It looks like it. Is that the way to drop a friend? Do the faults with which you reproach me justify this conduct? I propose peace; let us both forget the past. Send me news. Remember you have told me a thousand times that you will always be my friend. Despite appearances I cannot believe that you are no longer so.' The tension was relieved when the news arrived that Rhadamanthus had been suffering from the gout.

Walpole's letters to his friends reveal a deeper affection for Mme du Deffand than the few which have survived to herself. When his cousin Conway was about to visit Paris at the close of 1774 he was requested to 'take a great deal of notice of this dear old friend of mine. . . . She loves me better than all France together, but she hates politics and therefore to make her talk you must tell her it is to satisfy me. On this foot she will talk with the utmost frankness and with amazing cleverness.' In thanking Conway for his kindness he added: 'My intention is certainly to see her again if I am able. I have truly all the affection and attachment for her that she deserves from me.' In the following summer he resolved on a final visit. 'I did not think I should have so much resolution again,' he wrote, 'but my dear old blind woman has begged it and I cannot refuse, though I feel how terrible the parting will be, since I cannot expect to see her again. She is almost seventy-nine. In fact her lamp burns as bright as ever but I am sure mine grows dim.' Her proposal that he should occupy an apartment in the Convent of St Joseph was roughly declined, but the visit of two months was a time of unclouded happiness. 'I found my dear old woman so well and looking so much better than four years ago,' he reported, 'that I am transported with pleasure. Her soul is immortal and forces her body to bear it company. My journey has done me good. I have thrown off fifteen years. If possible my old friend is more worth visiting than ever, and so far from being ashamed am I of coming hither at my age that I look on myself as wiser than one of the Magi when I travel to adore this Star of the East.' Never had he had such a strenuous time, for invitations had poured in. 'I have been kissed so much by ladies', he complained, 'that my cheeks are covered with rouge.' When he left Paris in October, 1775, she wrote: 'Adieu, ce mot est bien triste. Souvenez-vous que vous laissez ici la personne dont vous êtes le plus aimé, et dont le bonheur et le malheur consistent dans ce que vous pensez pour elle.'

The five remaining years of her life were sweetened by his weekly letters. Her soul, she declared, did not grow old. To her last moment she would feel the need of loving and being loved, though that confession was a secret for him alone. She compared herself to a garden and him to a gardener. Periodical reproaches no longer wounded her so deeply, for she knew that his heart was gentler than his pen. Though she frequently complained of boredom she could still count on the faithful comradeship of the adorable Duchesse de Choiseul, the best of women and the best of friends. It was a delight to welcome Voltaire when he returned to Paris to die in a blaze of glory at the age of eighty-four. They had exchanged news, views and compliments for many years. 'Only your correspondence makes life endurable,' she had written; 'I should like a letter every day.' 'Vous êtes la personne de ce siècle,' he gallantly replied, 'le plus selon mon goût et selon mon coeur.' Her diary records a never-ceasing flow of foreign visitors, among them Burke, Benjamin Franklin, Fox, whom she described as clever but totally lacking in good sense, Gibbon, whom she found charming, and the Emperor Joseph, whose unassuming demeanour and eagerness to learn won general respect. Among her younger women acquaintances were Mme Necker, who had no enemies, and Mme de Genlis, who had more brains than character or heart.

The last letter, dictated on August 22, 1780, hinted that the end was near and added the simple words: 'Vous me regretterez, parce qu'on est bien aise de se savoir aimé.' Now, in the gathering twilight, Walpole allowed his heart to speak. 'Should she be capable of hearing it', he wrote to his nephew in Paris, 'I entreat you to tell her—but I do not know how to express how much I love her—my impatience and uneasiness increase every hour.

Would it be possible to give her the medicine I left with her, if
only five or six grains? I would give the universe to have her try
it. . . . I loved her most affectionately and sincerely. I admired
her infinitely and my gratitude is without words.' When all was
over he wrote to their common friend, the Duc de Guines. 'I have
suffered an irreparable loss. The friendship which Mme du
Deffand lavished upon me was as much above my merit as it was
dear to my heart.' She left him her books, papers and a gold box
with a portrait of Tonton, her adored little dog, who was provided
with a home for his old age at Strawberry Hill. But why did he de-
fer these tender phrases till they could no longer comfort her hun-
gry soul? If he had some small excuse for rebuking her occasional
exuberance, she possessed a far better title to complain that he
stinted his favours. There were faults on both sides, but her record is far the best. 'The total impression of him which these letters produce is very damaging,' is the considered verdict of Lytton
Strachey. It is his own fault for so obstinately suppressing his
nobler self. She gave most because she loved most.


### V. Mme Necker

OF the four leading *salonnières* of eighteenth-century France Mme
Necker alone enjoyed a happy domestic life. Mme Geoffrin, Mme
du Deffand and Mlle de Lespinasse sought fulfilment in a circle of
friends far dearer to them than any family ties. Suzanne Curchod,
on the other hand, married a man worthy of her affection and respect. As a cultivated and intelligent girl she was naturally delighted to exchange the provincialism of Geneva and Lausanne for
the stimulating atmosphere of Paris, where she played her part as
the wife of a wealthy banker and Minister of the Crown; but she
was never dazzled by the glitter and never forgot the country of
her birth. Whereas the other women created and maintained their
salons by their unaided efforts, she owed her position and her
celebrity to the husband she adored. At a time when successful
marriages were rare in the higher social circles of France, the
Necker household was an oasis of peace. The system by which
girls of good family were assigned like merchandise in their tender

years to a stranger for whom they cared nothing was unknown in the less sophisticated social climate of Switzerland. Though both Necker and his wife had some French blood in their veins, they belonged rather to Switzerland than to France, not least because they were neither Catholic nor *Philosophes* but pious Protestants. The pretty Vaudoise bore transplantation well, but she was never completely acclimatised in the most critical society in Europe, and many people thought her too stiff for the rôle of a Parisian *salonnière*.

Born in 1739, the only child of the pastor of Crassier in the Pays de Vaud and of a Huguenot mother, Suzanne grew up in an atmosphere of affection, austerity and culture. 'La Suzette' was not only the *belle* but the pride of the little village, for her passion for learning equalled her beauty and her charm. Her father, a classical scholar, taught her Latin, and she picked up the rudiments of science and philosophy. During her three years of student life at Lausanne she took the lead without an effort among the comrades who competed for her smiles. As chance would have it an English lad named Edward Gibbon arrived in Lausanne in the summer of 1753 at the age of sixteen. When he joined the Roman Church after a year at Oxford his father transferred him to the safe keeping of a Protestant pastor to be cured of what he later described as 'my childish revolt against the religion of my country'. The process of reconversion lasted a year, at the end of which he reported home: 'I have at length good news to tell you. I am now a good Protestant and heartily glad of it.' After further study and reflection, however, be adopted the prevailing ideology of the century of Hume and Voltaire. Despite the difference in nationality, tradition and temperament, Gibbon, at the age of twenty, fell in love with the pastor's daughter, aged eighteen. 'I saw Mlle Curchod,' he noted in his diary in June, 1757. 'Omnia vincit amor et nos cedamur amori.' Two months later he records a visit of two days to Crassier. In October he broke his journey from Geneva to Lausanne, and in November he spent six days in the quiet parsonage.

Thirty years later, at the height of his fame, Gibbon recalled the first and last romance of his life in the usual grandiloquent style of his Memoirs. 'I need not blush at recalling the object of my choice; and though my love was disappointed of success, I am rather proud that I was once capable of feeling such a pure and exalted sentiment. The personal attractions of Mlle Curchod were embellished by the virtues and talents of the mind. Her fortune was humble but her family was respectable. In the solitude of a sequestered village her father bestowed a liberal and even learned education on his only daughter. She surpassed his hopes by her proficiency in the sciences and languages; and in her short visits to some relations in Lausanne her wit, beauty and erudition were the theme of universal applause. The report of such a prodigy awakened my curiosity; I saw and loved. I found her learned without pedantry; lively in conversation, pure in sentiment, and elegant in manners; and the first sudden emotion was fortified by the habits and knowledge of a more familiar acquaintance. She permitted me to make her two or three visits at her father's house. I passed some happy days there, and her parents honourably encouraged the connection. In a calm retirement the gay vanity of youth no longer fluttered in her bosom; she listened to the voice of truth and passion, and I might presume to hope that I had made some impression on a virtuous heart. At Crassy and Lausanne I indulged my dream of felicity; but on my return to England I soon discovered that my father would not hear of this strange alliance, and that, without his consent, I was destitute and helpless. After a painful struggle I yielded to my fate. I sighed as a lover, I obeyed as a son. My wound was insensibly healed by time, absence, and the habits of a new life. My cure was accelerated by a faithful report of the tranquillity and cheerfulness of the lady herself, and my love subsided in friendship and esteem.'

Gibbon's version held the field till the archives at Coppet were utilised by Suzanne's descendant Vicomte d'Haussonville in his delightful volmes *Le Salon de Mme Necker*, and the whole surviving correspondence was published in 1929 by D. M. Low in his edition of Gibbon's Journal. Beginning as a boy and girl affair, it developed into a warm attachment on both sides. 'Je vous ai connu, mademoiselle,' he wrote, 'tout est changé pour moi. Une félicité au dessus de l'empire, au dessus même de la philosophie, peut m'attendre.' He signed himself 'Le fils du roi Moabdar,' and she responded with 'Limerline'. That they enjoyed their meetings and correspondence and looked forward to marriage is clear enough, but a firm engagement was impossible without the approval of the

N

parent who held the purse-strings. When his son returned to England in 1758, on the eve of his twenty-first birthday, after an absence of almost five years, he was confronted with a veto which he knew could never be overcome. His capitulation was conveyed in a letter of August 24, 1758. 'Je ne puis commencer! Cependant il le faut. Je prends la plume, je la quitte, je la réprends. Vous sentez à ce début ce que je vais dire. Épargnez-moi le reste. Oui, mademoiselle, je dois renoncer a vous pour jamais. L'arrêt est porté, mon coeur en gémit, mais devant mon devoir tout doit se taire.' His father was kind but firm. 'Marry your foreigner. You are independent.[1] But before doing so remember that you are a son and a citizen.' The chastened lover retired to his room, and after two hours for reflection he informed his father that he was ready to sacrifice the happiness of his life. 'Puissiez-vous, mademoiselle, être plus heureuse que je n'espère d'être jamais. Ce sera toujours ma prière, ce sera meme ma consolation. Je me rappellerai toujours Mademoiselle Curchod comme la plus digne et la plus charmante des femmes ; qu'elle n'oublie pas entièrement un homme qui ne méritoit pas le désespoir auquel il est en proie.'

Gibbon's letter was a blow not only to her affections but to her pride. 'L'inclination que j'avais pour vous,' she replied, 'était si pure, c'était la vertu et la tendresse réunies, mais une tendresse bien délicate, vous êtes le seul homme pour qui j'ai versé les larmes, et que tant d'autres me paroissent insipides. J'aurais abandonné avec plaisir, je pense, ma langue, ma patrie, mes connaissances, pour suivre quelqu'un que j'aurois cru incapable d'abuser de ma confiance. Je ne sais si cette lettre vous paraîtra extravagante; ce n'est point le stile d'un roman, c'est celuî d'un coeur ulcéré.' Her shrill cry of distress evoked no response, but Gibbon's step-mother, with whom he was on excellent terms, wrote to say that she had intercepted the letter and would intercept others if they came. Despite this warning Suzanne wrote again, reporting that her sleep was affected and that her gaiety had given place to black depression and sometimes to tears. This time Gibbon responded with a long and affectionate letter. 'Je vous retrouve partout. Un sentiment mêlé de douceur et d'amertume s'élève dans mon coeur. J'essuye une larme qui m'échappe. Il faut céder a la necessité.' A postscript suggested that it would perhaps be

---

[1] He had just been promised £300 a year.

prudent to drop their correspondence, though that was not his wish, and he supplied a London address to which she could write. She reluctantly accepted the situation and only begged for four letters a year. 'Je suis bien loin d'imaginer rompre tout commerce, toute liaison.'

Suzanne's admirers, with Comte d'Haussonville at their head, have presented her as the injured innocent and Gibbon as the unfeeling friend. Her critics reply that she was consumed by ambition and that she displayed a lack of dignity in her reluctance to let him go. Doubtless her feelings were mixed. Possessing the deeper and the warmer nature she was bound to suffer most. But Gibbon also had a heart, and he paid her the compliment of never asking another woman to bear his name. When he published his *Étude de la Littérature* three years later, he despatched a copy in January, 1763, to his old friend. When she consulted him about seeking a post abroad, he replied that the position of a companion was very uncertain in England, as elsewhere, politely adding that it would be impossible for anyone to withhold their esteem and very difficult not to grant their friendship. Though on all essential occasions she would find in him a friend who would regard a request as a favour, he feared that a correspondence involved danger as well as pleasure to them both.

When Gibbon revisited Lausanne they met by accident at Ferney as guests of Voltaire, and his behaviour was so icy that on the following day she let herself go. 'I will not threaten you again with the divine wrath as I did in the first moment, but I can assure you that one day you will regret your irreparable loss in forgetting for ever the too tender and too frank heart of Suzanne Curchod.' His decision, as she was soon to recognise, was in the the interest of both. Born to be an old bachelor, he could never have given her the love and tenderness she craved; and her affectionate nature would have grated on a man who, like Horace Walpole, rationed his emotions. That all sentiment on his side had disappeared is suggested by the entry in his journal on the day he received her shrill indictment. 'I have had a letter of the most unexpected character from Mlle C., a dangerous and artificial girl.' Yet the arrow had found its mark. 'At this air of candour and these sentiments of tenderness and frankness I felt regret and remorse.' Even now it was not the end of their acquaintance, for his journal records a few contacts at Lausanne. 'I hear Mlle Curchod has come,' he noted on February 14, 1764. 'The indifference with which I receive the news makes me feel I am completely cured.' Two days later he visited her with a friend, and 'talked with all the liberty of people who had occasionally met'. Five days later he wrote: 'I visited her. Her mind has gained greatly. I took her to a big reception.' A week later he accompanied her to see Voltaire's *Zaire*, where her sobs attracted attention; but he notes with a touch of malice that when she removed her handkerchief there was no trace of tears. Neither of them guessed that in a couple of years they would meet as equals in a smart Parisian drawing-room and become good friends for life.

On the death of her father, Suzanne and her mother quitted·the parsonage and settled in Geneva, but the widow's pension was so meagre that her daughter was compelled to give lessons. Moultou, a friend of Rousseau, found her pupils and introduced her at Ferney to Voltaire, who called her *la philosophe*. Three years after the loss of her husband Mme Curchod died and Suzanne found herself at the age of twenty-two alone in the world, hating the profession by which she earned her daily bread. In three years she had lost her fiancé, her parents and her home. At this moment the situation was transformed by an invitation from a young and wealthy Protestant widow of a French officer who had come to Geneva to consult Tronchin, the most fashionable doctor of his time. If she would devote four or five years to the education of her son, she was informed by Mme de Vermenoux, a pension would be her reward. Moultou, in whose house they had met, advised the plunge into an unknown world, since she could always return to her country if the experiment failed. It was the story of Julie de Lespinasse over again, except that Suzanne had plenty of friends and that Correvon, a young lawyer, was eager to offer her a home.

The first report from Paris sang the praises of her employer, but the discovery that she must buy expensive clothes was a shock. She knew that she had only to ask for payment of her bills, but this she felt would be undignified. A loveless marriage, she confided to a Swiss friend, would go against the grain, but in her acute embarrassment even that expedient would be preferable to her present plight. While she was worrying about her future the problem was solved by a happy accident. Among the visitors to

the drawing-room of Mme de Vermenoux was a young banker
named Jacques Necker. His father, a German lawyer from Kustrin,
had been called as Professor of Law to Geneva, where he married
into the family of a Huguenot refugee. Leaving the University at
the age of sixteen, his eldest son became a clerk in the Paris bank
of Vernet, a Swiss friend of his father. On the retirement of his
chief some years later he was supplied with money to found a
bank in partnership with Thelusson, the nephew of Vernet.
Thelusson managed the business in London, leaving Paris to
Necker. The firm flourished, partly by loans to the State, partly
by dealings in grain, and at the age of thirty-two Necker was a rich
man. He was courting Mme de Vermenoux before her journey to
Geneva, and she promised him a reply after her return. When he
called to learn his fate he received no encouragement, and promptly
turned his attention to the penniless governess. 'I like Necker
very much,' she reported in July, 1764 to Moultou, 'both for his
mind and his character.' In the early autumn he visited Geneva
for business reasons without declaring himself, and she wondered
whether he ever would. 'If our brilliant dream fades away', she
wrote to the same understanding friend, 'I shall marry Correvon
next summer. He is always persecuting me, and all his relatives
with him. That will allow me to spend two months with you every
year, and thus my life would be sweeter.'

All doubts were set at rest when Necker solicited a private interview. His letter is lost, but her reply is preserved. 'Je resterai chez
moi toute la soirée et je fermerai ma porte.' Matters were
speedily arranged and there was no reason to wait. Mme de Vermenoux made no trouble and before long she reported to Moultou,
the friend of both, that the fame of her late governess was growing
day by day. The news of her marriage to a rich banker of excellent
repute six months after her arrival delighted her Swiss friends with
the exception of Correvon, who made no effort to conceal the
bitterness of his defeat. 'I note that you regarded me merely as a
wretched *pis aller* and that you eagerly embraced the first opportunity to settle down in Paris or elsewhere.' After flinging these
reproaches at her head he allowed his better nature to speak. 'But
why mar your joy in recalling the past? I forgive you very sincerely, Mademoiselle and my dearest friend, for all your doings,
and I pray God with all my soul to bestow His most precious

blessings on you, on your dear husband, and on all your posterity. I beg you not to forget me entirely and to grant me a steady friendship. Believe me when I say that it would afford me infinite pleasure to give you proofs of mine, which will only end with my life.'

The young couple were as happy as they expected and deserved. 'I marry a man', wrote the bride, 'whom I should regard as an angel did not his attachment to myself prove his human weakness.' To Moultou's congratulations the bridegroom replied that he could not be happier. 'Is money to determine our judgment? What a pitiable attitude! To acquire a virtuous, lovable and sensible wife: is not that a good bargain for a man whether or not he sits on money-bags?' Though he had infinitely less personality and far less culture than Suzanne, he was not less respected for his character than for the business ability which was to carry him to the heights of power and fame. Each provided what the other lacked. Without his money there could have been little entertaining, and without her womanly charm the intellectual *élite* would have turned their steps elsewhere.

In an age when Paris was the best school of conversation in Europe, the host was celebrated for his silence. Necker, reported Moultou when he visited the capital in 1778, overwhelmed him with kindness, but he seemed to shut himself up with his thoughts. 'A man who does big things has no need to talk about them.' To speak frankly, in society he was distinctly dull. 'A noble heart and a venerable character, but not a soul of fire' is the verdict of Sorel. His wife encouraged him to embark on a public career, and at his wish she undertook the management of his landed property. In 1768 the Republic of Geneva appointed him its Minister at Paris, a post which gave him access to Choiseul, the Foreign Minister, and to the Court. He became a Director of the French East India Company, published an *éloge* on Colbert, attacked Turgot's free trade policy in his *Essai sur la législation et le commerce des grains*, and in 1772, at the suggestion of his wife, handed over his share in the management of the bank to his brother. On the fall of Turgot in 1776, though a foreigner and a Protestant, he followed him in the most onerous post in the State. At the age of forty-four he had reached the summit of his career. The story of his five years in office, his effort to fund the National Debt swollen by the claims of the American War, the publication in 1781 of the comprehensive

*Compte rendu* on the economic situation of France, and his dismissal belongs to the annals of France.

Whatever may have been his shortcomings in the days of his courtship, Gibbon made the *amende honorable* in his Autobiography. 'In her lowest distress she maintained a spotless reputation and a dignified behaviour. A rich banker of Paris had the good fortune and the good sense to discover and possess this inestimable treasure; and in the capital of taste and luxury she resisted the temptations of wealth as she had sustained the hardships of indigence. The genius of her husband has exalted him to the most conspicuous station in Europe. In every change of prosperity and disgrace he has reclined on the bosom of a faithful friend. His private fortune enabled him to support a liberal establishment, and his wife, whose talents and virtues I had long admired, was admirably qualified to preside in the conversation of her table and drawing-room. As their friend I was introduced to the best company of both sexes, to the foreign ministers of all nations, and to the first names and characters of France.'

Though completely unpolitical in temperament and upbringing, Mme Necker rejoiced in the opportunity for service opened up for her husband. 'He has only a single passion, a single idea,' she wrote to a Swiss friend; 'the public weal. You cannot imagine the confusion and activity of my life. I can only draw breath when I keep my door closed almost by force.' Having known poverty at first hand, nothing gave her keener pleasure than to help the less fortunate. She supported many good works—prison reform, the care of foundlings, the nursing of the sick—and she founded a small hospital which continued to bear her name long after her death. The most welcome of her reforms was her insistence that every patient should lie in a separate bed. In this field of service she found a partner in the kindly Christophe de Beaumont, Archbishop of Paris.

The salon began in a purely cultural setting. The hostess was at home on Fridays, so as not to clash with the Monday and Wednesdays dinners of Mme Geoffrin, the Tuesday receptions of Mme Helvétius, or the sumptuous entertainments on Thursdays and Sundays of Baron d'Holbach; for the literary lions were too much in demand for them to be immured in a single cage. Abbé Morellet relates in his Memoirs that she invited him, Marmontel and the

Abbé Raynal to help her to organise a salon. She possessed good looks, great intelligence and extensive knowledge. The conversation, he declares, was good though at times a little constrained by her strict religious views and many subjects were taboo, but in matters of literature she was in her element. Necker rarely appeared, not merely because he was busy but because he never pretended to care for the things of the mind. Only rarely did he break his silence to direct a little thrust at the *Philosophes* and the writers. She teased him for his *gaucheries* and his silence, though always in a respectful manner. 'Every Friday I am with you in spirit,' wrote the Abbé Galiani from Naples after ten years in the city where he had left his heart. 'I arrive and sit at your feet, with Thomas, and Morellet, and Grimm, and Suard and my dear Comte de Creutz. After dinner over the coffee all talk at the same time. The Abbé Raynal agrees with me that Boston and British America are lost for ever, while Creutz and Marmontel agree that Grétry is the Pergolesi of France. M. Necker finds it quite all right, makes his bow, and off he goes.' He was indeed scarcely less out of place in his wife's crowded salon than the unfortunate M. Geoffrin. But with his rapid rise to power a political element was automatically added which differentiated it from the other salons, for a Minister of Finance was always worth cultivating under the *Ancien Régime*. In addition to the spacious establishment at Paris, he rented the Château de Madrid, built by Francis I after his release from Spain, at the end of the Bois de Boulogne to avoid the summer heat; and later he purchased the Château de Saint-Ouen with beautiful grounds on the bank of the Seine. It was within easy reach of the capital, but since few of their visitors possessed a carriage, the hostess often fetched them and sent them home in her own. She had learnt something of the technique of entertaining from Mme Geoffrin, the first *salonnière* to welcome her. Mme du Deffand, though not unfriendly, never cared much for the Neckers. 'Le mari a beaucoup d'esprit,' she reported to Horace Walpole. 'La femme est roide et froide, pleine d'amour-propre, mais honnête femme.' Her stiffness, which was mainly the result of nervousness, was noticed by many who met her. Before creating her, complained Mme du Deffand, God had soaked her in a tub of starch.

We owe the fullest account of the new *salonnière* to the lively pen of Marmontel, who met her at a ball, young, good looking, blooming, dancing badly but with zest. 'Hearing my name she came to me with an air of naïve delight. "When I arrived in Paris," said she, "one of my wishes was to know the author of the *Contes Maraux*: I hope we shall meet again." Calling her husband she exclaimed, "Necker, add your invitation to mine to M. Marmontel to do us the honour of paying us a visit." Necker was very polite, and I went. Thomas was the only man of letters they knew before myself, but soon Mme Necker, taking Mme Geoffrin as her model, chose her own society. As a stranger to the ways of Paris she lacked the accomplishments of a young Frenchwoman. In her ways as in her talk one missed the air and the tone of a woman trained in the school of the arts and formed in the school of the world. Without taste in her attire, without ease in her carriage, without attraction in her breeding, her mind, like her face, was too set to have charm.'

After censuring the provincialism which she never completely overcame, Marmontel proceeds to list the qualities which won for her general respect. 'A virtuous education and solitary studies had given her all that culture could add to excellent natural abilities. In matters of the heart she was perfect, but her thought was often vague and confused. She seemed to see certain things through a fog which magnified their dimensions, and then her expressions were exaggerated to a degree which would have caused a smile had one not known it to be naïve. In her case taste was less a sentiment than a product of opinions collected and tabulated. Even when she did not quote names it would have been easy to tell who and what had formed her judgment. In literary style she only cared for elevation, majesty, pomp; for quotations, nuances, variations of colour and tone, she had little use. Having heard tell of the *naïveté* of La Fontaine and the artlessness of Mme de Sévigné, she spoke of them from hearsay but without conviction. The charm of the impromptu, of facility, of letting oneself go, was beyond her. Even in conversation familiarity displeased her. I was often amused to observe how far she carried this fastidiousness. One day I mentioned some customary expressions which I maintained were admissible in an elevated style, but she rejected them all as unsuitable. Racine, I rejoined, had been less austere, for he had employed every one of them, and I quoted some passages. But her opinion once formed was impregnable, and the authority of

Thomas or Buffon was for her an article of faith. With her everything was precise and severely circumscribed: even her amusements had their reason and their method. One saw her wholly occupied with her attentions to her society, eager to welcome her guests, careful to say to each what would give most pleasure; yet everything was premeditated and nothing flowed spotaneously from its source.'

The merciless Marmontel proceeds to explain why the hostess seemed to him like a fish out of water, never quite sure of herself. 'It was neither for us nor for herself that she took such pains: it was for her husband. To introduce him to us, to win our sympathies, to sing his praises in society, to spread his fame: such was the principal purpose of her salon. But the salon and the dinner had to be for him a recreation, a spectacle, for he was only a cold and silent onlooker. Except for a few pointed interjections he left it to his wife to keep the talk going. She did her best, but she had nothing very entertaining to say: never a sally, never a piquant phrase, never anything to stimulate the company. Nervous and ill at ease, directly she saw the conversation lagging she sought the cause in our eyes. Sometimes she was naïve enough to complain to me. Madame, I replied, one is not always at the top of one's form. Is M. Necker always amusing? Her attentions and obvious desire to please us would not have overcome our dislike of dinners arranged merely to entertain her husband; but here, as so often elsewhere, the members of the circle, enjoying each other's company, dispensed the host from the duties of amiability and the guests from taking notice of him. When Necker became a Minister, people who had not known him in a private station attributed his silence and gravity to arrogance inspired of his new position, but I can testify that he had had exactly the same grave and silent manner when he was only in Thelusson's bank. He received the company with civility but without cordiality or any pretence of friendship. His daughter has said of him that he knew how to keep people at a distance. Had this been true it would have indicated a ridiculous pride. The simple truth is that a man accustomed to the mysterious operations of a bank, immersed in commercial calculations, knowing little of society, mixing little with his fellows, reading very little, only superficially acquainted with subjects outside his profession, was bound by discretion and dignity not to

give himself away. He talked freely and at length of what he understood, sparingly of everything else. In this he showed his good
sense and he was never arrogant. There was nothing winning
about him. He never tried to make me feel he was my friend, and
I certainly was not his. Yet he showed me as much consideration
as I could expect from a man so coldly polite, and I highly respected
his talents and his abilities.' Mme Necker, concludes Marmontel,
had her favourites, and he was among them. 'Not that our minds
or tastes were in tune. I frankly opposed my simple and commonplace ideas to her lofty conceptions, and she had to descend from
these inaccessible altitudes to establish contact with me. Yet, in-
docile as I was and more dominated by the senses than she would
have wished, she liked me none the less.' The greatest attraction
of her salon was the company of the Ambassadors of Naples and
Sweden, Galiani and Creutz, of whose society he could never have
enough.

Though Marmontel was too much of a Frenchman and a
*Philosophe* to suit a Swiss Puritan, his testimony cannot be wholly
disregarded. That as an *habitué* of all the salons he found the atmosphere of Mme Necker's circle least to his taste is not surprising;
and we may accept his verdict that, of the four *salonnières* she was
the least fitted for her *métier* by training and nationality, temperament and ideology, and that she derived the least satisfaction from
the performance of its duties. The born *salonnière* should feel—
and make every one of her guests feel—that she is fulfilling herself.
There should be no sign of strain, no hint of effort. *Summa ars
celare artem.*

Among the earliest foreign visitors was one of her oldest acquaintances. 'I have seen Gibbon,' she reported to a friend, 'and
it gave me immense pleasure. Not that I still retain any feeling for
a man, who, I believe, does not deserve it. Never has my feminine
vanity had a more complete or honourable triumph. He spent two
weeks in Paris and visited me every day. He has become gentle,
humble, bashful.' Gibbon's report to his friend Lord Sheffield
breathes equal satisfaction. 'The Curchod I saw at Paris. She was
very fond of me and the husband particularly civil. She asked me
every evening to supper. Afterwards he goes to bed, and leaves
me alone with his wife. It is making an old lover of mighty little
consequence. She is as handsome as ever and much genteeler;

seems pleased with her fortune rather than proud of it.' After being introduced to Parisian circles it was Gibbon's turn to play the host when they visited England in 1776 with their precocious ten-year-old daughter Germaine. When the six happy weeks were over he wrote: 'In thinking of the delightful moments with Mme Necker in Suffolk Street, all the English ladies seem colder and stiffer than before.' Henceforth, both in Paris and later in Switzerland in their closing years, their steady friendship brought satisfaction to them both.

In the field of literature Mme Necker could hold her own with the brightest intellects of France. She had always loved good books, read Milton and Pope in the original, and translated Gray's Elegy. Among the early *habitués* at her weekly dinners were Diderot and d'Alembert, Grimm and Marmontel, Helvétius and Morellet, Raynal, Suard and La Harpe. Mme Clairon would occasionally act in her drawing-room after she had left the stage. Bernardin de Saint-Pierre read *Paul et Virginie* before publication, and it was there that the plan to commission a statue of Voltaire was conceived. The Abbé Morellet she had known before her marriage as a friend of Mme de Vermenoux. 'C'est un ours mal léché,' she reported to Moultou. 'But he has candour, probity, a thousand good qualities, and enough religion to suspect that there may be a God, and sometimes to admit it to his friends if he can count on their discretion. I like him, and I think God will pardon him his incredulity, which does not spring from his heart.' Though Mme Necker detested the ideology of the *Encyclopédistes*, she recognised that it was impossible to launch a literary salon without them; but there was little affection on either side. 'Il y a ici une Mme Necker,' wrote Diderot to Sophie Volland, 'jolie femme et belle esprit, qui raffole de moi. C'est une persécution pour m'avoir chez elle.' Closer acquaintance led to admiration of a woman who 'combined the purity of an angelic soul with perfect taste'. Diderot was on his best behaviour in a salon where irreligion and indecency were taboo.

When Moultou, her guardian angel, expressed his anxiety lest the *libres-penseurs* might undermine her faith, she hastened to reassure him. 'Can you suspect me for an instant? I imbibed my sentiments at my birth. I see certain men of letters, but as I at once told them my principles, these things are never mentioned in my

house. At my age, and in such an agreeable setting, it is quite easy
to set the tone. I live, it is true, among a crowd of atheists, but
their arguments have never touched my mind, and if they ever
reached my heart they only aroused horror. I have atheist friends,
why not? They are unhappy friends.' Fortunately, she explained,
their high character corrected the impression of their principles;
were it otherwise, their society would be unwelcome. Some critics
have described Mme Necker as a prig, but in the France of Louis
XV a little austerity was not amiss.

Marmontel was not very profound, but he sensed from the first
that his hostess would never qualify as a thorough-going *Parisienne*.
On one occasion, when about to sit down to dinner, Grimm's
observations on some religious controversy evoked a lively reply
from the sensitive hostess; and when he held his ground she for
once lost control of her nerves and burst into tears. The same
evening she sent the offender a letter of apology which brought
tears to his eyes. It was for him, not for her, he replied, to apolo-
gise for touching on a delicate subject, and he admired her spirited
reaction. The incident increased his liking and respect, and during
his prolonged journey to Prussia and Russia in the company of
Diderot he and his hostess maintained a regular correspondence.

Mme Necker never wore her heart on her sleeve and she needed
time to make new friends. Among celebrities none held such a
place in her heart as Buffon, the celebrated author of the *Histoire
Naturelle* and Director of the Jardin du Roi, now the Jardin des
Plantes. Meeting her when he was sixty-seven, the grave and lonely
widower was attracted at first sight. Scores of his affectionate letters survive, and hers, though more reserved, reveal her pride in
his friendship. 'M. de Buffon is inimitable in everything,' she reported. They strolled together in the Jardin du Roi and at St
Ouen, and she visited him several times in Burgundy. Like a
daughter nursing her father, she sat at his bedside in the last few
days of his life, bathing his head, and recording with satisfaction
his declaration: 'I die in the religion of my birth.' A no less rewarding partnership existed with 'le vertueux Thomas', a tedious
writer but a loyal and helpful friend. English visitors were always
welcome, above all her oldest friend. 'As a woman of talent and
fortune,' reported Gibbon to his step-mother in April, 1777, 'she
is at the head of literature in Paris. The station of her husband

procures her respect from the first people in the country, and the reception I shall meet with in her house will give me advantages that have fallen to the share of few Englishmen.' His expectations were fulfilled. 'I live very much with them,' he wrote two months later, 'dine and sup with them whenever they have company, which is almost every day, and whenever I like it.' Though too great a man for snobbery, Gibbon appreciated success, comfort, culture and the society of the intellectual *élite*.

In addition to the literary lions Mme Necker's menagerie contained some of the Ambassadors whom we have met elsewhere. The Abbé Galiani, the wittiest of them all, wrote her long letters from Naples when he was recalled after a blissful decade at Paris, which he described as the only years when he was truly alive. As in all the salons except that of Mme du Deffand, the men outnumbered the women. Some wives, among them Mme Diderot and Mme Marmontel, did not fit in, and the only *habitué* who brought his partner to the Friday gatherings was Suard. Ladies of the aristocracy were chiefly to be found at the table of Mme du Deffand, but the friends of Mme Necker included the Maréchale de Luxembourg, long the oracle of *bon ton*, Mme d'Houdetot and, above all, the Duchesse de Lauzun, who had been deserted by her husband and was to perish by the guillotine.

The most arresting figure during the later phases of Mme Necker's salon was a member of her own family. Born in 1766, the precocious Germaine from the age of ten sat on a stool at her mother's feet, listening intently to the clever talk and before long taking her part. On approaching the hostess the guests greeted the child with a compliment or a joke, and she answered with easy grace. Mme de Genlis, who prided herself on her pedagogic wisdom, regretted that the girl spent most of her time in the drawing-room, surrounded by all the stars. Mme Necker, temperamentally more of a wife than a mother, took greater interest in her husband than in their only child, and as the most dazzling conversationalist of her time emerged from the schoolroom the clash of personalities was inescapable. There was more *rapport* between father and daughter, but in truth she inherited little from either parent. She possessed no trace of her mother's beauty or piety and little of her father's stability. Religion never touched her heart. She confessed to yawning in church, and the morality in which she was reared

was discarded when she sailed away under her own flag. Bursting
with mental and physical energy, she was resolved to think her
own thoughts and shape her own career. While still in her teens
it was clear to everyone that France of the *Aufklärung*, not the city
of Calvin, was her spiritual home. Throughout the years of exile
her thoughts were to turn instinctively to Paris as the eyes of the
pious Moslem in the direction of Mecca.

In one respect alone was she willing to receive counsel from her
parents. After William Pitt, whom the Neckers had met at Fontainebleau, had been considered, and after an offer from an im-
pecunious Prince of Mecklenburg had been politely rejected,
the coveted heiress bestowed her hand on Baron de Staël-Holstein
after years of haggling about the terms. To improve his chances
the young diplomat persuaded Gustavus III to promise him the
reversion of the Swedish Embassy in Paris, and shortly afterwards
Creutz, the popular Ambassador, vacated the post. The aristocratic bridegroom secured the magnificent dowry of 650,000
francs, and the bourgeoise bride gained the coveted status of an
Ambassadress. The marriage contract was witnessed by the King
and Queen, and a fortnight after the ceremony she was presented
at Court. There was no trace of affection on either side, and no
one expected it to be a success. If any excuse for such a commercial transaction is needed in an age and a country where love
marriages in high society were the exception, it must be remem-
bered that the Protestant faith of the family limited the field of
choice, and that Germaine Necker, fretting at the increasing tension with her mother, longed to spread her wings. In her new
official position and with her incomparable gifts there was no
difficulty in forming a circle which quickly outshone the *clientèle* of
her mother. 'Quite the first salon of Paris,' was the verdict of
Gouverneur Morris, the Ambassador of the United States, in
1789. Passionately interested in politics and herself an ardent reformer, Mme de Staël welcomed the moderates who inaugurated
and directed the Revolution till the fiery Jacobins swept them aside.
Though men of letters in plenty were to be found at her receptions,
her circle was as predominantly political as her mother's was
mainly literary. The earliest political salons in France and in
Europe were those of Mme Roland and Mme de Staël.

Necker's dismissal in 1781 left his prestige intact, and, like

Choiseul a few years earlier, he dreamed of a return to power. His expectation was widely shared, and the throng in his wife's draw-ing-room was as great as ever. So formidable a rival was he deemed by his blundering successors in the Ministry of Finance that in 1787 he was banished forty leagues from the capital for attacking Calonne. A year later, in August, 1788, when the situa-tion was rattling from bad to worse, he was recalled to office. His first recommendation was to summon the States General and to double the representation of the Tiers État, since the large sums needed could be raised in no other way. The pace of the move-ment was too hot for Court circles, which held him to be mainly responsible for the decline of the authority of the Crown. It was the old story of the victim of self-indulgence complaining of the doctor who had been summoned too late. The chief grave-diggers of the *Ancien régime* were Louis XIV, Louis XV and Marie Antoinette. On July 11, 1789, Necker was ordered to leave France, and three days later on the historic July 14, partly in con-sequence of his banishment, the Bastille was stormed. The vacillating King promptly recalled him, and for a brief space he was the hero of the crowd. His popularity quickly ebbed when he failed to ride the storm, and in September, 1790, his political career was at an end. 'Too honest, perhaps, for a Minister,' was the ver-dict of Gibbon, who knew him well.

During these bewildering changes of fortune Mme Necker's health was steadily deteriorating and her work in Paris was done. It was no time for leisurely discussions of literature, and the politically-minded members of her circle flocked to the receptions of Mme de Staël. Many of the old *habitués* were dead, and the spacious château of Coppet, which had been purchased in 1784, stood ready to welcome her. The faithful Moultou was still alive, and old friends, such as Gibbon and Bonstetten, were within reach. Necker, still at the height of his powers, was deeply shaken by his fall. 'With all the means of private happiness within his power,' reported Gibbon to Lord Sheffield, early in 1791, 'he is the most miserable of human beings. The past, the present and the future are equally odious to him. Mme Necker maintains more external composure.' Some months later he sent a more cheerful report. 'In my last excursion to Geneva I frequently saw the Neckers. He is much restored in health and spirits since the publication of his last book.' The success of his apologia, *De l'Administration de M. Necker, par lui-même*, encouraged him to use his pen. His *Réflexions offertes à la Nation Française*, published in the autumn of 1792, vindicated the character of the blameless King and vainly pleaded for his life. A year later his treatise *Du Pouvoir exécutif* gave renewed expression to his liking for the English constitution which he shared with Mirabeau.

Poring over the correspondence of his great-grandmother, Comte d'Haussonville was surprised to detect a vein of sadness, despite the happiness of her marriage and the devotion of her friends. One reason was that she was rarely without pain and anticipated an early death. Another was that the pastor's daughter had never really changed her skin. Paris, 'that centre of corruption', as she described it, had been a marvellous experience, but it had drained away her vitality. The piety of her parents' parsonage meant infinitely more to her than the challenge of the *Encyclopédistes* or the clarion call of the Rights of Man. Yet the crowded years in Paris had left deep furrows. 'Of course one can and ought to be happier elsewhere,' she confessed to a friend; 'but for that one should not have tasted this enchantment which, though it does not bring one happiness, forever poisons all other modes of life.' It was her misfortune that neither France nor Switzerland provided the full satisfaction for which she craved. In her last days she wrote *Réflexions sur la Divorce*, denouncing the new French law and pleading for the indissolubility of marriage. Though the name of her husband was not mentioned, it was her final tribute to the partner whose rock-like steadiness of character had made life possible in a rôle for which she had not been born. Passing away in 1794 at the age of fifty-five, she had lived long enough to learn of the execution of the King and Queen and of many of her old guests. With her brilliant daughter she had little in common except a love of literature and devotion to the head of the family. If the one had too little temperament, the other had too much. While Mme de Staël belonged in every fibre of her being to France, her austere parents seem to have drifted almost inadvertently out of a quiet Swiss backwater into the main stream of European history, returning to the land of their birth when the turbid waters burst the dykes. To stand up to the tornado of the Revolution demanded a tougher fibre than they possessed. Their

o

supreme achievement, in the picturesque phraseology of Sainte-Beuve, was their magnificent gift to France of Mme de Staël. The Swiss doves had launched an eagle into the stormy world.

*Bibliographical Note.* The best introduction to the intellectual life of eighteenth-century France is still to be found in the twenty-eight volumes of Sainte-Beuve's *Causeries du Lundi.* The Marquis de Ségur's biography of Mme Geoffrin, *Le Royaume de la Rue St Honoré*, is a classic. Her correspondence with Stanislas, King of Poland, was edited by the Comte de Muy. For Mme du Deffand see Ferval, *Mme du Deffand*; Lucien Perey, *Le Président Hénault et Mme du Deffand*; Lion, *Le Président Hénault*; President Hénault's *Mémoires*; Ségur, 'Mme du Deffand et sa Famille', in his *Esquisses et Récits.* Her letters to Horace Walpole should be read in the five volumes of the Yale edition edited by W. S. Lewis. Her correspondence with the Duchesse de Choiseul was edited in three volumes by St Aulaire in 1865, and was utilised by Gaston Maugras in *Le Duc et la Duchesse de Choiseul*, 2 vols. The best biography of Julie de Lespinasse is by Ségur. Shorter lives by Camilla Jebb and Naomi Royde Smith are of interest as feminine interpretations of one who was *toute femme.* The complete text of the celebrated love letters, *Correspondance de Mlle de Lespinasse et le Comte de Guibert*, was edited by his descendant Comte de Villeneuve-Guibert in 1906. A selection, translated by K. P. Wormeley, contains Guibert's *Éloge d'Élise* and other tributes. D'Alembert's literary portraits of himself in 1760 and Julie in 1771 were published in Joseph Bertrand's *D'Alembert*, ch. 8. Comte d'Haussonville's *Le Salon de Mme Necker*, 2 vols., is an affectionate tribute, based on the family papers at Coppet, by her great-grandson. Corbuz, *Mme Necker*, and Chapuisat, *Jacques Necker*, are useful. Necker's five years at the Ministry of Finance are described in Ségur, *Au Couchant de la Monarchie*, Vol. II. New light has been thrown on Mme Necker's friendship with Gibbon, briefly described in his Memoirs, by the publication of his correspondence and a youthful Journal. The début of Mme de Staël is narrated in Lady Blennerhassett's masterly biography, Vol. I, and more briefly by Albert Sorel in the *Grands Écrivains* series.

# 3

## VOLTAIRE AS HISTORIAN

### I. *Charles XII and Peter the Great*

VOLTAIRE, declared Gibbon, his neighbour at Lausanne, was the most extraordinary man of the century. The greatest figure in the literature of all ages, the most astonishing creation of the author of nature, the most representative of Frenchmen, echoed Goethe. Centuries would be needed to produce his equal, exclaimed Diderot. 'Ce n'est pas un homme, c'est un siècle,' exclaimed Victor Hugo. 'Le plus bel esprit de ce siècle,' was the verdict of President Hénault. Taine compared him to a fountain whose waters never ceased to play. No writer before or since has occupied such a commanding position in Europe or exercised such immediate and enduring influence. He possessed a larger *clientèle* during his lifetime than any man of letters before Bernard Shaw. French publications could count on readers all over Europe, since French was the *lingua frança* of the Intelligentsia in every land. Few foreigners could enjoy *Hamlet* or *Faust* in the original, and even in the best translations the magic disappeared. The attention of the world had been focused on French culture and the *Ville Lumière* by the galaxy of genius during the seventeenth century and by the immeasurable prestige of *Le Roi Soleil*. Of this accumulated capital Voltaire was a grateful beneficiary, and in the sixty years of his literary activity he contributed even more than he had received. Leaping into fame with his early plays and poems, he grew in stature and authority till he became the uncrowned king of the Republic of Letters. In addition to the Académie Française he was a member of the Royal Society and of the Academies of La Crusca, St Petersburg and Berlin. His acquaintance was craved by princes no less than by literary aspirants, and his letters passed like current

coin from hand to hand.  Everyone coveted his praise and dreaded
the lash of his tongue.

Voltaire's interests extended far beyond the frontiers of *belles-
lettres*, and his patronage was solicited for many causes.  During
the ferment of the *Aufklärung*, when tradition and authority were
challenged with even greater vigour and over a wider field than
in the hectic century of the Reformation, the Goddess of Reason
was enthroned and the sage of Ferney was recognised by friend
and foe as the High Priest of the cult.  His legacy was the principle
of free inquiry.  While Chateaubriand complained that he had
rendered incredulity fashionable, Quinet hailed him as the
angel of extermination sent by God against His sinful Church.
As a satirist he ranks with Aristophanes and Juvenal, Aretino and
Swift.  As a factor in the intellectual climate of modern Europe his
place is with Machiavelli and Rousseau, Burke and Adam Smith,
Darwin and Marx.  That he made Paris and France in his image is
the verdict of Sainte-Beuve.  A soldier in the army of humanity,
he was a builder as well as a destroyer, and many of the things he
attacked deserved to die.  'The spirit of intolerance sank blasted
beneath his genius,' declares Lecky.  'Wherever his influence
passed the arm of the Inquisition was palsied, the chain of the
captive riven, the door flung open.  He died leaving a reputation
that is indeed far from spotless, but having done more to destroy
the greatest of human curses than any other of the sons of men.'
Whatever the changes in literary fashion, political ideals, academic
methods and religious beliefs, Voltaire can never be ignored.
*Candide* is as immortal as the *Essais* of Montaigne, the *Pensées* of
Pascal, the *Maximes* of La Rochefoucauld and the *Fables* of La
Fontaine.  The undying interest in the most eminent Frenchman
of the eighteenth century is illustrated by the international enterprise of a complete and critical edition of his letters, more extensive
in bulk and more widely ranging in the list of his correspondents
than his two most serious competitors, Erasmus and Horace
Walpole.

In the evolution of modern historiography the sixteenth century
was the age of doctrinal controversy, the seventeenth of massive
erudition, the eighteenth of flowing narratives.  With the single
exception of Gibbon, Voltaire was the leading historian of his
age, and it is only the masterpieces of these two supermen which

are still widely read. Hume and Robertson retained their popularity till the middle of the nineteenth century, and Montesquieu's *Considérations sur les causes de la Grandeur et de la Décadence des Romains* inaugurated the sociological approach to history, but the twentieth century leaves all three in dignified retirement on the topmost shelf. *The Decline and Fall of the Roman Empire*, the most impressive achievement in the whole range of British historical scholarship, was too voluminous and in the later portions too dull to make a wide popular appeal. The *Siècle de Louis XIV*, on the other hand, a work of manageable dimensions, retains its vogue as an unrivalled panorama of the golden age of the French Monarchy. Equally popular is the *Life of Charles XII*, the earliest biography of a ruler in any language which still fascinates readers two centuries after its birth.

During the middle decades of his tempestuous career Voltaire's principal occupation was the study of history. Most of his plays had historical themes, and the *Henriade*, which took Europe by storm, was based on considerable study of the life and times of his favourite hero. In these early works, however, history was merely the raw material of literature, and it was not till he was gripped by the epic of Sweden's warrior king that he embarked on a course of reading which ultimately furnished him with a wider knowledge of world history than any Frenchman, perhaps any European, of his time. Of his major historical writings all but one are of interest and value. *The Life of Charles XII* contained material derived from a number of eye-witnesses. *The Life of Peter the Great* utilised documents supplied by his daughter the Tsarina Elizabeth. *The Age of Louis XIV* was enriched by the confidences of many survivors of the *Grand Siècle*. *The Age of Louis XV*, though necessarily more reticent as the work of the Historiographer of France, possessed the authority of a keen contemporary with many contacts in the highest circles. *The History of the Parlement of Paris*, for which documents were placed at his disposal, was a substantial contribution to the constitutional history of France. The *Essai sur les Moeurs*, at once the most comprehensive and the most individual of his historical writings, provided the first readable survey of the evolution of mankind on the basis of the evidence available in the middle of the eighteenth century. *The Annals of the Empire*, from Charlemagne to the Thirty Years War, on the other hand, is

nothing more than its title implies—a work of reference commissioned by a German Princess which might have been written
by any literary hack. 'Gardez-vous de lire ce fatras', wrote the
author to a friend; 'il est d'un ennui mortel.'

The corpus of Voltaire's historical writings makes an impressive
show, amateur though he was. 'A great historian,' declares Émile
Faguet, 'one of the fathers of history.' *Homo sum*, he might have
echoed, *nihil humani a me alienum puto*. Every phase in the slow
ascent of man, however primitive or uninviting, seemed to him
worthy of attention. While Gibbon's interest began with the
classical world, Voltaire commanded a far wider perspective by
including the civilisations and ideologies of the East. While
Bossuet, with his closed mind, had presented a geographically and
chronologically limited section of the human record as the implementation of a divine plan, Voltaire envisaged the whole drama as
a progressive liberation of energies, an instinctive urge towards a
fuller and more satisfying life. There is no trace of determinism
in his approach. He never suggested that progress towards enlightenment, which he prized above all things, was automatic. His
vision of *homo sapiens* groping his way towards civilisation,
organisation, humanisation, was the forerunner of the doctrine of
collective creation formulated by Herder and the Grimms, Savigny
and Eichhorn. The story of mankind, he was well aware, was infinitely more than a string of events.

Next to his courageous attempt to interpret the fortunes of man
as the unfolding of a mighty drama of effort and experiment, Voltaire's most significant contribution to historical study was his
challenge to the dead hand of tradition. In politics he was a liberal
conservative, in scholarship an iconoclast. Probability, declared
Bishop Butler in a famous phrase, is the guide of life, and Voltaire
unflinchingly, indeed gleefully, applied the maxim to the testimony
of the past. Though *Quellenkritik*—the expert analysis of sources
—was the child of the nineteenth century, a few pioneers, from
Lorenzo Valla and Père Simon to Vico, Beaufort and Astruc, had
pointed the way. The 'Donation of Constantine' had been exposed
as a colossal fake, the legends of Livy had been challenged, and
some of the elements which went to the making of the Old Testament had been sorted out. Without claiming to be an expert,
Voltaire brought his razor-edged intelligence to bear on a multi-

tude of marvels which embellished the narratives of the past, particularly those connected with the Jews and the Christian Church. Though the conception of the uniformity of nature only became an axiom of science and historical reconstruction in the nineteenth century, he adopted it as a working hypothesis. Is it likely to be true? Could this really have occurred? Such was his instinctive reaction to stories which contradicted the general experience of mankind. Like the other leaders of the *Aufklärung*, he was unaware that there were more things in heaven and earth than were dreamed of in their philosophy, and that the exceptional was not necessarily the impossible. Nevertheless it was a useful service to let a stream of cool air into the stuffy chambers where unreflecting chroniclers mechanically repeated from generation to generation the legends invented or accepted by their predecessors. Neither the longevity of a tradition nor the range of its acceptance, he argued, provided the slightest guarantee of its factual truth. Erudition had proved insufficient to reconstruct an intelligible picture of the past, for scholars were frequently as credulous as illiterate laymen. The free play of reason, arbitrary though it might sometimes be, was required to sift the grain from the chaff. The first duty of the historian was to apply the criteria of his own time to the jumbled testimony of bygone days. At the shrill blast of his trumpet many legends collapsed like a house of cards. Complacent credulity aroused his mockery and scorn. No eighteenth-century historian brushed away so many cobwebs from the temple of Clio.

*The Life of Charles XII*, written during his residence in England and published at Rouen in 1731, was not only the earliest of Voltaire's historical writings but his favourite child. He had grown to manhood during the years in which the dare-devil exploits of the King of Sweden reverberated through Europe. The swaying fortunes of the struggle between 'the Lion of the North' and Peter the Great were watched with hardly less interest than the campaigns of Louis XIV against the ring of enemies which his ambition had provoked in the West. Voltaire was never too absorbed in his literary triumphs to spare attention for the passing scene, and he was always eager to acquire information from performers on the public stage. He was particularly indebted to the gentle Stanislas, ex-King of Poland, to whose duodecimo Court of Lunéville he

paid frequent visits. Other well-informed contemporaries who
furnished information included Bolingbroke, the Duchess of
Marlborough and Marshal Saxe. All available printed authorities
were used, among them *The Wars of Sweden* by Defoe, masquerading as 'a Scots gentleman in the Swedish service'; and Count
Poniatowski, a Polish friend of the King, allowed him to read his
unpublished Memoirs.

The book won immediate success. The theme was a godsend
to any writer who knew how to handle it—swift action, a European stage, a colourful hero, unpredictable developments, a tragic
conclusion. Voltaire could tell a story as skilfully as he composed
an epitaph. Written for the general public, there is no overloading
with detail and there is not a dull page. Though the author seldom
comments on events it is easy to detect undertones. That he so
frequently and so exclusively salutes his courage and austerity suggests that he finds little else to admire. The whole work might
serve as a tract against war under cover of a biography. Throughout life he detested violence in every form and pitied the innocent
victims of the men of wrath. No celebrated biography is less disfigured by hero-worship, and from time to time his indignation
flares up. 'King Stanislas told me that a Russian officer, a friend
of his, surrendered to and was shot by a Swedish General. Worst
of all was that the King wrote the order in his own hand to break
Patkul, the Russian Ambassador to Augustus of Saxony, on the
wheel. Every lawyer—and every slave—feels all the horror of this
barbaric injustice.'

Beginning with a brief sketch of Sweden and Finland, the climate and the people, Voltaire passes to the dynasty which made
Sweden a Great Power. Gustavus Vasa, the father of his country, Gustavus Adolphus, Charles X and Charles XI, three doughty
warriors, prepared the way for Charles XII, 'perhaps the most
extraordinary man who ever lived'. When the precocious lad was
asked what he thought of Alexander the Great, he expressed a
wish to resemble him. Ascending the throne at fifteen he crowned
himself, like Napoleon, only to find Denmark, Poland and Russia
blocking his path. Throughout life the Slav colossus of the North
was never far from the thoughts of Voltaire, who briefly outlines
the realm of the Romanoffs. The existence of that immense country, he exclaims, was not realised by the West before Peter the

Great, and it was not an agreeable discovery. The Russians, less civilised than the Mexicans in the time of Cortez, were the slaves of masters as barbarous as themselves. All the more memorable was the achievement of the superman who built a capital, trained an army, created a navy and broke the power of the Church. When Charles scattered his troops at Narva, Peter prophetically remarked: 'I know the Swedes will long continue to be victorious, but in time they will teach us to beat them.' Since Poland was a mere pawn on the chessboard, the author analyses the elements of weakness and laments the plight of that unhappy State, whose constitution was the laughing-stock of the world. 'The nobility have scarcely elected a King before they fear his ambition and plot against him.' The implicit invitation to her neighbours to fish in troubled waters was joyfully accepted, and the elective throne became the challenge cup of Europe. The War of the Polish Succession, in which Russia championed the claims of Augustus, Elector of Saxony, while Sweden supported Stanislas Lecszynski, was merely an aspect of the wider struggle between Stockholm and St Petersburg for the hegemony of Northern Europe.

The young King left his capital in 1700 at the age of eighteen and never entered it again. He dedicated himself to the art of war, renouncing wine and women, schooling himself to hunger, sickness and cold, and sharing every hardship with his troops. His hairbreadth escapes confirmed his belief in predestination: fate, it seemed clear, was reserving him for higher things. At the age of twenty-two he selected Stanislas for the Polish throne, and this part of the narrative is enriched by reminiscences of the fallen ruler who loved to recall his early days. For instance, his baby daughter, afterwards the wife of Louis XV, was missed in the turmoil of war and was found in a village. 'This is the story I have often heard him tell.' The fumes of victory went to the head of the first teetotal King. 'Success became too familiar to him; he said it was more like hunting than fighting, and complained of never having to contest a victory.' After the laurels of Narva, a second Rossbach, nothing seemed impossible to his seasoned troops. 'He even despatched officers to Asia and Egypt to make plans of the cities and to report on the strength of these countries. If anyone could overthrow the Persian and Turkish Empires and then go to Italy, it was he. He was as young as Alexander, but he was more indefatigable and more temperate. Perhaps the Swedes were better soldiers than the Macedonians. But such plans, which are called divine when they succeed, are regarded as chimaeras when they fail. His sole pleasure was in making Europe tremble.'

The tide turned at Pultowa, where the King, drunk with military glory and crazed with ambition, met the punishment he deserved. Peter's proposals for peace provoked the haughty reply: 'I will treat with the Tsar in Moscow.' Counting on the aid of Mazeppa, the rebel chief of the Ukraine, he scorned advice. 'Their victories had filled the Swedes with such confidence that they never inquired about the enemy's numbers, but only about their location.' The description of the battle, as fiercely contested as Blenheim and Ramillies, is a spirited performance. 'All who have served with the Swedes,' comments the biographer, replying on first-hand testimony, 'know that it is almost impossible to resist their initial onset.' The Russian ranks were speedily broken, quickly rallied, and finally scored a resounding victory. Charles escaped to Turkey, a General without an army, since his troops had surrendered in droves as the Russians had collapsed at Narva. In a few hours the warrior King lost the fruit of nine years' campaigning and a score of battles. The captured Cossacks were broken on the wheel, a hideous practice prevalent in many parts of the Continent.

Voltaire grasped the epoch-making significance of Pultowa as clearly as his twentieth-century readers. 'The battle was fought on July 8, 1709, between the two most famous monarchs in the world: Charles distinguished by nine years of victory, Peter by nine years of training his troops to an equality with the Swedes. The former was celebrated for having given away the dominions of others, the latter for having civilised his own; Charles loving danger and fighting merely for the sake of glory, Peter shirking no difficulties and making war only from calculation; the Swedish King liberal from a generous temperament, the Russian never generous except with some object in view; the former sober and temperate in an extraordinary degree, naturally brave and only on one occasion displaying cruelty, the latter retaining the roughness of his education or his race, as terrible to his subjects as he was fascinating to strangers, and addicted to excesses which shortened his days. While Charles bore the title "Invincible" which he might lose at any moment, Peter had already received the title "the Great", which no defeat could forfeit since he did not owe it to his victories.' The biographer leaves his readers in no doubt as to the real hero of the book.

The few remaining years were an anti-climax. Treated as an honoured guest by the Turks, Charles had ample leisure to dream and to scheme. He longed to enlist the might of the Ottoman Empire in another round of his boxing match with Peter, for he still believed in his star. His protégé Stanislas had lost his throne after Pultowa, but might he not be restored when the tide of victory turned? The picture of the *ménage* at Bender is enriched by the testimony of acquaintances, among them a Portuguese doctor Fabricius living in Constantinople, an envoy of Holstein, and Count Poniatowski. The Turks chivalrously provided food and cash, money was sent from France, and the captive King borrowed from merchants at Constantinople. 'Many people journeyed from the capital to see him. The Turks and the neighbouring Tartars came in crowds. All honoured and admired him. His rigid abstinence from wine and his regularity in attending public prayers twice daily spread the rumour that he was a true Mussulman.' For the first time he had leisure to read, and he found solace in the heroes of Corneille and Racine. All proposals for peace with Russia and his return to Sweden were rejected out of hand, and when the Turks at last requested him to leave their country the ungrateful guest staged a sanguinary resistance. Marching north he was soon in the thick of the fight once more, defending Stralsund to the last and perishing by a shot from an unknown hand— perhaps by a member of his own forces—at the siege of Frederikshall at the age of thirty-six.

The biographer's verdict, severe though not unjust, needs comparatively little revision after two centuries of research. The best of his English biographers, Nisbet Bain, describes the book as brilliant and attractive, but adds that Charles was more of an Intellectual than Voltaire admits. Despite certain heroic qualities to which unstinted homage is paid, he is presented as a pocket Attila, storming over northern and eastern Europe without any constructive aims. Living in the moment, he was incapable of creation and indeed had no desire to create. Hegemony passed to the Tsar, who made a better use of it, for he employed his successes for his country's good. If he conquered a town, the best artisans were transferred to St Petersburg. The customs, arts and sciences of any place he took were imported to enrich and elevate his own country. Thus of all conquerors he had the best excuse for his conquests. Sweden, on the other hand, lost all her foreign possessions, and had neither trade, money nor credit; her veteran warriors were killed or died of want. More than 100,000 remained in the vast Russian Empire, and as many more had been sold to the Turks and the Tartars. The male population was visibly diminishing, yet their hopes revived when they heard that their King had arrived at Stralsund. The country youth crowded to enlist, leaving the land without cultivators. He thought his subjects were only born to follow him to war, and he had schooled them to think so too. He enlisted many fifteen-year-olds. In numerous districts there were only old men, women and children; sometimes the women ploughed unaided. A people thus loaded with taxation would have revolted under any other King, but even the most miserable peasant knew that his master was faring even worse. So great was their veneration that they could not hate him: one could not help blaming him, admiring him, pitying him, or aiding him. All his actions were almost incredible. He carried the heroic virtues to a point at which they became faults. His eminent qualities were a nightmare to his country: he was an extraordinary rather than a great man. His life should be a lesson to kings, teaching them that a peaceful and happy reign is better than so much glory. Like other adventurers, crowned and uncrowned, he dug his own grave, forgetful of the maxim that politics —of which war is a function—are the art of the possible. No contemporary observer realised more fully than Voltaire that the final collapse of Swedish imperialism was an event of minor significance compared with the emergence of Russia as a Great Power.

Voltaire was fascinated by the towering figure of Peter the Great, and he returned at intervals to the epic struggle for the mastery of the North. A half-length portrait, entitled *Anecdotes sur Pierre le Grand*, written in 1748, is notable for the tribute to the Genevese Le Fort who met the young ruler in 1695 and encouraged him to break with the prejudices of the past. Without the Genevese, he declares, Russia might still be in a state of barbarism. The reformer of such a backward country could only build in brick, but elsewhere he would have built in marble. Merciless he was, but cruelty was traditional at the Russian Court.

When a full-length biography was suggested by the Russian Court during the later years of the Tsarina Elizabeth and official materials were offered for his use, Voltaire accepted the invitation with pleasure. That it was commissioned by the daughter of the hero to some extent clipped the author's wings, and the portrait of the superman could hardly be expected to reproduce every wart on his swarthy countenance. The story of Charles XII had been one of private virtues and public vices; with Peter it was the reverse. Rulers of good character, however, like Charles I, Charles XII and Louis XVI are judged by their public performances, not by their observance of the Ten Commandments. Yet the book is no mere official panegyric, and the final verdict differs little from that of the earlier portrait. While Charles envisaged life as a military campaign, Peter dedicated himself to the more rewarding tasks of the political architect. Never did their biographer doubt who was the better ruler and the greater man. Published in 1759, the *Histoire de Russie sous Pierre le Grand* breathes a warmer tone than the life of Charles XII. With the warrior King the whole plan was wrong; with the Tsar merely some of the methods. There was naturally a good deal of repetition in the narrative of the wars, but there was also new material on internal developments. For the first time the West was enabled to visualise the greatest of the Romanoffs not only as the creator of modern Russia but as a living personality, part genius, part savage. There had been travellers and travellers' tales, but little was known of the reforms which had revolutionised the life of the country and wrought a permanent shift in the balance of power on the European chessboard.

Compared to the Chinese and Indians, the oldest civilisations with a span of over 4,000 years, the Russian people, as Voltaire reminds his readers, had arrived late and had made more progress in fifty years than any other nation by its own efforts in five hundred. Though still underpopulated, it possessed as many inhabitants as any Christian state. Of the 24 millions—the latest figure supplied from official sources—most were serfs, as in Poland, many parts of Germany, and, until recent times, in nearly all Europe. Wealth was reckoned not in money but in slaves. Since the chief need was population, Peter wisely attempted to limit the number of monks. From the standpoint of national survival those 13,000 drones were lost to the State, and the 720,000 serfs whom they possessed were out of all proportion to their needs. This abuse, added Voltaire in a later edition, was only corrected by the Empress Catherine, who deprived the clergy and monasteries of these odious privileges, and strove to turn them into useful citizens. The religions of the Empire, as numerous as the races, included Muslims and primitive pagans. The Christian dissidents from the Orthodox Church, such as the Raskolniks, were left in peace, but Peter expelled the Jesuits as a political danger to the State.

At the close of his introductory chapters Voltaire pays preliminary homage to the mighty Muscovite whose achievements had fascinated him since his youth. Writing in the middle of the Seven Years War when Russian armies were in the field, he declares that Russia owed her influence in Europe to him alone. Of all the celebrated legislators he alone was fully known, for fables had clustered about all his predecessors. 'We enjoy the advantage of writing truths which would be regarded as fables were they not well attested. In the largest of states everything had to be made. At last Peter was born and Russia was transformed.' Voltaire always admired pioneers.

Though he never visited Russia, Voltaire approached his task with a lively sense of its extent and resources. It was larger than all the rest of Europe, he began, larger than the Roman Empire, larger than the dominions of Alexander the Great. So vast a territory required a population to match, but to make it as populous and productive as the countries of western and southern Europe could need centuries of labour and a succession of supermen on the throne. He records with satisfaction that of the thirty-five churches in the new capital five were allotted to Catholics, Calvinists and Lutherans— five temples erected to the spirit of tolerance, an example to other nations including his own. The admixture of race is stressed, and the showman takes Siberia and the Far East in his stride. His interest in religious beliefs and practices finds full scope as he summarises the reports of visitors to those distant lands. The Kamchatkans, for instance, possessed a mythology but no religion; demons and sorceresses took the place of gods. Yet backward communities were not unteachable. Culture and the arts had been established with such difficulty in Asia, and the edifice had so often been overthrown, that it was surprising that the majority were living above the Tartar level.

The biographical sketch begins with the death of Alexis in 1677 at the age of forty-six, and the provisional partnership of Sophie, his daughter by his first wife, and her brother Ivan, an epileptic imbecile. Peter, the precocious child of a second marriage, grew up among horrors. Like his half-brother Ivan he suffered from convulsions, but he possessed a cool and powerful brain. He taught himself German and Dutch. Ships and shipbuilding, a boyish passion, remained the chief delight of his adult life. At the outset of the reign he inaugurated commercial relations with China. Whenever China crosses the stage Voltaire salutes his favourite nation.

Peter's visit to Western Europe at the age of twenty-five is described with admiration. His half-brother dead and his odious half-sister a prisoner of state, he felt that he could safely leave his kingdom and seek lessons abroad. He worked and lived like an artisan in the shipbuilding yard at Sardam, learned to perform operations, to make clocks and to cast cannons, corrected Dutch maps of Russia, studied astronomy, finished his training in shipbuilding at Deptford, and invited foreign technicians to settle in Russia. He returned by Vienna and Warsaw. Not till Joseph II half a century later did a ruler undertake journeys for such strictly utilitarian aims.

The first searching test was the revolt of the Streltsi, or palace guards, who were believed to aim at the elevation of Sophie during the absence of the ruler. Though in itself a small affair, it indicated a core of opposition to the foreign models and foreign instructors whom Peter felt to be essential for his plans. Yet throughout his reign he took care to keep the higher controls in Russian hands. Like the Japanese of the Restoration era, he employed foreign experts to train his subjects and for no other purpose. The savage punishments of the Streltsi cast a shadow over the fame of the young ruler, but they notified potential malcontents that they would receive short shrift if they raised their hand against the State. Like Sultan Mahmoud, who slaughtered his Janissaries in the nineteenth century with equal unconcern, he believed that the interests of his backward country demanded totalitarian rule. A further step towards autocracy was the abolition of the Patriarchate, the creation of the Holy Synod under a Procurator responsible to the Crown, and the diversion of large ecclesiastical revenues to the payment of troops. Every blow at the power and pretensions of the Churches—whatever the Church and whatever the creed—is greeted by the biographer with applause.

The long war with Sweden fills a smaller space in the annals of the Tsar than that of the King, for in Russian history it was merely an incident. Though the panic at Narva left Charles the first man in Europe, Peter never doubted that Russia's turn would come. His heroic labours for national recovery resemble the efforts of Frederick the Great after the Seven Years War. He imported live-stock, created a textile industry and developed the Siberian mines. In addition to building a new capital, he constructed fortresses from Cronstadt and Archangel in the north to Kiev and Taganrog in the south. How much was at stake at Pultowa was fully grasped by the biographer. 'I have read the letters of several Ministers who shared the general view that Charles would win; but his death would mean only one hero less in the world. That of Peter would involve the ruin of all his achievements, useful as they were to the whole human race, and the relapse of the largest empire into the chaos from which he had begun to extricate it.' Both rulers were under fire. Pultowa, concludes the biographer with something like a shout of triumph, meant the happiness of the vastest empire in the world. The note is a little too shrill, but it is true enough that a Swedish victory would have stimulated the Swedish bull's pathological urge to gore his neighbours.

While the knight-errant blandly ignored the lessons of experi-ence, the practical idealist was eager to learn. His visit to Paris in 1717 aroused even more interest than his earlier sojourn in the West, for he was now at the summit of his fame. No ruler ap-proached him in ability and achievement. He desired to see every-thing with his own eyes and to test objects with his own hands. He was a mechanic, an artist, a geometrician. 'The Academy dis-played its choicest treasures, but none so rare as himself.' He cor-rected mistakes in maps of his territories. He accepted member-ship of the Academy, and began a correspondence on experiments and discoveries with those members of whom he wished to be a col-league. 'We must go back to Pythagoras to find such travellers, and they had not quitted an empire in order to learn.' Embracing the statue of Richelieu he exclaimed: 'Great man! I would have given half my territories to have learned from you how to govern the other half.' Once again he invited experts to Russia to instruct his subjects.

The later chapters are dominated by the fate of Alexis, the first of the dynastic tragedies which darken the story of eighteenth-century Russia. The heir to the throne, the son of Peter's first wife Eudoxia Lapouka, never knew happiness, for his mother was immured in a convent when he was six and his father had no time for the nursery. His marriage in his seventeenth year to a Brunswick princess, who died in childbirth, brought no ray of sunshine into his life. Inheriting his mother's dislike of foreign advisers, he fell under the influence of ecclesiastical and civilian reactionaries. Voltaire had collected a good deal of information about the frustrated lad in addition to the official material provided for his use. The clergy emerge as the villains of the piece. The books provided for his education seemed to him to condemn his father's revolutionary work. 'Priests were leaders of the malcontents, and he submitted to their will. They convinced him that the whole country was outraged, that his father, who was often ill, would not live long, and that the nation would welcome expressions of his disapproval.'

Voltaire, like a conscientious historian, sympathises with both parties in the dynastic feud. He has equal understanding for the ruler's consuming anxiety as to the permanence of his work and for the heir's sour disapproval of the new pattern of the realm. The tension increased when in 1711 the Tsar divorced his wife and married Catherine, his Lithuanian mistress, who presented him with two daughters, potential competitors for the throne. It was in vain that Alexis was entrusted with various administrative tasks and was sent to complete his education at Dresden, for by this time the feud was too bitter to be healed and too notorious to be hushed up. Warned by his father that he must change his course or forfeit the throne, the unhappy heir renounced his claim. To a second warning, 'Improve, or enter a monastery,' he replied that he would become a monk.

The drama entered its final stage when Peter visited the West in 1717. Alexis fled to Vienna with his mistress and thence to Naples.

P

He was coaxed back by the solemn oath of his father that he would not be punished. He was removed from the line of succession, which passed to his infant son, and his associates were tortured to death. The biographer, like the Greek chorus, looks on and cries, 'The pity of it all!' 'The Tsar had to decide between the interests of nearly eighteen millions and a single individual incapable of governing them.' Some charges were denied by Alexis, but he admitted others, excusing himself on the ground of anger and drink. In confession he had expressed a wish for his father's death. His confessor had replied: 'God will pardon you; we wish it too,' and admitted under torture that the statement was correct. 'We must not judge the laws and customs of one nation by those of others,' comments Voltaire. The Tsar had the undoubted right to punish his son with death for his flight; that he acted with deliberation and full publicity indicated his conviction of the justice of his cause. He allowed the Bishops to decide after a trial of five months, during which Alexis was interrogated several times. Though he had never thought of parricide, a unanimous sentence of death was pronounced for having left Russia without permission— a curious anticipation of the attempted flight and punishment of Prussia's Crown Prince Frederick in 1730. So confident was the Tsar that he was discharging his duty that he ordered the publication and translation of the proceedings. A commissioned biography was hardly the place to record that Alexis was flogged to death, and Voltaire dutifully reproduces the fairy tale of apoplexy which was served out to Russian embassies abroad.

The closing years of the reign were not the least memorable. Peter was the first modern ruler to seize the possibilities of applied science, and he founded the Academy of Science as an instrument of national policy. 'The arts flourished,' writes Voltaire, 'manufactures were encouraged, the navy was enlarged, the armies were well supplied, the laws were observed.' He enjoyed his glory in full, and resolved to share it with his low-born second wife, the only woman—perhaps the only human being—he ever loved. In 1724 he placed the crown on her head at Moscow and married his daughter Anne to the Duke of Holstein. But there was always some skeleton in the Imperial cupboard. In 1722 Catherine was proclaimed successor to the throne and in 1724 was crowned Empress Consort. After the coronation, however, her husband suspected her—probably without reason—of a *liaison* with a young chamberlain, and the latter's sister, one of her ladies, was charged with financial misdemeanours. The chamberlain was executed and his head, preserved in spirits, was deposited in the apartments of the Empress. His sister was punished with the knout. 'These severities which outrage our customs,' comments Voltaire, 'were perhaps necessary in a country where observance of the law seemed to demand a terrifying rigour. The Empress asked mercy for her lady-in-waiting which was refused. When in his anger he smashed a Venetian vase, she remarked: 'You have broken an ornament of your palace. Do you think that will make it more beautiful?' Partially appeased, the Tsar reduced the blows of the knout from eleven to five. This and similar incidents gave rise to the suggestion that his agonising death was due to poisoning. 'Mere malicious rumours,' exclaims the biographer: the Persian campaigns had overtaxed his strength. In the winter of 1724–5 he suffered from an abscess and other ailments, and was often delirious. Claims for the succession could be made for his grandson Peter, the child of Alexis, and for his eldest daughter Anne, Duchess of Holstein; but the influence of Menschikoff, the all-powerful Minister, placed his widow Catherine on the throne without a hitch.

The book concludes with an impressive catalogue of the reforms of the master-builder. He introduced textile industries, constructed canals, organised the police, repressed begging, decreed uniform weights and measures, imported foreign artisans, worked the iron, gold and silver mines, built forts, improved the maps. Sometimes he took the spade himself and carried heavy burdens on his back. Commercial relations were established with Persia and China, and an Orthodox Church was built in Pekin. In the sphere of legislation he studied foreign practice; the code he began to compile was completed by his daughter and reflected the mildness of her reign. His governing principle was that service counted for more than birth. The biographer dwells with special satisfaction on the religious reforms. He abolished the Patriarchate because he wished the executive to be supreme in every sphere; the Holy Synod, chosen by the ruler, could only pass laws which he approved. The idea of competing authorities in a state seemed to him absurd. Though the Patriarch had not sworn obedience, the fourteen members of the Synod, who held senatorial rank, recognised their master who occasionally presided at their sessions.

Like Augustus in Rome, Peter found a Russia of brick and left it of marble. Inheriting a sprawling, semi-oriental monarchy, dominated by the great nobles and the Church, he left it a centralised autocracy, the prototype of the Enlightened Despotisms of eighteenth-century Europe. After the conclusion of the long war with Sweden the Senate of the Holy Synod conferred the titles of The Great and Emperor on the most influential personage of Eastern Europe since Constantine. 'Half hero, half tiger!' exclaims Voltaire in the life of Charles XII. Soft-pedalling is to be expected in official biography, but the final tribute is more than mere flattery. That his work endured tells its own tale. 'Europe had recognised that he loved glory, but that he used it to do good; that his faults never weakened his great qualities; that he coerced nature, his subjects, and himself, on land and water, but coerced in order to adorn.' A graceful compliment is added to the daughter who had commissioned the work. 'Extreme rigour was necessary at that time towards the lower class; but when manners changed the Empress Elizabeth buttressed by clemency the work which her father had begun by his laws. This indulgence has been carried to a point without precedent, that during her reign no one should be put to death; and she kept her word. She is the first sovereign to respect human life. Malefactors have been condemned to the mines and public works. Thus their punishments are rendered useful to the state—an arrangement as wise as it is humane. Everywhere else the criminal is executed without stopping crime.' Life had always been cheap in Russia, and Peter's volcanic rages left it cheaper still. For Voltaire, as for ourselves, the best measuring rod for civilisation was the degree of respect for the body and soul of the individual citizen, in other words, for the rule of law. Confronted with this exacting test neither the Swedish gladiator nor the Romanoff master-builder deserves high marks. The century of the common man was still far away.

## II. *The Ancien Régime*

So long as mankind retains interest in the *Grand Siècle*, the *Roi Soleil* and his degenerate successor, in the poets, the preachers and the captains of the *Ancien Régime*, Voltaire's surveys of two long and eventful reigns will continue to be read. As a youthful eye-witness of the closing years of Louis XIV and a keen observer of the whole span of Louis XV, he records his own impressions and utilises the oral as well as the written testimony of men and women who had stood close to the heart of events. The second work is of less interest, partly because the recorder had to be more reticent and partly because there was infinitely less glamour and glory to describe. Yet the *Age of Louis XV* deserves more attention than it usually receives. In these two books the history of France from the death of Richelieu to the eve of the French Revolution is interpreted by the brightest intellect of the age. A third work, on the Parlement of Paris, traces constitutional developments from the Middle Ages to the writer's own time.

No Frenchman before the age of Sismondi and Thierry, Guizot and Michelet made such notable contributions to the history of his country as Voltaire. The first attempt was Mézeray's survey, carried down to the reign of Henri IV, which was published during the Fronde. The three folio volumes, and still more an abridged version issued in 1668, supplied the needs of readers for almost a century. While his use of the sources for the early centuries was uncritical, the value of the book increases as it approaches his own time. Economic and social conditions were sketched, and his independent judgment cost him his pension as Historiographer Royal. His sympathies were with the bourgeoisie to which he belonged and with the cool-headed *Politiques* who frowned both on the Huguenots and the *Ligue*. The next attempt was made by the Jesuit Père Daniel, who rejected some of the Merovingian fables accepted by Mézeray, and whose tributes to the rôle of the Monarchy earned him the coveted title of Historiographer Royal. After spending one hour in the archives he concluded that they were unnecessary for his task. A less ambitious attempt was the *Abrégé Chronologique de l'histoire de France* by President Hénault, the distinguished lawyer and discreet lover of Mme du Deffand, who was strongest in the field of institutions and was extremely careful not to risk his skin. None of the three possessed the slightest literary talent and none attempted to paint the life of the nation. France had to wait for Voltaire to produce a readable narrative, as England had waited for Hume.

'I consider Louis XIV as a benefactor of mankind,' wrote Voltaire to d'Argenson in 1740. 'I write as a man, not as a subject. I desire to portray the last century, not merely a prince.' Though the author was a cosmopolitan who felt equally at home in every civilised land, his book is a glowing tribute to the genius of France. Published in Berlin in 1751, it was revised in 1756 and assumed its final form in 1768. To please all his readers was impossible. 'Voltaire has sent me his book,' wrote President Hénault. 'The weakness of the first volume is that the King is unfairly treated. But the second volume makes up for it.' Émile Faguet, on the other hand, long afterwards complained of the glorification of Louis XIV. As a matter of fact Voltaire is a fairer judge than Saint-Simon into whose unpublished Memoirs he dipped during his last visit to Paris. He read everything available, published and in manuscript—Dangeau's voluminous journal, the Memoirs of Torcy and Villars, the papers of Louvois and Colbert. After the first edition he obtained from the Duc de Noailles the Memoirs or rather Memoranda of the King himself. Among the oral witnesses were Villars, Fleury, the Duc and Duchesse du Maine, and Caumartin, the helpful friend of his youth. He was also privileged to examine the archives in the Louvre. The finished portrait is not very different than that which has been painted by Lavisse.

The *Siècle de Louis XIV* opens with an exposition of the author's aim: to depict not merely the career of a celebrated ruler but the mind of man during the most enlightened age the world had ever seen. There had only been four happy periods when the arts ripened to perfection—classical Greece, the age of Caesar and Augustus, the Renaissance and seventeenth century France. The latest was the best, not indeed in artistic achievement but in the advance of reason. It was the more remarkable since it followed a period of barbarism and civil war. Yet the historian confines his eulogy to the lofty realm of the spirit, for the actions of rulers had not kept pace with the advance of mind. All ages were alike in criminal folly. The book is written in complete independence by a man who brings his own scale of values to the task.

Though justly proud of the cultural achievements of France, Voltaire, like Gibbon, Lessing and Goethe, was more of a European than a patriot. The vision of Europe as a cultural unit was continually before his eyes. Christian Europe, excluding Russia, he declared, was like a great republic divided into states, with a common substratum of religion and public law; for instance, the person of ambassadors was respected and prisoners of war were not enslaved. In a community connected by so many ties religious wars were a form of madness peculiar to Christians. Though attempts had been made to maintain a rough equilibrium, since Charles V the balance had inclined to the House of Austria. Detesting war as heartily as any of the Quakers whom he had met in England, he was too much of a realist to dream of a warless world. His sombre picture of France after the assassination of his hero Henri IV anticipates Vandal's celebrated denunciation of the Directory before the emergence of *le petit Caporal*. Though not quite so cruel and frenzied as the wars of the *Ligue*, when religious fanaticism was mated with political faction, the era of the Fronde is denounced as a welter of ambition and intrigue. France's greatest soldiers, Condé and Turenne, fought successively on both sides, and the climax of degradation was reached when the former enlisted the aid of the Spaniards against his fatherland. The disunion of the rebels was the salvation of the Court, but the dictatorship of the cunning Mazarin, who cared for nothing except money and power, was a shady episode. His principal achievement was to secure Alsace for France. Was he a great Minister? That, replies the historian cautiously, was for posterity to judge. When the young monarch came of age his day was over, and his death relieved a tension which was becoming unendurable.

Voltaire was a convinced royalist, for he thought little of the political capacity of the common man. But there was no unction in his attitude to Kings. His florid compliments to Frederick the Great and Catherine the Great were merely the current coin of the age, as they fully understood; awe was as foreign to his nature in the Courts of Europe as in the courts of heaven. Yet he was unstinted in his homage to born rulers of men, and the *début* of Louis

XIV stirs him to enthusiasm. For the first time since Henri IV there was a firm hand at the helm and tortured France was grateful for the boon. The prestige of the throne was quickly restored, Dunkirk was purchased from England, a fleet came into being. By 1665, at the age of twenty-seven, he had reached the summit of ambition. 'He was young and rich, well served and blindly obeyed, fearing no foreign ruler and eager to distinguish himself by foreign conquests.' The campaigns are described with spirit but without emotion. In the war with Holland the author's sympathies are with the Dutch, who fought heroically under William of Orange against desperate odds and kept up the struggle till the Emperor, the Great Elector and other princes came to their aid. Though he salutes the genius of Condé, Turenne and Vauban, he describes Louvois as more valuable to the King than any of his Generals.

The second interval of peace which followed the Treaty of Nimeguen in 1678 is described with more satisfaction than the victories in the field. Louis XIV ruled a nation happy in itself and a model to other states. He had added Franche Comté, Dunkirk and part of Flanders to France, naval bases were established at Brest and Toulon, and Strasbourg was acquired without drawing the sword. He would never have approved the devastation of the Palatinate which Louvois had ordered if he had witnessed the horrors it involved. With the turn of the century and the War of the Spanish Succession, however, the historian's tone becomes more severe and the arrogance of the monarch is roundly denounced. 'It was against him rather than against France that the Allies were leagued. The King deteriorated, not only in the shaping of policy but in the choice of his agents. Chamillart, virtually Prime Minister, was unfit for his post. The King held the reins too tightly; commanders in the field had often to ask leave before launching an operation, whereby favourable opportunities were sometimes unused.' In a word, *le Roi Soleil* possessed too much power. Voltaire had as little use for monarchical absolutism as for Divine Right: Limited Monarchy was far the best system. 'Elsewhere the people have blindly to acquiese in the designs of their Kings, but in England the King must acquiese in those of his people.' Thanks above all to Villars' belated victory at Denain the War of the Spanish Succession achieved its purpose by planting a grandson of the French monarch on the Spanish throne, though at the cost of prolonged and terrible suffering. Yet at the close of his stirring narrative the historian reiterates his admiration for the supreme practitioner of a difficult art. 'He possessed an elevation of soul which urged him to the accomplishment of great things in every sphere. The splendour of his rule was reflected in his most trivial actions.' The writer, who lived into the reign of Louis XVI, realised how far and how fast the French Monarchy had fallen, though he had no notion that it was so near to collapse.

The latter portion of the book is the most interesting because it is the most personal. The chapters entitled 'Anecdotes of the Reign', containing material collected from eye-witnesses, round off the portrait of the King. The earliest sign that he was born with a great soul was the victory over his passion for Marie Mancini. It was the fault of his mother and Mazarin that he had received no systematic education and had read little beyond the plays of Corneille. He should have been taught some history, especially of recent times, but the available manuals were almost unreadable. Yet he learned his *métier* quickly, and France was grateful for the dignity and brilliance of the Court after the horrors of civil war and the secluded life of his colourless father. A new era opened with his marriage fête in 1660 and those of his brother to his English cousin Henrietta in 1661. It is not the monarch alone who receives high marks. 'Nature herself seemed to take a delight at this moment in producing men of the first rank in every art,' but the ruler could hold his own with the best. 'He towered above everybody by the grace of his figure, the majestic nobility of his countenance, and the sound of his voice, at once dignified and charming. An old officer faltered when asking a favour, saying, 'Sire, I never trembled like this before your enemies.' Fêtes never interfered with his incessant labours. His generosity was unprecedented, not only to French writers, among them Racine, but to foreign scholars, though he knew too much of human nature to expect much gratitude. "Every time I fill a post I make a hundred people discontented and one ungrateful," he remarked.' His worst fault was sensuality. Few women could resist him, and even his genuine affection for the La Vallière synchronised with frequent infidelities. Her successor, the Montespan, was detested for her arrogance and pomp. The whole Court was a hot-bed of amorous intrigue, and Louvois indulged in several mistresses. Superstition was as rife as immorality. The Marquise de Brinvilliers was justly executed for poisoning her family, but there was much foolish talk about love potions and pacts with the devil. Medical science was in its infancy, and natural deaths, such as that of Henrietta, were attributed to crime.

Next to the monarch the most interesting portrait in the gallery is that of Mme de Maintenon, who was described to him, among others, by Cardinal Fleury. In a well-known study Döllinger saluted her as the most influential woman in French history, but that was not the view of her contemporaries. She rarely interfered, declares Voltaire, either to render a service or to make mischief. 'She had scarcely any feelings of her own, and her only care was to conform with those of the King.' There was no outward show of greatness. She was an agreeable and docile companion of the ruler who was more deeply attached to her than she to him. Though he admits that no marriage contract was drawn up, he asserts that the ceremony took place in January 1686 on the advice of the King's confessor, Père La Chaise, 'in a small chapel at the end of the apartments later occupied by the Duke of Burgundy'. The Archbishop of Paris pronounced the Benediction. Only the Confessor and two valets were witnesses.

The anecdotal chapters are followed by surveys of the administration, commerce and finance, arts and sciences, and ecclesiastical affairs. Though he never used the words *L'état c'est moi*, he was more entitled to do so than any of his predecessors or successors on the French throne. He read every document that he signed. His most enduring achievement was the creation of a navy. 'He had defects and made grave mistakes, but if those who condemned him had been in his place would they have equalled his achievements? No one has surpassed him as a monarch. He was aware of his faults though unable to correct them. "I have been too fond of war," he confessed in a memorandum for his son; "do not imitate me in that, nor in my extravagance." Though his life and death were alike glorious he was not mourned as he deserved. His eminent qualities and his noble deeds eclipsed all his faults. He was never ruled by his Ministers, and he did more good to his country than twenty of his predecessors together.'

France, we are reminded, was weak in historians and com-
posers but pre-eminent in literature and painting, architecture and
sculpture. To these creative activities Louis XIV gave more encouragement than all his predecessors added together. A brief
digression on the Arts and Sciences in Europe enables the author
to pay tribute to England. Since the Restoration, he declares with
his ignorant contempt for the Middle Ages, the English had made
greater progress in all the arts than in all previous times. Milton
was the glory and wonder of the age. Dryden and Pope were
admirable, Swift a better Rabelais, Addison's *Cato* a masterpiece,
Newton and Locke the leaders of science and philosophy. Leib-
nitz is saluted as perhaps the most universal genius in Europe,
Galileo as a giant. Looking round the Continent Voltaire proudly
concludes: 'We have shown that during the last century mankind,
from one end of Europe to the other, has been more enlightened
than ever before'. There spoke the High Priest of the *Aufklärung*:
not territory, nor power, nor riches were the test of progress, but
enlightenment and the arts of peace. None of his contemporaries
could have produced so widely ranging a survey of intellectual
life. Though the humanities were his special province, he was
deeply interested in science. He knew enough physics to understand Newton, and he had carried out experiments in chemistry.

The concluding chapters on the Protestant churches and the
Catholic heresies are among the most characteristic in the book.
The Church in France, contrary to general belief, was not wealthy;
there were no Prince Bishops as in Germany and Austria, and a
good deal of money flowed away to Rome. The Gallican Articles
of 1682, strictly limiting the authority of the Vatican, are naturally
approved by the old foe of Ultramontanism. The revocation of
the Edict of Nantes, on the other hand, was one of the greatest
calamities, not only for the victims but for France. The Protestants, who formed about a twelfth of the population, were loyal
and useful citizens who had taken no part in the Fronde. Fifty
thousand families left the country in three years, and the total loss
amounted to half a million. Voltaire had met Huguenot exiles in
England and Holland, among them Cavalier, their best-known
chief. Though his sympathies were always with the oppressed, he
admits that there were fanatics among them, and fanatics of every
colour he abhorred.

The feud between Jansenists and Jesuits is treated with scant sympathy for either side. While the disputes of the classical philosophers were peaceful, those of the theologians were always violent and often led to bloodshed. Voltaire hated the Jesuits as much as Arnauld himself, not merely for what they taught, but for what they had done. They were indeed completely discredited by the murder of Henri IV, the Gunpowder Plot and the *Lettres Provinciales*, which contained as much Attic salt as *Tartuffe*. Pascal, however, was unfair in saddling the whole Order with the extravagances of a few Spaniards and Flemings; he might have detected similar monstrosities among Dominican and Franciscan casuists. The Jansenists receive gentler treatment, though their doctrine of grace, derived like that of Calvin from Augustine, was part of 'the wretched controversies of the Schoolmen'. The piety of Port Royal is acknowledged, but the Jansenist movement fizzled out with the convulsions and miraculous cures at the tomb of the Abbé Paris. The Bull *Unigenitus*, issued on the eve of the death of Louis XIV, registered the triumph of the Jesuits and of Father Le Tellier, his Confessor, who had persuaded him that the best means of atoning for his sins was to hammer the heretics.

From Jansenism to Quietism was but a step. Mme Guyon, declares Voltaire, wished to be the Saint Theresa of France. 'The ambition to have disciples, perhaps the strongest of all ambitions, obsessed her mind. Though herself a light weight, she secured the patronage of Mme de Maintenon and of Fénelon, tutor to the King's grandsons, 'the most brilliant figure at the Court.' Like a man in love, he condoned all her faults and she hailed him as her son. It is a tribute to the Archbishop of Cambrai that the arch enemy of the clergy felt his fascination, and he regrets that the big battalions were on the other side. Mme de Maintenon, hating discord, withdrew her protection, and Bossuet was called in to dissect the writings of Mme Guyon. When he denounced them she was sent to Vincennes, and now he demanded that Fénelon himself should condemn his friend. When the Archbishop published a milder version of Quietism in his *Maxims of the Saints* Bossuet pronounced it heretical, and the King requested condemnation by the Pope. Fénelon recanted, a humiliating procedure which Voltaire himself, forced to more than one face-saving surrender, cannot condemn. No ecclesiastic in the portrait gallery is painted in such glowing colours. 'His personality and *Télémaque* won him the veneration of Europe. He was universally beloved.' Despite the charm of this radiant figure, the historian dismissed the mystics as 'the alchemists of true religion'. The whole controversy is exhibited as a storm in a tea-cup. 'These disputes, which long claimed the attention of all France, are over. One marvels at the rancour and bitterness they caused.' At the end of his journey through the longest reign in French history, Voltaire draws a lesson from the other side of the world. Jesuit missions had been permitted entry at the close of the sixteenth century, but they were soon forbidden as the effect of innovation was feared. The Eastern peoples had never despatched missionaries to Europe, and the mania for proselytising was a disorder of recent times. The beginning of wisdom was to live and let live. Different peoples—and different persons—had differing traditions and varying needs. The simpler a religion the less there was to quarrel about. All theologies and philosophies were guesswork. What mattered most was conduct, and in the field of morals the West had little to teach the East.

There is very little propaganda in the *Siècle de Louis XIV*, but the articles of the author's creed stand out as clearly as the Ten Commandments: intellectual enlightenment, the encouragement of the arts and sciences, religious toleration, mild laws, sound finance, the avoidance of war, and above all a spirit of humanity. Neither idealising nor despising the average man, Voltaire believed that on such lines the sum of happiness, both for individuals and nations could be vastly increased. England had made him a *Philosophe*, and to the end of his days he preferred her political system to the inefficient autocracy of Versailles. 'If one religion only were allowed in England,' he wrote in his *Lettres sur les Anglais*, 'the Government might well become arbitrary. If there were only two, they would be at one another's throats. Since there are a multitude, they all live happy and in peace.' The division of power was the secret of harmony and success. 'The English alone, by a series of struggles, have at last established that wise system where the Prince is all powerful to do good and is restrained from doing evil, where the nobility is great without insolence, and where the people share in the government without confusion.'

The *Précis du Siècle Louis XV* is planned on a less comprehensive scale. Appointed Historiographer of France in 1746, Voltaire commenced his official duties with a narrative of the War of the Austrian Succession which was submitted for approval to d'Argenson, Minister of War. Other portions of the reign were described at intervals in later years, and revision continued till the close of his life. The book is enlivened by material from such prominent actors in the drama as Marshal Villars, the Duc de Richelieu and the Duchesse du Maine. The curtain rises on the Regency, when gaiety returned in a flood after the gloom of the declining years of Louis XIV. The Regent died of his debaucheries in the prime of his life. 'We laughed at his death as we had laughed at his government, for the French are accustomed to laugh at everything.' Yet he was not wholly contemptible. 'His only faults were his passion for pleasure, his liking for innovations. Of all the descendants of Henri IV Philip of Orleans most resembled him in his valour, his kindliness and his lack of pose, but he possessed a richer culture.' The chief sensation of the Regency was the crazy scheme of the Scottish adventurer John Law, who founded a bank and a Mississippi Company, assumed control of the national resources with the title of Controller General, and issued paper money in a flood. In the pursuit of his vaulting ambitions he was naturalised and became a Catholic; for a brief space Paris was at his feet. 'I have seen him entering the Palais Royal followed by Dukes and Peers, Marshals and Bishops.' When the bubble burst the magician fled from France. 'I have seen his widow at Brussels, as reduced as she had once been proud and triumphant at Paris.'

The portrait of Cardinal Fleury, the King's tutor, who held the reins for twenty years after the death of the Regent, is painted from personal acquaintance. 'If any mortal was ever happy, it was Fleury', who retained health and power till his death at the age of ninety. He was moderate, mild, conciliatory, economical, a lover of peace, and in consequence less criticised and less envied than the flamboyant Richelieu and the greedy Mazarin. Like his contemporary Walpole he disliked adventures and wisely allowed war-weary France to lick her wounds. 'It was a happy time for all the nations which vied in commerce and the arts and forgot its past calamities.' Though no superman and lacking elevation, Fleury gave his countrymen what they needed and craved. The long peace was interrupted by the War of the Polish Succession, in which France vainly backed Stanislas for the throne, while the

Emperor and Russia championed Augustus III, Elector of Saxony. A far graver enterprise was the War of the Austrian Succession, in which Fleury joined as regretfully as Walpole embarked on the Spanish war of 1739. The account of the campaigns, enriched by the unpublished record of Frederick the Great, provides the fullest treatment of any aspect of the reign. A long digression describes the romantic escapade of the young Pretender in 1745, details of which the author derived from an eye-witness of the expedition. Having seen England flourishing and contented under the Hanoverians, he extends his sympathy to the prince but not to his cause. London, he could testify, was full of traders and sailors who were far more interested in maritime successes than in events beyond the Rhine. A full account of Anson's voyage round the world was rewarded by the gift of a gold medallion with the hero's head from his grateful family.

Voltaire turns with relief to the eight years of peace between the devastating struggles of the Austrian Succession and the still fiercer flames of the Seven Years War. 'Commerce flourished from St Petersburg to Cadiz. The arts were held in honour. All the nations were in touch. Europe was like a large family reunited after disagreements.' Fresh misfortunes, however, seemed to be heralded by earthquakes in Portugal, Spain and Morocco. In Lisbon, where one third of the city was destroyed and 30,000 lives were lost, the Portuguese thought to secure God's mercy by burning Jews and other innocents. The catastrophe left an abiding impression on the historian who embodied his reflections in the most moving of his poems and the most popular of his tales.

Though he had quarrelled with Frederick before the outbreak of the Seven Years War, Voltaire pays unstinted homage to his military abilities. 'Louis XIV was admired for resisting Germany, England, Italy and Holland in union. We have witnessed a more extraordinary event: an Elector of Brandenburg standing alone against the House of Austria, France, Russia, Sweden and half the Empire: a prodigy attributable to the discipline of the troops and the superiority of the captain. Luck can win a battle; but when the weak resists the strong for seven years in open country and repairs the gravest misfortunes, that is more than mere luck.' In this respect the war was without precedent. The second King of Prussia was the only ruler who possessed a treasure and the only one who,

having introduced real discipline into his armies, had created a
new power in Germany. The father's preparations enabled the
son to seize Silesia. France's military record, by contrast, was
lamentable and Rossbach was a panic, not a battle. She was
equally unsuccessful in India, where the conflict of British and
French brought misery on the gentle inhabitants. 'The Indians
would have been the happiest people on earth if they had not been
known to the Tartars and to ourselves.' The author's knowledge
of the East was scanty, but his lifelong interest in its teeming
peoples shines out again and again. Far worse than the defeat of
the French army in Asia was the breaking of Lally on the wheel.
Stirred to the depths by such an atrocity he strove to clear the
memory of the unfortunate General, and the news of the vindica-
tion of his honour was brought to him long afterwards on his
deathbed. Scarcely less poignant was his grief at the execution
of Admiral Byng for his inaction at Minorca, which, foreigner
though he was, he had striven to avert. 'In vain Marshal Richelieu
sent the author a declaration justifying the Admiral. It reached the
King of England, and Byng despatched his thanks to the author
and to Marshal Richelieu.' Voltaire's lifelong detestation of
cruelty, irrespective of the victim's nationality or creed, is the
most attractive feature of his character. He even spares a crumb
of sympathy for Damiens, who jabbed at the King when he was
entering his carriage at Versailles. It was merely a political demon-
stration, explained the assassin, without intention to kill. He
thought his action would be pleasing to heaven: that was what he
had heard all the priests say. 'This wretch was just a crazy fanatic.
The only accomplices of these monsters are the fanatics whose hot
heads unwittingly kindle a fire which consumes feeble and dis-
torted minds.' Though he only inflicted a skin wound, Damiens
was broken on the wheel, while his innocent father, wife and
daughter were banished.

The real criminals in the case, as Voltaire saw it, were the priests,
of whom the Jesuits were the worst. They had always been a
danger to the safety of kings, and long ago Aquinas had proclaimed that the Church might depose unfaithful princes. Monks
had only possessed power owing to the blindness of the laity,
and with the coming of the eighteenth century eyes had at last
begun to open. A religious Order which had made itself hated by

so many nations deserved its fate. To the general surprise the Protestant King of Prussia retained them for his schools. 'He thought them useful and was not afraid of them. He regarded Calvinists, Lutherans, Papists, Ministers of the Gospels and Fathers of the Society of Jesus with equal disdain, while establishing universal toleration as an axiom of government. He was more interested in his army than in his colleges, knowing that with his soldiers he could control the theologians, and not caring whether a Jesuit or a pastor taught Cicero and Virgil to the young.' A chapter subsequently addded on the suppression of the Order warmly applauds the wisdom and courage of Clement XIV, who had demonstrated that it was as easy to destroy monks as to create them. 'It raises one's hopes some day to diminish this crowd, useless alike to others and themselves, who vow to live at the expense of workers and who, though formerly very dangerous, are now considered merely ridiculous.' The thought of a swarm of idle celibates in states requiring a larger population and every available pair of hands filled him, as it filled Frederick, with contempt.

On reaching the closing phase of the reign the historian selects two topics for special treatment—the acquisition of Corsica and the conflict with the Parlement of Paris. Writing after the death of Louis XV he criticises that unworthy monarch as he would not have dared during his life. Choiseul, the greatest political figure of the reign, who had added Corsica to France, had been banished at the instigation of the du Barry. 'Louis XV was too much inclined to regard his servants as tools, to be broken at his pleasure. Exile is punishment, and only the law should punish. It is deeply regrettable when a sovereign punishes men whose offences are unknown, whose services are known, and who have public opinion on their side, which is more than their masters can often claim.' Though he had no love for the Parlement of Paris, he denounced the banishment of magistrates as illegal. Though never a democrat he believed in the separation of powers as wholeheartedly as Montesquieu himself.

A chapter on Laws, added when the author was seventy-five, preached the humanitarian gospel of which he was the most eloquent champion in Europe. He had welcomed Beccaria's epoch-making treatise on *Crime and Punishment*, and had earned the

Q

applause of the world by his protests against the savage treatment of Calas and La Barre. All the most cultivated men in recent times, he declared, felt the need for milder laws, yet no great nation had disgraced itself by assassination and major crimes more than his own. The horror of the trial of the Knights Templars had been staged by priests with the approval of the Pope. Men had been governed like wild beasts by wild beasts, except perhaps during a few years under St Louis, Louis XII and Henri IV. The more civilised they became the more they detested barbarism, of which so much still survived. Torture, which had been abolished in England, parts of Germany and recently Russia, was worse than death, and should be reserved for the Chastels and Ravaillacs, since the whole kingdom was interested in discovering the accomplices of such monsters. The confiscation of a criminal's property, on the other hand, was an abomination, for it punished the innocent children. 'Everywhere we witness contradictions, severity, uncertainty, arbitrariness, and the venality of the magistracy in France is unique.' He returned to the subject in a closing chapter entitled 'Progress of the Human Mind in the Century of Louis XV'. There had been great advances in the science of government, of which jurisprudence was a vital branch. 'The bar has often recognised the universal jurisprudence, derived from nature, which transcends all conventional laws and mere authority, dictated as they often are by caprice or need of money.'

Writing in 1768 at the age of seventy-four, the sage of Ferney detected rays of light spreading across the sky. The Academies encouraged youth by competition for prizes. Disease was coming under control, the Duke of Orleans had inoculated his children, and when Louis XV died of smallpox his grandsons were treated. Man learned by experience, however belatedly. Scientific discoveries opened up new vistas. The *Encyclopédie*, in which experts in many fields had collaborated, was the glory of France; it would have been of still greater value but for the fetters imposed by authority and the persecutions its contributors endured. Living till 1778 he witnessed the dawn of a new reign and greeted it with a cheer. 'All that Louis XVI has done since his accession had endeared him to France.' Little could he foresee that the century of reason, of which he was the most celebrated spokesman, would end in a deluge of blood.

Voltaire covered a portion of the same ground and reiterated some of his political convictions in his sixth and last historical work, *Histoire du Parlement de Paris*, published pseudonymously at Amsterdam in 1769. It was an inflammable topic, and the author had no craving for a martyr's crown. The title page carried the words 'par l'Abbé Big . . .,' but it was easier for a camel to go through the eye of a needle than for the most celebrated of European writers to conceal his identity. The book was written at the instigation of the Ministry, then engaged in open conflict with 'Messieurs', as the members of the High Court were called. Though it is no shrill indictment of a venerable institution, the factual record helped to undermine what little was left of its prestige. The Parlement tried to prevent its circulation, and the booksellers who sold it were threatened with dire penalties. Despite the attempt at suppression, an eighth edition appeared in the following year. The decision to burn the book frightened the author into a repudiation of his offspring by a letter to *Le Mercure*. To produce such a book, he explained, it would have been necessary to toil in the archives: this he could not have done, since he had lived far away from Paris for twenty years and had busied himself with widely different tasks. He never scrupled to lie when his physical safety was at stake, and he concealed the fact that friends in Paris sent him material.

The Preface contains reflections on the task of the historian. Students should shed all prejudices so far as human frailty allows. They should remember that no government and no institution remains unchanged: the Empire, England, France, for instance, were utterly different to what they had been. The science of history was the measurement of change. All that we know with certainty is that everything is uncertain. Very few laws, civil or ecclesiastical, had retained their original form; for instance, there were neither Prince Bishops nor Cardinals in the early Church. The administration of justice exhibited a similar record of change. No society could exist without laws and law courts, but after the collapse of the Roman Empire in Gaul there was no law except that of the strongest. 'The centuries from Clovis to Charlemagne are merely a tissue of crimes, massacres, devastations, the foundation of monasteries, which arouse horror and pity.' The thesis of the book is the same as that of the *Essai sur les Moeurs*: the instinctive struggle of mankind towards enlightenment despite the resistance of secular and ecclesiastical tyrants.

The larger portion of the book is devoted to the Middle Ages, and the subject is so broadly treated that it almost amounts to a history of France. The first Parlements were assemblies of fierce warriors in arms and had nothing in common with the modern tribunal except the name. When Hugh Capet followed the Carolingians the anarchy became even worse, every feudal lord seizing all he could. The country was divided into seigneuries, and the great lords reduced most of the towns to servitude. The Kings themselves were scarcely more powerful than the nobility which made such laws as they pleased for their domains. Hence the difference of local customs, all equally ridiculous. In this ocean of barbarism the Kings summoned Parlements of the upper barons, bishops and abbots, which formed the Estates of the nation. The mass of the people had no share, for most of the towns and all the villages were in a state of slavery.

The historian wrings his hands over the tyranny of the few, the exploitation and miseries of the masses, who were almost as helpless as dumb animals. The whole book is a plea for the reign of law as the only barrier against misrule. It is above all the misdemeanours of the Church which excite his anger and contempt: the more backward the population, the more power it gained. All Europe, except the Eastern Empire, groaned under this misgovernment. How could so many different nations live in such degrading servitude under about sixty to eighty tyrants who had other tyrants under them, and who in combination made up the most detestable anarchy? 'I can only answer that most men are imbeciles, that it is easy for the successors of the conquerors, Lombards, Vandals, Franks, Huns, Burgundians, being in possession of castles, armed from head to foot on armoured horses, to keep the population under their yoke. The masses, possessing neither horses nor arms and immersed in earning their livelihood, believed they were born to serve.' Since every feudal lord administered justice on his domains according to his pleasure, all Europe lived in anarchy. Spain was divided between Mussulmans and Christian Kings, Germany and Italy were in chaos, the quarrels of the Emperor Henry and Pope Gregory VII inaugurated five hundred years of civil strife by a new Papal jurisprudence which turned

Christendom upside down in order to dominate it.  The Pontiffs profited by the ignorance and confusion to sit in judgment on Kings and Emperors, who often invited them to arbitrate.  Amid this barbarism the bishops established a monstrous jurisdiction, and the ecclesiastics, being almost the only literates, controlled the affairs of Christian states.  The barbarian invasions brought terrible evils, but the usurpations of a greedy and intolerant Church were much worse.  If a testator omitted a legacy he was deprived of Christian burial, his will was annulled, and the Church seized what it thought he should have given.  The most atrocious of its crimes was the trial of the Templars, in which fifty-nine Knights were burned to death in Paris; though the Church pretended to abhor bloodshed it evidently did not feel the same objection to fire.

The newly created Parlement played no part in this unique trial, an eternal witness to the ferocity of Christian nations almost till our own times.  Anything was better than anarchy, and the Parlements, as Courts of Appeal, performed a useful service.  The first of them, instituted at Paris by Philip the Fair in 1302, was followed by Toulouse and Grenoble, Bordeaux and Dijon in the fifteenth century, Aix, Rouen and Rennes in the sixteenth, Pau and Metz, Besançon and Douai in the seventeenth.  The youngest of the family was instituted at Nancy only fifteen years before they were all swept away by the French Revolution.  Taken as a whole their record was no more creditable than that of the Monarchy and the Church.  For Voltaire the Middle Ages were a melancholy epoch of anarchy, suffering and superstition, a discreditable intermezzo between the glories of the classical world and the Renaissance when the goddess of reason returned to a benighted earth.

On reaching the sixteenth century the historian of the Paris Parlement found himself on familiar ground.  Mercenaries were hired, judgeships were sold, the wars of religion began.  The horrible practice of condemning citizens to death for their beliefs, a grim legacy of the Middle Ages, continued; though there was no Inquisition, the Vaudois were burned and the horrors were no less than in Spain.  France was a vast charnel-house.  The Chancellor L'Hôpital, leader of the *Politiques*, a man after Voltaire's own heart, shone out like a beacon in the storm.  He was almost the only member of the King's Council who sincerely desired peace; but scarcely had he issued an edict of pacification than Catholic and

Protestant divines alike preached a gospel of murder and a call to arms. The Guises and their *Ligue* were too strong for him, the Duke and his brother the Cardinal were murdered, and Henri III, the last of the degenerate Valois, soon joined them in a bloody grave.

Once again Voltaire pays homage to Henri IV. Using the Memoirs of Sully, the voluminous journal of Pierre l'Estoile, and the copious narrative of de Thou, he pronounces him the greatest of French Kings. The Prince of Orange, Gustavus Adolphus and Charles XII would have been more inflexible in their religion, but Henri of Navarre possessed more humanity and more political flair. His conversion, though a sacrifice of pride, was the price of peace. The Edict of Nantes proclaimed that there must no longer be any legal discrimination between Catholics and Huguenots; all could be good Frenchmen. Though the Parlement of Paris accepted him as King it was deeply divided, and attempts on his life were made. He was the greatest man of the age, and the last decade of his reign was the happiest era the Monarchy had ever known. Yet the wisest of rulers was no paragon in his private life, and his attempt to seduce the Princesse de Condé, a married woman and a member of the Royal Family, tarnished his name.

The survey of his successors repeats the verdicts of the *Siècle de Louis XIV*. The Regency was a time of chaos, weakness and coups. Concini, the Italian favourite of Marie de Medici, was murdered with the young King's consent, and his widow was executed. There were a few wise men, such as L'Hôpital and de Thou in the political arena, Montaigne and Charron in the world of thought; but the flicker they had kept alight had gone out. Louis XIII— ailing, ignorant and lazy—had to choose between an unloved mother and a detested Minister. He chose the latter because the ship of state needed a pilot. The portrait of the great Cardinal is severe though not unjust. Ungrateful, ambitious and tyrannical though he was, he rendered immense services to France. Ignored by the Iron Cardinal, the Parlement became omnipotent when the authority of the executive collapsed after his death. Mazarin was an even worse financier than Richelieu, his knowledge being limited to the methods of piling up a fortune. 'He was the first man in the world for intrigue and the last for everything else.' His one merit was that he was less vindictive than Richelieu and never shed blood. Moreover he played a useful part in defeating the Fronde, that ridiculous revolt in which Condé became the bane of France. When the young King took the reins firmly into his hands, the Parlement gave no further trouble for a hundred years.

Once again, under Louis XV, it strove to limit the power of the crown, and once again it deserved to fail. It had tried his patience for years, for it always seemed jealous of the royal authority. Voltaire was no friend of monarchical absolutism, but he preferred it to the selfish pretensions of the jurists. Their power was broken by Chancellor Maupeou, and new Parlements were nominated, the members being paid by the crown instead of buying their place. The book closes on a cheerful note, like the *Siècle de Louis XV*, for a new ruler was on the throne. 'All the Parlements were reformed, and it was hoped, though in vain, to reform the jurisprudence as well. The changes should have gone further, but they honoured the King who ordered them, the Ministry which framed them, and the Parlement which accepted them, and France witnessed the dawn of a wise and happy reign.' Blissfully unaware of what was in store for his countrymen, Voltaire died a happy man.

### III. *The Story of Civilisation*

THE *Essai sur les Moeurs* is the largest and the most personal of Voltaire's historical works. While the other histories and biographies provide only occasional glimpses of his ideology, the survey of world history vibrates with his unique personality. To use a convenient adjective, it is as Voltairean as *Candide* itself. All his writings, declared Grimm, breathed love of virtue and a generous passion for human welfare, but in none was this passion more articulate. He has no use for 'drum and trumpet' history, and the military spirit fills him with disgust. Unlike the Abbé Saint-Pierre, he propounds no scheme for the prevention of war, for he was too much of a realist to expect radical changes in human behaviour. His hopes centred in the *élite*, those of Rousseau in the common man. All progress had been the work of gifted pioneers who followed the light of reason and humanity. Here we find not only his considered estimate of institutions, celebrities and world-shaking events but his interpretation of the human drama in all its length and breadth. It was the first attempt of the kind. Bossuet's *Discours sur l'histoire Universelle* was a majestic theological tract, its scope strictly limited as regards both time and place. Since God always arranged the programme and pulled the strings of the puppet show, history was merely the implementation of the divine will. Blindly accepting Ussher's dating of the Creation in the year B.C. 4004, he built the first stages of his edifice round the Chosen People and the second round the Catholic Church. Voltaire, on the other hand, embraced the whole world so far as it was then known, and traced the ascent of man from primitive times till the century in which he was born. He was the first to envisage the story of civilisation as a connected whole of enormous length and to map out the main stages. The barrier between sacred and profane history was broken down. The outstanding merit of the book is its majestic design. Mere annals no longer sufficed. Like the *Siècle de Louis XIV*, but on an ampler scale, it is a blend of politics and culture. Though an amateur by the side of such giants of erudition as Scaliger and Ducange, Mabillon and Muratori, he possessed a wider range of knowledge, a broader perspective and a more original mind. 'I wish to discover what society was like, how people lived, what arts were cultivated, rather than to renew the tale of so many miserable conflicts, the commonplace of human misdoings.' The Supreme Being, having created the world, left man to work out his destiny: history was the record of his efforts. The book anticipates both the spaciousness and the superficiality of Wells' *Outline of History*, but surpasses it in the recognition of the significance of great men. 'A great but most unequal work', declares Faguet, and few readers will be inclined to dissent.

The 'only begetter' of the treatise was Mme du Châtelet, 'the divine Émilie,' who enjoyed Voltaire's society and shared his intellectual pursuits in her quiet house at Cirey for thirteen years. Her masculine intellect turned to science and mathematics, and her translation of Newton's *Principia* revealed her as more than a Parisian bluestocking. She complained of being bored by the current manuals which provided raw materials without illumination. 'I have enjoyed the history of the Greeks and Romans,' she declared, 'but I was never able to finish a detailed record of our modern nations. I find little but confusion—a multitude of minor events without connection, a thousand battles which settled nothing. I renounced a study which overwhelms without enlightening the mind.' Here was a challenge which her friend felt unable to decline. It was for the journeyman to collect the materials, for the architect to plan the house. The growing demand for historical instruction was proved by the success of the *Universal History*, a cooperative enterprise in sixty volumes published in London 1736–65. The Preface claimed that it was by far the most comprehensive work of the kind ever offered to the public. The best known contributor was George Sale, the translator of the Koran, who wrote on the East, and the principal novelty was the inclusion of Asia and Africa, not as a mere background to the history of Europe but in their own right. Since there was no trace of national bias or religious propaganda the enterprise was widely welcomed. There were several translations and abridgments, one of them by Heeren, the High Priest of the Göttingen historical school.

'You wish to overcome your disgust for modern history since the decline of the Roman Empire,' wrote Voltaire in the Preface, 'and to form a general idea of the nations which inhabit and desolate the earth. You only seek in this immensity what deserves to be known—the mind and customs of the leading nations illustrated by facts. My object is not to record in which year an insignificant prince succeeded a barbarian ruler in an uncivilised state. Just as one should know the principal actions of the sovereigns who made their peoples better and happier, so we should ignore the common type of kings. We have to select. History is a vast storehouse from which we take what we need, but we must choose wisely. The illustrious Bossuet stopped at Charlemagne, dismissed the Arabs as barbarians, and attributed everything to the Jews. He ignored the ancient East, the Indians and the Chinese, though we were nourished by their products, clothed in their fabrics, and instructed by their moral fables.' Voltaire had no intention of immediate publication, and he constantly bore in mind what seemed likely to appeal to his friend. A few copies were made of the elaborate Introduction, which he called *Discours Préliminaire*, one of which, found among the booty taken by the Austrians at the battle of Soor in 1745, was published at the Hague under the title *Abrégé de l'Histoire Universelle*. It was an old manuscript he had given to Frederick in 1739, explained the author, a first draft, and the edition was full of errors. The work was expanded when he settled in Switzerland and was published in 1769 under its familiar title, which had been suggested by Montesquieu.

'You would like philosophers to have written ancient history,' begins the Preface addressing Mme du Châtelet, 'because you wished to read it as a philosopher, seeking useful truths, and you say you have only found useless errors. Let us try to enlighten ourselves together, to disinter some precious monuments beneath the slag heaps of the centuries.' The first task was to inquire whether our globe, as we knew it, resembled its former state. Probably it had undergone as many transformations as our human communities. The sea had covered immense spaces now occupied by mighty cities and bountiful harvests. Everywhere the waters had receded or advanced. Were not the sands of the North African and the Syrian desert once the basin of the sea? Could we not say the same of the southern shores of the Baltic ? Was not Sicily once a part of Italy? Had not parts of Frisia and Southern France been under the waves? Ravenna had been a busy port. Perhaps 'Atlantis' had existed and disappeared. Passing from the earth to its occupants, the historian suggests that the legends of satyrs and centaurs, half man, half beast, may have embodied traditions of sub-human types which had long disappeared. There had probably been little change in the span of life. There is for once a touch of Rousseau in the remark that life was healthier and happier before the growth of large cities and powerful empires. Much time had been needed to build a society, to construct a language, to frame laws. Warm climes were the first to be inhabited because they provided most food: in northern lands it would have been easier to find a pack of wolves.

More important than material factors were the thoughts of men. With the emergence of societies a few gained leisure to reflect. Belief in hell and a future life originated in Egypt, and Plato first conceived of an immaterial spirit. Wisdom was a plant of slow growth. The knowledge of a God, creator, rewarder, avenger, is the fruit of reflection. All peoples were once as they are today in many parts of Africa, America and the islands—lacking the notion of one God, omnipresent and eternally existent. Atheists they were not; they could not deny the Supreme Being because no such idea entered their mind. Some adored the heavenly bodies, trees, even serpents. The earliest deities were invented as protectors against disaster. Primitive religion was the child of fear. There were many varieties of belief but also much imitation. Sun-worship was widely spread, and great men were held to be gods or the sons of gods. The majority of mankind had been and would long remain imbecile, and the most foolish were those who sought to find some sense in their ridiculous fables. Nature being everywhere the same, men had necessarily adopted the same truths and errors in the attempt to explain what their senses perceived: for instance, thunder was attributed to a superior being in the air. The world was full of mysteries and our ancestors groped about for a key. The serpent was often a symbol of immortality, shedding its skin and thereby renewing its youth. Dreams seemed to lift a corner of the curtain. Since there were good and evil deities, the latter had to be propitiated. It was a gloomy picture of childish superstition and chronic fear. Man had been always much the same: the differences were less than the similarities. There was no need for a social contract, for there had always been some embryo of society. Though God had provided an organ of reason, we had made little use of it. Yet some progress there had been: one of the greatest achievements had been the development of language from the inarticulate cries of animals.

After this thoughtful survey of primitive man Voltaire passes to the earliest organised communities. In some respects there was certainly an advance, but the lot of man was little improved, for in most cases he set out on the wrong road. If anything could be worse than anarchy, it was the yoke of priests. Most ancient states—India, Persia, Egypt—were governed, or rather misgoverned, by theocracies which abused their powers. 'When a nation has chosen a tutelary deity, it has its priests who control the mind of the community in the name of their god. Hence the human sacrifices which have disgraced almost the whole world. Theocracy has carried tyranny to the most horrible excesses to which human madness can attain: the more such a régime claimed to be divine, the more abominable were its actions.' Nearly all nations have sacrificed children to their gods. China was a shining exception, for theocracy was unknown.

In the survey of ancient civilisations, their customs and beliefs—

Chaldeans, Persians, Syrians, Phoenicians, Scythians, Jews—the latter receive the lowest marks. Everything was miraculous in the history of the Hebrews. The Chinese, who had no need of priests, were a far better model. 'Their religion was simple, wise, impressive, free from all superstition and barbarism. Confucius introduced neither new opinions nor new rites. He was neither inspired nor a prophet, merely a wise magistrate who taught ancient laws. We speak sometimes, very incorrectly, of his religion. He had none but that of all the Emperors, the tribunals, and the first sages: he merely enjoined virtue, and preached no mystery. His countrymen were not atheists.' Voltaire quotes approvingly an inscription on the temples: ' To the first principle, without beginning and without end. He has made everything, governs everything, is infinitely good and just, illumines, sustains, directs all nature.' Not a word about survival, rewards or punishments, for they had no wish to affirm what they did not know. The historian believed that in China he had found the simple and sufficient Deism and the doctrine of the good life which he had always taught.

In comparison with this satisfying faith there was little to admire in Egypt. 'I do not challenge the story of the Hebrew books, which I duly revere', declares Voltaire with his tongue in his cheek; 'I am merely surprised that Herodotus, Manetho and the Greeks do not mention the passage of the Red Sea.' The Pyramids were symbols of despotism and vanity, servitude and superstition. Egypt's most significant contribution to mankind was the belief in survival. Greece, too, was a land of fables, almost every one of which was the origin of a cult, a temple, a festival. The philosophers could shed little more light than the priests. 'Plato's reputation does not surprise me. All the philosophers were unintelligible—he as much as the rest, but he was the most eloquent. There was much nonsense in his teaching but also some very fine ideas.' The Greeks had so much intelligence that they abused it, yet, to their honour, the governments did not interfere with thought. Athens admitted all the foreign deities and dedicated an altar to the unknown god. Like all the nations, they recognised a supreme God—Zeus—as others recognised the sun, moon or stars. While China realised the limits of human knowledge, Greece revelled in futile speculation. 'Man only loves the extraordinary and the impossible.' The more incredible the miracles, the more readily are they believed. Voltaire underestimated the Greeks as much as he overestimated the Chinese, for all speculation seemed to him mere waste of time. No *Philosophe* took less interest in philosophy. He saw the surface of things with his sharp eyes but did not probe underneath.

No chapter of ancient history received so much attention as that of the Jews, but the idea that a race with such a record could be the Chosen People filled the historian with anger and disgust. It was in large measure a story of massacres and miracles. All peoples have had their prodigies, but we are only expected to swallow those of the Jews. 'Let us confess that, humanly speaking, these horrors revolt reason and nature. But if we consider Moses as the instrument of the Deity we can only adore in silence.' Such sentences were inserted like mascots to diminish the danger to life and limb in an intolerant age. Of Rome only a hasty sketch is supplied to the fall of the Western Empire and the centuries of gloom. Rome's best legacy was her laws. In all countries noble souls and good lawgivers were to be found and the latest of them was Peter the Great.

The larger work, like the spacious *Discours Préliminaire*, begins in the East. Why should we ignore the spirit of these nations whom our traders have visited? The East was the cradle of the arts and had given everything to the West. The picture of China is fuller than in the Introduction, and the appreciation no less generous. To her we owed silk, printing, paper. 'All the vices existed there as elsewhere, but they were better kept within bounds by the laws. Obedience to the laws and adoration of a Supreme Being was the religion of the Empire and the Intelligentsia. The ethics of Confucius were as pure, as austere, as human as those of Epictetus. Atheists they were not. The vices of India, in like manner, were of a milder character than ours. The work of Mohammed is described as the greatest and the most rapid revolution in history, greatly superior to that of the Jews since the Arabs brought the arts and sciences to the West. Nothing was new in Islam except the Prophet himself. Simple Monotheism and resignation to the will of God proved attractive in many lands. Its teaching had no need of mystery and it alone forbade games of chance. The Prophet was a formidable and awe-inspiring man who established his dogmas by his courage and his arms, yet his religion became tolerant. The divine institutes of Christianity preached the pardon of offences, yet that holy and gentle religion had become the most intolerant and barbarous of all. Voltaire admired the early Christians and their simple life. No hierarchy existed for over a century; Bishops began under Ignatius; there was no evidence that Peter visited Rome, and the early Popes were as legendary as the early Kings of France. No Roman Emperor wished to force the Jews to change their religion, and the Christians enjoyed a large amount of liberty. Diocletian, a fine soldier and a just lawgiver, deserved a better reputation, for he only persecuted after twenty years of toleration and then only for reasons of state.

For Voltaire the history of the Christian Church was a tragedy of degeneration from the teaching and practice of its founder. *Corruptio optimi pessima.* 'Our holy religion' was disfigured by pious frauds and impudent inventions: the Bollandist *Vitae Sanctorum* swarmed with them. 'So many errors, so many disgusting absurdities, with which we have been inundated for seventeen centuries have failed to harm it.' Constantine cuts a sorry figure, and the biography of Eusebius, his Court historian, was full of fables. He murdered members of his family, and the transfer of the capital sacrificed the West to barbarian invasions. The triumph of Christianity was followed by vengeance and atrocities. The 'Donation of Constantine' was a ridiculous imposture, but it had been accepted for centuries. Julian was a far better man. If anyone could have rejuvenated the Empire or retarded its fall it was he, but it was beyond his strength. He was not a soldier of fortune, like Diocletian and Theodosius. He was liked by his troops and was a fine General. No Emperor, not even Marcus Aurelius, was a juster ruler, and no philosopher was more sober or more moral. He reigned by the laws, valour and personal example. But his task was impossible. The Empire was plagued by barbarians and torn by religious disputes. There were more monks than soldiers—70,000 in Egypt alone. Christianity opened the doors of heaven but destroyed the Empire. The sects fought each other and they all attacked the old religion of the state—false and ridiculous, no doubt, but under which Rome had marched from victory to victory for ten centuries. 'Passing from the history of the Roman Empire to that of the peoples who tore it to pieces in the West is like leaving a proud city for a desert. Twenty barbarous jargons succeeded the noble Latin tongue, wise laws were replaced by savage customs, the fine roads decayed. A similar revolution occurred in the human mind: Gregory of Tours, the Monk of St Gall and Fredegarius are our Polybius and Livy. The most insensate superstitions prevailed. The monks became lords and princes, possessing slaves who dared not complain. All Europe submitted to this enslavement till the sixteenth century and only emerged at the price of terrible convulsions.'

The weakest portion of the whole work is the picture of the Middle Ages, which Voltaire approached with the same pitying contempt as Gibbon; the Ages of Faith were for both the Ages of Darkness, though Voltaire managed to discover a few gleams of light. The Christian Church had made a good start, but its sublime moral precepts had been overlaid by speculations which no one could understand. With the ascent from the catacombs to temporal power simplicity was laid aside. Orthodoxy usurped the place of morals, and the priests imprisoned the mind of Europe in an iron cage. 'Notre crédulité fait toute leur science,' he had written in his early drama *Oedipe*, and he applied this sweeping condemnation to ecclesiastics of every age and creed. The Roman Church, wealthy, worldly and intolerant, unworthy representative of the gospel of love, was the worst offender. Natural religion was enough for him, and in his opinion it should be enough for everyone. Dogmas were not only superfluous but the worst foes of faith, for how could we hope to express the divine in formulas and ritual? The simpler a religion the more it appealed to him. For this reason he preferred Islam to Christianity and Confucius to both. The intellectual life was his province, and he ruled it like a king. The spiritual life was beyond his range.

The Eastern Church was little better than the West, and it was torn asunder by the Iconoclastic controversy. Monasteries served a useful purpose as places of refuge for those who sought a quiet life. The reign of Charlemagne, like that of Constantine, was one of the greatest proofs that success is held to cover injustice and to confer glory. With his Thirty Years War with the Saxons, his massacres and his forced conversions, he could only be described as a brigand: Christianity was cemented by blood. While he founded the Vehmgericht, more abominable than the Inquisition, the Khalif, Haroun-al-Raschid, greatly surpassed him in justice, culture, and humanity. 'The Church has made a saint of this man who shed so much blood, who despoiled his nephew, and was suspected of incest.' The Franks had always been barbarians, and barbarians they remained after their conversion. Their laws were a blend of ferocity and superstition. 'Imagine deserts where wolves, tigers and foxes devour a few timid cattle: such was Europe for many centuries.' False Decretals found acceptance; Bishops were temporal lords with their lands and serfs, and sometimes they marched to battle. The only ray of light in this dark world was the Benedictine Order which preserved books by making copies. A new method of gaining power was invented when Confession began in the sixth century, for priests thus learned secrets which they could turn to account. One of the most despicable institutions of the Middle Ages was the Ordeal.

The history of the great events of this world, laments Voltaire, is the history of crimes: there was not a century which the ambition of laymen and ecclesiastics has not filled with horrors. Nothing is so enduring as superstition. So obsessed was he with the barbarism of the Middle Ages that he failed to recognise that the Christian Church saved more than it destroyed and was the main civilising agency in Europe for a thousand years. The glories of Gothic art meant nothing to the eighteenth-century mind. The millennium from Augustine to Machiavelli was a lamentable interruption in the march of mankind which had begun in Asia and had been carried forward by Greece and Rome. Progress towards enlightenment and humanity had to be fought for at every inch of the way by an *élite* who dared to cast off the stifling yoke of tradition and to think for themselves. The age of authority was inevitably the age of darkness, for only the unfettered use of reason, man's noblest faculty, can guide us onward towards the light.

Voltaire breathes a sigh of relief when amidst these horrors he meets some great man who rescues his country from servitude. 'I know of no one more deserving of respect than Alfred the Great, if all that is told of him is true. He ordered books from Rome, could read Latin and studied history. His place is in the front rank of heroes useful to the human race which, without these extraordinary persons, would always have remained like wild beasts.

The Normans were brigands and pirates, the Moors were cruel, but no more cruel than the Christians, and they fostered the arts and sciences. The Byzantine Empire of the eighth and ninth centuries was a scandal. Except Julian and two or three others, which of the Emperors did not disgrace the throne by abominations and crimes? The Eastern Empire was wider, had larger resources and was more powerful than that of the West, but on the moral plane there was little to choose between them. In the annals of the Papacy the sisters Marozia and Theodore were the dregs of humanity. Everyone carried arms and quarrelled over the spoils. The Albigenses, the Vaudois, the Lollards, were accused of heresy and vices as a pretext for seizing their property. You will notice that in all disputes between Christians since the birth of the Church Rome has always favoured the doctrine which most completely subjected the human mind and annihilated reason. I only speak historically, leaving aside the inspiration and the infallibility of the Church which are outside the domain of history. Yet its record was not wholly vile. It had often condemned savage customs, and despite all the scandals there has always been more decency and dignity there than elsewhere. There was scarcely a monastery in which good men were not to be found. When free and well governed it could give lessons to others. Among its merits was the recognition of talent regardless of birth. In the long line of Popes the proudest were the men of the lowest class.'

On reaching the Crusades the historian lays about him with a big stick. The Pope promised forgiveness of sins if men indulged their dominant passion of pillage, and though they carried the Cross the Crusaders were mere vagabonds. 'This epidemic fury proved that the human race was to be spared no curse.' Jews were massacred *en route*. Compared with this horde of undisciplined adventurers Saladin stands out as a pillar of light, chivalrous to his defeated foes. The sack of Constantinople in the Fourth Crusade was the crown of iniquity, and it opened the door into Europe for the Turks. Far the best of the Crusaders was St Louis, who receives unexpected and extravagant praise. 'He seemed destined to reform Europe, to render France civilised, victorious, the model for mankind. His piety did not unfit him for his royal duties nor did his wise economy prevent liberality. He combined deep policy with exact justice—perhaps the only sovereign to

R

deserve such praise.' Prudent and firm in council, intrepid in war, merciful, no human being came nearer perfection. Yet this paragon had a bee in his bonnet: he longed to go on a Crusade and attacked Egypt with no other excuse than that it was not a Christian land. He was taken prisoner, ransomed, and spent four years in Palestine. Even now he had not enough crusading, and on his return to France he began to plan a new adventure which ended with his death in Tunis. The Crusades were the tomb of countless Europeans, the cause of vast expenditure, a crescendo of folly and fanaticism. Even more atrocious, though on a smaller scale, were the persecutions of the Albigenses, the establishment of the Inquisition, and the trial of the Knights Templars on vague charges with the unavowed purpose of seizing their property.

From the madness of the Crusades and the cruelties of the Church Voltaire turns with relief to Switzerland as a blessed island of peace, which had preserved the simplicity and poverty of primitive communities in a greater degree than any other land. Never had a people fought longer or better for its liberty which it seemed likely to preserve. Equality prevailed: not of course the equality of servant and master, artisan and magistrate, plaintiff and judge, but the equality by which the citizen is subject to the law alone and which defends the weak against the strong. They had no need of a professional army, no itch for aggression. Their mountains were their ramparts, every citizen a defender of the fatherland. There were very few republics in the world, and they owed their liberty to their rocks and the protecting sea. Unfortunately men were rarely worthy to govern themselves.

With the fifteenth century Voltaire reverts to his usual whipping boy, the Church. The Great Schism made it the laughing-stock of Europe and the Council of Constance disgraced itself by a hideous crime. The authority conferred by superior culture gave the clergy and the Orders power which they used for their own interests. Yet the vices arising from opulence and the disasters which flow from ambition reduced most of them to the level of ignorance of the laity, and learning was left to the Universities of Bologna, Paris and Oxford. The doctrines of Wycliffe, largely anticipating the Protestants in his attack on confession and indulgences, transubstantiation and ecclesiastical opulence, had reached Bohemia where the lighted torch was carried forward by

Huss and Jerome of Prague. The guilt of their death, which led to the fierce Hussite Wars, must be divided between the Emperor Sigismund, who violated a safe-conduct, and the Church which practised the burning of heretics.

If *La Pucelle*—a satire not on the Maid but on the superstitions which had gathered round her name—was the worst of Voltaire's literary offences, he made partial amends in the *Essai sur les Moeurs*, which speaks of her with admiration and respect. France was in chaos. It was necessary to resort to a miracle. A gentleman of Lorraine, Baudricourt, believed that he found in a young barmaid in Vaucouleurs a person suited for the rôle of inspired warrior. 'This Jeanne d'Arc, generally thought to be a shepherdess, was a young inn servant, possessing sufficient courage and intelligence to undertake this enterprise which became heroic. She was examined by women who found her a virgin, and by doctors of the University and councillors of Parliament who declared her inspired. Whether she deceived them or whether they were clever enough to enter into the artifice, the crowd believed and that sufficed. The King was crowned, the foreigner driven out, the Maid wounded, taken prisoner and burned. A man such as the Black Prince would have honoured and respected her courage. The Regent Bedford thought it necessary to encourage the English. She feigned a miracle and Bedford pretended to believe her a sorcerer. Accused of heresy and magic, this heroine was worthy of the miracle she had feigned. Having saved her King, she would have had altars in the heroic times when men raised them to their liberators. It is not only cruelty which causes such deeds, but also the fanaticism of blended ignorance and superstition, which has been the malady of nearly every century. Burnings for sorcerers were not uncommon. Let the citizens of the great city where the arts of pleasure and peace reign today, and where reason begins to prevail, compare these times and complain if they dare. That reflection is suggested by almost every page of this history.'

At the close of his survey of the Middle Ages, Voltaire pronounces judgment on their cultural achievements which, seen through the spectacles of the *Aufklärung*, he could hardly be expected to approve. The *Divina Commedia* is described as a queer poem, but with natural beauties in which the author rises above the standards of his century and his subject. Petrarch is more to his taste. Scholastic theology, on the other hand, a bastard daughter of the philosophy of Aristotle, often mistranslated and misunderstood, damaged the cause of reason more than the Huns and Vandals. The Flagellants excite particular scorn. That there were no police tells its own story. Great virtues were to be found in all states, on the throne and in the cloister, among knights and ecclesiastics, but no nation can be happy without the reign of law. Liberty began in the towns, and when Philippe le Bel created the States-General and the Parlement of Paris, the people began to count for more.

The fall of Constantinople in 1453 evokes no regrets. The Byzantine Empire, shattered by the felon blow of the Fourth Crusade, had become a welter of cruelty, weakness and superstition. Mahommed II, a good linguist and a lover of the arts, was wiser and more civilised than was generally believed, and the Sultans were no more cruel or despotic than many Christian rulers. He allowed the Greeks to choose their Patriarch and to retain some of their churches at a time when no Christian ruler would permit a mosque in his capital. A digression on the Jews in Europe combines a rebuke to their persecutors with dislike of their ways. 'This people should interest us, since we derive from them our religion and many of our laws and customs; but they had always been greedy moneylenders, who regarded usury as a sacred duty.' Even the thieving gypsies have a chapter to themselves in this panorama of the fifteenth century.

On reaching the threshold of modern times Voltaire enters on more familiar ground. Since real civilisation, in his opinion, only emerged in seventeenth-century France, he stresses the dark spots on the Renaissance sun. Florence and Milan under the Medici and the Sforzas were a hotbed of assassination and poisoning, superstition and debauchery. He pronounces no opinion on the stories of incest and poisoning in the Vatican of Alexander VI, but he has no doubt that Caesar Borgia was a monster. The first Medici Pope, Leo X, possessed the merit of loving classical culture, but the prelates lived like voluptuous princes and everyone was bent on having a good time. He is not impressed by Savonarola, half-impostor, half fanatic. 'We regard with pity these scenes of horror and absurdity, to which we find no parallel among the Greeks, the Romans or the barbarians. It is the fruit of the most

infamous superstition which has ever brutalised mankind and of
the worst of governments. We have only recently emerged from
this darkness, and light does not shine everywhere. Even the
brain of Pico della Mirandola, that prodigy of learning, was confused.' France fared even worse than Italy, for it could boast of
little culture. The elaborate portrait of Louis XI, the first French
ruler to call himself *Le Roi très Chrétien*, is darkly coloured. Yet,
despite his cruelty, his iron cages and his superstition, he did some
good, preferring little men to the nobility and effecting many
improvements. His reign was the transition from anarchy to
tyranny. 'Barbarism, superstition, ignorance, covered the face of
the earth except in Italy. It was the interest of Rome that the
peoples should be imbecile. The impudent charlatanism of the
doctors matched the imbecility of Louis XI, which in turn was
commensurate with his tyranny. But this was true of almost all
Europe.' The best energies of the sixteenth century mind went
into literature. Guicciardini was the Italian Xenophon. *Orlando
Furioso* was in every way superior to the *Odyssey*, though both
exhibited the same fault—undisciplined imagination. Tasso's epic
on the Crusades possessed more interest, variety and grace than
the *Iliad*. In painting, architecture and music Italy surpassed the
Greeks, and in sculpture she was not far behind. In Shakespeare
there was far more barbarism than genius.

Voltaire's cool appraisement of the Reformation is equidistant
from that of both Catholics and Protestants: it was neither a disaster nor an emancipation of the mind. For their respective doctrines and controversies he felt nothing but contempt. Luther's
rôle is minimised, for the forces behind him were greater than the
man. 'If one had told him he would destroy the Roman religion
in half of Europe, he would not have believed it. He went further
than he intended.' A vital factor in the Reformation was the dislike of the financial exactions of Rome. Though the historian has
no love for the Wittenberg reformer, he applauds his courage.
'One can only laugh in pity at his treatment of the Pope—as if to
say: Little Pope, you are an ass.' He was right to reject sacerdotal
celibacy but wrong to condone the double marriage of Philip of
Hesse. The Anabaptist revolt arouses the detestation which the
historian felt for violence and fanaticism in every camp. Yet the
conflagration quickly burned itself out. 'The Anabaptists, who

began with barbarism, ended in gentleness and wisdom,' by which he means that they became pioneers of religious toleration. Since the sects were all equally mistaken there was no moral justification for one to persecute another. 'The Papists ate God for bread,' he sneers, 'Lutherans bread and God, the Calvinists bread but not God.' Such hairsplitting speculations were unworthy of civilised beings. In an autobiographical fragment written in the third person in 1776 he declares that 'M. de Voltaire always fought atheists and Jesuits.'

Among the Reformation Fathers Zwingli finds most favour, and the Zurich Senate wisely approved his rejection of the Real Presence. 'Happy people, which in its simplicity left the decision to its magistrates on a subject which neither they nor Zwingli nor the Pope could understand.' The magistrates of Berne, after listening to the debates, followed suit. Switzerland, to which the author owed so much, is described as the steadiest of nations. Calvin, on the other hand, was a tyrant by temperament, and the historian's blood boils at the thought of the murder of the Spanish doctor Servetus who was passing through a foreign city. 'They differed about the Trinity, and theological hatred is the most implacable of all.' The austere fanatic who dominated Geneva would himself have been burned had he remained in France. If the same sanguinary spirit had always presided over religion, Europe would be a great cemetery. Where Calvin burned one the Spanish Inquisition burned its thousands.

Though Voltaire admired the tolerant land where he had spent three happy years, he denounces Henry VIII as a cruel tyrant, a barbarian, a slave of his caprice. The judicial executions under Edward VI and Mary were also a horror. Elizabeth soiled a fine reign by the murder of Mary Stuart. Yet to canonise the latter was a fanatical imbecility: she was merely the martyr of her adultery, the murder of her husband, her own imprudence. The Virgin Queen was a successful ruler but not a great character. 'Her people were her prime favourite; not that she really loved them, but she felt that their safety and glory depended on treating them as if she did.' Infinitely worse than the execution of Mary Stuart was the Bartholomew Massacre—'that abominable tragedy, half the nation slaughtering the other half, dagger and crucifix in hand', with Charles IX shooting at his subjects from the windows of the Louvre. That orgy of blood was followed by the chaos of the religious wars. The Court under Henri III was a sink of intrigue, debauchery and superstition. The King moved about with his minions. Catherine de Medicis brought an astrologer from Italy, sorcerers plied their trade, and wax figures were pricked in the heart to hasten the death of rivals and foes. The Protestants were at any rate austere.

Spain under Philip II was even worse off than France under the degenerate Valois, and the comparison of that besotted ruler to Tiberius was not undeserved. The gravest of his crimes was his treatment of his subjects in the Low Countries, to whose courage and endurance eloquent tribute is paid. 'His bloody despotism was the cause of their greatness. The Flemings are good subjects and bad slaves. The mere dread of the Inquisition made more Protestants than all the writings of Calvin, for this people is not prone to innovation or unrest. There are proud spirits whose quiet fidelity is stimulated by difficulties. Such was the character of William the Silent and of his descendant William III. He possessed neither troops nor money to resist a monarch such as Philip II, but the persecutions supplied his needs. The blood of Egmont and Horn was the cement of the Republic.' The fanatic on the Spanish throne rewarded the assassin of the heroic Prince of Orange. The morals, the simplicity and the equality of the Republic resembled Sparta. No episode in modern history except the reign of Henri IV excites the historian to such enthusiasm.

Voltaire's pulse always quickened at the mention of Henri IV. No Jesuit, he declares with Père Daniel in his mind, could write history faithfully: the King was amorous but not effeminate. Gabrielle d'Estrées, the most colourful of his mistresses, called him 'mon soldat'. Brave and generous, he was the only man who could save his country. His humanity after victory should win all hearts. He had only the justice of his cause, his courage, and some friends to sustain him. He had to fight Spain, Rome and France simultaneously. The *Ligue* was a gang of fanatics. Since they were taught that heresy is the leprosy of the soul, Henri III was a leper who ought not to rule. The conversion of the hero, recommended as it was by friends who remained Protestants, is approved for the sake of the unity and prosperity of France. 'If he had not been the bravest prince of his time, the most clement, the most upright, the most honourable, his kingdom would have been ruined. France needed a prince who knew both how to wage war and to govern in peace, who was acquainted with all the wounds of his state and could supply the remedies, and she found him in Henri IV. He wished every peasant to have a fowl in the pot on Sundays.' With the aid of Sully's wonderful finance he reduced taxes, paid off debt, repaired roads, reformed justice, instituted the lace industry. Above all, the rival religions lived at peace with one another. He was the greatest figure of the age, the arbiter of Europe. Yet several attempts were made on his life, and he was wounded by Chastel in 1594. Regicide was approved by the Jesuits and their teaching was carried out by Ravaillac. The King only became dear to the nation after his death when his loss was increasingly felt. The more his career was studied in the Memoirs of Sully and others who had known him, the more he was beloved. The reign of Louis XIV was a far greater age, but Henri IV was much the greater man. Each day added to his glory, and the love of the French people for the best of their rulers became a passion. 'By a mild and firm administration he kept all the orders of the state together, all the factions quiescent, the two religions at peace, the people in plenty. Thanks to his alliances, his treasure and his arms, the balance of Europe was in his hands.' All these advantages were lost under the Regency of his widow and their son Louis XIII, pious, mild, scrupulous, suspicious, but quite unable to stretch the bow of Ulysses. Of Richelieu there is only an unflattering sketch, and we are told that he was among the lovers of Marion Delorme. At this point the historian lays down his pen, for the story was continued in greater detail in *Le Siècle de Louis XIV*.

The significance of the *Essai* was promptly recognised at home and abroad. 'I have followed Voltaire,' testified Robertson in his celebrated survey of Europe before Charles V; 'he exhibited not only salient facts but the conclusions to be drawn.' The impact on the mind of the French Intelligentsia is most eloquently described in Condorcet's *Vie de Voltaire*, written shortly after his master's death. 'The *Essai* will always delight for its range of subjects, the limpid style, the love of truth and humanity, the profound ideas. It is the record not of the centuries but of what one wishes to know. Few works are more useful for sound education. We learn to despise superstition, to dread fanaticism, to detest intolerance, to abhor tyranny. He was the brightest ornament of the *Encyclopédie*, the noblest monument ever designed by the mind of man. He was one of the very small number of men in whom the love of humanity was a veritable passion. We owe to him a conception of history vaster and more instructive than that of the ancient world. In his writings it has become, not a list of events or revolutions, but a picture of human nature itself, the philosophic embodiment of the experiences of all nations and ages. He introduced true criticism, showing that the natural probability of events must be kept in view, and that the philosophic historian must not merely reject miracles but assess the motives of belief in those which deviate from the common order of nature. We shall always remain his debtors for freeing history from the heap of marvels accepted without proof. He demonstrated that the absurdities of polytheism were never more than the faith of the masses, and that belief in one God, common to all peoples, did not require a supernatural revelation. He also showed that all peoples recognised the great principles of morality, becoming purer as men became more enlightened. The sentiment of active goodness and benevolence dominated him throughout life.'

Voltaire would have desired no other tribute. He had his failings and limitations, but the core of the man was sound. Like Anatole France, satirist and humanitarian, he loved his fellows and strove for their happiness according to his lights. Far more than the elder Mirabeau he deserved the title *l'ami des hommes*. Since God has given us reason, 'as He has given feathers to birds and fur to bears,' it was our duty to use it in the service of mankind. After the opening phase in which he lived for the delights of literature and society, he became a reformer, preaching the gospel of enlightenment, not merely as an intellectual luxury of the *élite* but as the guide to everyday life. To such enlightenment historians, scientists, and the great religious teachers made their specific contributions. The historian, like the statesman, worked with a practical end in view. Who before Voltaire, asked La Harpe, had conceived the sublime idea of demanding from the centuries what each had done for mankind, of tracing, amid the chaos of revolutions and crime, the slow and painful steps of reason and the arts? No one else before the nineteenth century except Condorcet attempted such a task. Though the *Essai sur les*

*Moeurs* cannot be classed with the *Decline and Fall of the Roman Empire*, the *Wealth of Nations*, the *Critique of Pure Reason*, and the *Reflections on the French Revolution*, among the supreme achievements of the eighteenth-century mind, it yields to none in the novelty and amplitude of its design.


IV. *The Philosophy of History*

In addition to his major historical works, Voltaire published a multitude of historical sketches and studies which form a large part of the four volumes of the *Dictionnaire Philosophique* and the ten volumes of the *Mélanges* in the latest edition of his writings. Many of them merely abridge or expand what he had said elsewhere, but there is also a good deal of new material. The first impression of the reader is the wide range of knowledge, unapproached by any of his contemporaries, his vivid interest in every aspect of human activity, past and present. The second arresting feature is that he is never content with the task of a recorder, and that he applies his measuring rod of reason and human welfare with confident assurance to each object in turn. Though not the earliest thinker to reflect on the processes and the lessons of the ages, he was the first to apply the scale of values elaborated by the *Aufklärung* of which he was the recognised oracle; and he was the inventor of the phrase 'the philosophy of history'.

Voltaire's attitude must be studied against the background of European thought since the end of the Middle Ages. Though the word *Aufklärung* was a German invention, the school which it denoted originated in France. The cult of reason, the pride in enlightenment, the buoyancy of spirit which dominated the middle decades of the eighteenth century, was the culmination of tendencies which dated back to the Italian renaissance, when the climate of thought began to shift from the theocentric to the anthropocentric approach. A new and vivid interest in the mind and body of man, his triumphs and his potentialities, came into being after the long and almost unchallenged reign of Augustine. The secularisation of thought which has coloured the modern era had commenced, but the process was not and could hardly be expected to be continuous. The sixteenth century was not the first act of a new drama but an intermezzo between two sharply contrasted eras. Luther's mind was as theological and medieval as the approach of Machiavelli and Rabelais was empirical and modern. The world of today, in which the Christian Church no longer occupies the centre of the stage, dates from the scientific discoveries and the rise of the bourgeoisie during the seventeenth century. For the first time since the civilisations of Greece and Rome the state and the citizen moved into the front place, and man began to feel confidence in his power to shape his destinies. The rivulets of modernism were swelling into a mighty stream. 'The establishment of perfect liberty of thought and discussion,' declares Bury in his *History of the Freedom of Thought*, 'may be considered the most valuable achievement of modern civilisation.' It was at any rate the mother of science and scholarship.

The various factors which contributed to the secularisation of thought provided the substructure for a philosophy of history. The classical world had produced historians of the first rank, but they knew too little of the past and present of any civilisations but their own to gain perspective. Ebb and flow, regional advances and retrogression, were a familiar experience, but even the greatest thinkers of the pre-Christian era failed to envisage a developing civilisation obeying ascertainable laws. Unable to peer far back or far around they lacked incentive to gaze into the future. The Intellectuals of the Middle Ages had a longer span behind them, but they knew little about it and felt little desire to learn. The author of *De Civitate Dei* was more concerned with the salvation of a section of the human family in another world than with the fortunes of the whole of mankind on earth. The Middle Ages, of which Bossuet was the last majestic echo, visualised history as a succession of events shaped by the hand of God for the fulfilment of His purposes. So long as the notion of an all-controlling Providence remained without challenge, the idea of progress as a human achievement shaped by a combination of material factors and spiritual energies was impossible. Christianity had supplied history with meaning by teaching that it led up to a goal, but the process was regarded as the ultimate responsibility of God, not of man.

The crucial difference between the ideology of the Middle Ages and the climate of the modern world was that the latter entertained a loftier opinion of the powers of man, a deeper appreciation of the opportunities for self-realisation and happiness afforded by his life on earth, independently of another existence in another world. The substitution of a robust belief in man's progress towards perfection by the exercise of his mind and will for the traditional teaching of external control of his destiny could hardly take place before the eighteenth century, when the anthropocentric conception had had several generations to take root. Though the process may be broadly described as a shift from a supernatural to a naturalist interpretation of history, the new philosophy of progress—that mankind is advancing in the right direction and is likely to continue his advance—also contained an element of faith. How many assumptions there were in the philosophy of the *Aufklärung* which transcended the bounds of pure reason or experience, how an exaggerated optimism in regard to the nature of man succeeded the pessimism of the Middle Ages, is more fully realised in the twentieth century than in the nineteenth, which has been labelled the Century of Hope.

The conception of an advance towards enlightenment, which formed the core of Voltaire's philosophy of history, was worked out by a succession of thinkers of the seventeenth century before it became the dominant creed of the Age of Reason. Bacon heads the list with the argument that the modern era was the old age of humanity and therefore possessed longer experience and riper wisdom. Descartes, mathematician and metaphysician, joined in the challenge to authority, proclaiming the supremacy of reason and the uniformity of nature, and Cartesianism has been described as a Declaration of the Independence of Man. Despite the transcendentalism of Pascal and Bossuet, the empirical spirit continued its march, and Newton's discovery of the reign of law in the physical universe seemed to many to destroy the hypothesis of external intervention.

By the close of the seventeenth century reflection on the problem of progress had become general and gave rise to the celebrated controversy on the respective merits of the Ancients and Moderns. The tournament was opened by Perrault, who argued for the superiority of the latter, on the ground that they inherited the

wisdom of the ages and were continually adding to the treasure-
house of mankind. Writing when Louis XIV was at the height of
his prestige, he asserted that the race had advanced so far towards
perfection that there were not many things for which he and his
contemporaries need envy future generations. The man of letters
was vigorously supported by Fontenelle, the man of science, who
scouted the hypothesis of degeneration, on the ground that as the
modern world had moved beyond the limits of the ancient through
the increase of experience, so posterity would assuredly witness a
further advance. Humanity had known a period of youth but
would never experience the decline of old age. Admiration of the
ancients in no way involved the thesis that man had reached the
limits of his endeavour. Even more uninhibited in his championship of the doctrine of indefinite progress was the Abbé Saint-
Pierre. Best known to posterity as the author of the first detailed
plan for the organisation of perpetual peace, he was regarded by
his contemporaries as one of the boldest thinkers of the opening
decades of the eighteenth century. If the seventeenth had been
above all the age of science, the eighteenth was the age of sociology, inaugurated by Saint-Pierre, developed by Montesquieu,
Rousseau, and Adam Smith, and culminating in Herder and
Burke. Man had the right and the duty to seek individual happiness and social well-being, and enlightened reason was his only
guide. A Deist who did not believe in the occurrence of miracles,
Christian or non-Christian, the Abbé never doubted the capacity
of *homo sapiens* to work out his own salvation. His *Observations on
the Continuous Progress of Human Reason*, published in 1737, reminded his readers that the race had had only seven or eight
thousand years to develop its powers. Civilisation was in its infancy, and the future offered limitless possibilities. Progress had
begun with the Greeks, had been interrupted by wars, superstition and intolerance, and was only resumed when the broken
threads were picked up during the sixteenth century. Superstition
was now declining and wars could be averted by his proposals for
perpetual peace. Give man a chance and he would seize it with
both hands. Living before Rousseau began to preach democracy,
Saint-Pierre taught that wise government and just laws could
mould society to a fairer pattern.

When Voltaire focused his attention on the study of history in middle life, he inhaled the bracing air of the *Aufklärung*. The keen-est intellects in France, with the exception of Rousseau, were in general agreement that man was in large measure master of his fate, that civilisation was a good thing, that conditions of life could be improved, and that there were no insuperable obstacles to a further advance. Humanists and humanitarians, the High Priests of the Enlightenment were thrilled by the thought of the power of reason when the fetters of tradition were struck off and the fear of penalties for new opinions was removed. No transcen-dental philosophy of history was required, for there were no final causes, no original sin, no need for a divine revelation, no infal-lible Church. Man should use his wits, study, criticise, experi-ment, judging everything by its actual or potential service to humanity. The Utilitarian approach proclaimed by Bacon was adopted by the *Philosophes*, who in turn prepared the way for Bentham. Their task was to create an intellectual atmosphere which would sooner or later compel governments to think only of the happiness of their people. Political revolution was not in their programme, for the age of democracy in France did not dawn till 1789. There was no objection to autocracy if the ruler was bene-volent and understood his trade.

The message of the *Philosophes* was set forth at greatest length in the *Encyclopédie* planned in 1745, announced by Diderot in a pros-pectus in 1751, and published in seventeen volumes 1751–65. The first two instalments were denounced by the Church and suppressed as hostile to authority and religion. Booksellers were forbidden to sell them, but there was no veto on the continuation of the enterprise. A volume appeared each year, the seventh coming down to G in 1757. Beginning with 2,000 subscribers, the sales rose to 4,000, but the opposition waxed with the success. In 1759 the Government forbade the sale of the seven volumes and the printing of any more. At this stage d'Alembert withdrew, ex-plaining to Voltaire that vexation had worn him out. The stout-hearted Diderot remained at his post as sole editor, contributing many articles himself. Offers of shelter arrived from Berlin and St Petersburg, but the enterprise, with its large staff, was too big to be transplanted. The ten remaining volumes appeared *en bloc* in 1765, followed by ten volumes of plates. Yet it was not the *Encyclopédie* of the editor's dreams, for the timid Genevese printer had without authorisation omitted or mutilated everything which seemed to him likely to provoke the Government. Owing to the ban the copies were privately distributed, but the purchasers were ordered to surrender their copies to the police. Despite official sabotage the work was reprinted at Geneva and Lausanne and selections from the work appeared. No large-scale publication of the eighteenth century aroused so much antagonism or attracted such widespread attention.

The Bible of the *Aufklärung* furnished the first authoritative summary of human knowledge. The popularity of Bayle's *Dictionnaire Historique et Critique* had revealed the demand for information among the Intelligentsia of Western Europe, but its significance pales in comparison with the *Encyclopédie*. The former was the work of a single brain, the latter of a brilliant team. The former virtually ignored natural science, the latter eagerly welcomed the latest discoveries. The former breathed a mild scepticism, the latter a militant rationalism. The former was primarily a book of reference, the latter primarily a manifesto. Leslie Stephen's description of the eighteenth century as an age of sound common sense may have been true of England, but it was a very inadequate characterisation of France. The *Philosophes* were men who dreamed dreams and saw visions, rationalists who proclaimed a rival set of dogmas, crusaders determined to sweep away the accumulated rubbish of the past. Never before or since has such an enterprise exerted so profound an influence on the thought of the time, for its comprehensiveness rendered it as indispensable to statesmen and civil servants as to the Intelligentsia in every land. It helped to transform the authoritarian, aristocratic and traditionalist France bequeathed by Louis XIV into the bourgeois, critical yet self-confident nation which carried through the revolution of 1789. Human nature was conceived as infinitely impressionable, as capable of responding to the inspiring guidance of the *Philosophes* as it had long obeyed the blind leaders of the blind.

Voltaire's article on History appeared in the eighth volume of the *Encyclopédie* in 1765, after a long interruption caused by the withdrawal of the licence by the state. D'Alembert, who hated controversy, had resigned in despair, and Voltaire's contributions ceased in 1758. There were two reasons for withdrawing support from an undertaking which in its general purpose of spreading enlightenment commanded his entire sympathy. In the first place this fearless knight of the spirit was always apprehensive as to his personal safety. The assertion in the article on Geneva, published in 1757 in the seventh volume, that among the Genevese clergy were Deists and Socinians created an uproar in Swiss Protestant circles. It was wrongly attributed to Voltaire, for it was written by d'Alembert; but it was inspired by the veteran who had chosen Switzerland for his second fatherland, and who knew and cared far more about the matter than the scientist far away in Paris. Having quite enough on his hands with his formidable Catholic foes, he thought it wise to limit his risks by ceasing contact with the most explosive literary enterprise of the age.

The second reason for withdrawal was more plausible, for Voltaire was now busy with an Encyclopaedia of his own on a limited scale. The origin of the *Dictionnaire Philosophique*—in its final form the largest of his works—is sometimes traced to the supper-parties at Potsdam, when every subject in heaven and earth came up for review. The plan took shape in the little *Dictionnaire Philosophique Portatif*, containing seventy-three articles, published anonymously in 1764, during the interval between the first and the second phase of the *Encyclopédie*. The book grew under his hands till he was almost an octogenarian and eventually filled nine volumes. Its debt to the *Encyclopédie*, to which he frequently paid public tribute, is obvious. In this vast medley of wit and wisdom, learning and prejudice, there is as much history as philosophy. Though many articles are abridged or expanded from his earlier writings, the *Dictionnaire Philosophique* is as essential for our understanding of Voltaire as a historian as his purely historical works.

To the contention of the Church that man had fallen and needed redemption the *Philosophes* retorted that he had risen by his own efforts. They formed a new church with a new gospel—humanitarian, optimistic, materialistic. The whole enterprise was planned as an attack on obscurantism and the dead hand of the past, a plea for the unfettered use of reason and the reign of law. 'You have no idea of the influence which Voltaire and his great contemporaries had in my youth,' remarked Goethe to Eckermann in 1830, 'and how they governed the whole civilised world.' Next to Diderot, the editor of the *Encyclopédie*, and d'Alembert, his chief of staff, the most eminent though not the most frequent contributor was Voltaire. There is no evidence that he had been consulted about the enterprise, and he was the guest of Frederick the Great at Potsdam when the first two volumes appeared. Diderot he had never met, and his acquaintance with d'Alembert was slight, but the editor needed the prestige of his name. A few articles from his pen on minor topics appeared in the fifth volume. Not till d'Alembert visited him in Switzerland in 1756 was his interest seriously aroused and his collaboration assured.

By far the most important of his contributions was that on History. 'Herewith the article,' he wrote to d'Alembert in 1756. 'I fear it is too long. It is a subject on which it is difficult not to write a book.' History is defined as a record of facts purporting to be true. There is a history of opinions, which is merely a collection of human errors. The history of the arts is the most rewarding when it stimulates further invention. The earliest attempts were the stories of fathers to children, which are only to be believed if they do not affront plain common sense. With the passage of time the fable was embroidered and the truth was lost in a haze of superstition. All the stories of human origins which had floated down the ages were absurd. Who could believe that the Egyptians had been governed first by gods, then by demigods for many centuries before their first King? The legends of the Greeks and Romans, even of the Merovingians, were equally ridiculous. Prodigies should be recorded, not as facts as by Rollin, but as illustrations of human credulity. Since our acquaintance with the ancient world was extremely limited, imagination had had full play. We must not always ask for what was mathematically demonstrable and must content ourselves with the maximum of probability. Marco Polo's account of the size and population of China was disbelieved till it was confirmed by Portuguese navigators and by the unanimous testimony of a thousand eye-witnesses since the sixteenth century. That some events which at first sounded incredible had actually occurred was illustrated by the most dramatic incident in the epic of Charles XII. 'If only two or three historians had related how the King and his domestics fought against an army of Janissaries and Tartars in his house at Bender I should have suspended judgment. But having conversed with eye-witnesses and receiving no contradiction of the story,

s

one has to believe it, for it contradicts neither the laws of nature nor the character of the hero.' Probability and even improbability could be turned into certainty by adequate evidence, but nothing should find credence which plainly violated the ordinary course of nature. Festivals, however ancient, medals and monuments, however imposing, did not guarantee the truth of what they were designed to commemorate. The speeches attributed to ancient leaders were obviously fakes, and a historian had no more right to concoct orations than to invent facts. Faked memoirs, the latest example of which was attributed to Mme de Maintenon, were common, and of the 'ana' and anecdotes which were so popular only one per cent contained a grain of truth. The first test to be applied was inherent probability, the second the nature and volume of the evidence. The historian should steer an even course between scepticism and credulity.

If the first obligation was to sift the wheat from the chaff, the second was to differentiate between the important and the unimportant and to search for the teachings and warnings of the past. 'If you have nothing to tell us except that one barbarian succeeded another on the banks of the Oxus and Jaxartes, what is that to us?' The story of errors, crimes and misfortunes was useful particularly for rulers and their advisers. Thus the catastrophe of Pultowa proved the folly of invading the Ukraine without supplies. Insensate ambition brought its own punishment. One advantage of the study of modern history had been to teach rulers that from the fifteenth century there had always been a rally against a predominating Power. This system of equilibrium was unknown to the ancients. Another point to bear in mind was the usurpations of the Popes, the scandals of their schisms, the madness of their controversies, persecutions and wars and the horrors caused by this madness. If the young were not taught all these things, and if a few scholars were not aware of them, the public would still be as imbecile as in the time of Hildebrand, and the calamities of the past would inevitably recur since few precautions would be taken to avert them. 'Eliminate the study of history and we may see more St Bartholomew massacres in France and new Cromwells in England.' Bayle had been blamed for criticising David, but the man after God's own heart deserved to be shown up as a criminal. Bad actions should never be concealed or excused. Constantine,

Clovis and Henry VIII were monsters of cruelty. God had not compiled the history of the Jews, which was full of crimes. 'One must admit that if the Holy Spirit wrote this history He did not choose a very edifying subject.' The historian must be not only a recorder but a fearless judge.

Voltaire returned in 1768 to the theme of the duties and difficulties of the historian in a treatise entitled *Le Pyrrhonisme de l'Histoire*, which is included in the sixth volume of the *Mélanges*. Portions are reproduced from the article on *History*, but the detailed comments on historians, ancient and modern, which form the most valuable aspect of the work, are new. 'I desire neither an unmeasured scepticism nor a ridiculous credulity,' he began. The main facts in a narrative or a tradition might be true though certain details might be false. The historian must use his own discretion. 'As children we are taught a chronology which is demonstrably false. We are taught everything except how to think. Even the most learned and eloquent writers have sometimes embellished the throne of error instead of overthrowing it. Bossuet is a conspicuous example in his miscalled *Histoire Universelle*, which is only the record of four or five peoples, above all of the little Jewish nation, which was either ignored or justly despised by the rest of the world. We should speak of the Jews as we speak of the Scythians and the Greeks—one race among many; nevertheless he relates everything as if a Cornish historian were to say that nothing occurred in the Roman Empire except in the province of Wales. We know that Providence extends over the whole earth and is not confined to a single race. Bossuet was like an artisan who systematically sets false stones in the gold. Heresies, he declares, were foretold by Christ. There is no mention of heresy in the Gospels, since the word dogma never occurs. Christ proclaimed no dogma. For instance He never said that His mother was a virgin, and there is not a word in the Gospels which bears any relation to the Christian dogmas we know. Fleury's *Histoire Ecclesiastique* was equally misleading, like a mud statue adorned with some gold leaf. I have thrown away the mud and kept the gold.' The bulk of his history was soiled by fairy-tales which an old woman would nowadays blush to repeat, such as the miracles of Gregory Thaumaturgus, though he never says that he believes them. 'Is it to insult the human race, I had almost said to insult God Himself, that the Confessor of a king dared to relate these detestable absurdities?'

Passing from the moderns to the ancients, Voltaire renews his campaign against the Jews. Were the historical books of the Old Testament inspired? Was God really the historian of the Jews? After citing with gusto a number of miracles and crimes he concludes with his customary ironical grimace. 'Jewish history is the history of God and has nothing in common with the feeble reason of all other peoples.' Since the history of Egypt was not the history of God, and since her religion was largely the worship of animals, we were allowed to make fun of it. With the Greeks we were on firmer ground. Herodotus was reliable on what he had seen, not on what he had heard. Yet the significance of the Greeks and Romans should not be exaggerated, since they were young in comparison with the Indians and Chinese, Chaldeans and Egyptians. The Romans deserved study chiefly because they were our legislators, and their laws, like their language, were still in use. After the dissolution of the Roman Empire came the Middle Ages—a barbarous history of barbarous peoples who, in becoming Christian, did not become better. Yet the Roman historians must be read with critical eyes. Livy's stories were rightly treated as fairy tales, but what of Tacitus and Suetonius? Were the atrocities attributed to Tiberius, Caligula and Nero true? 'Must I believe the report of a single man, writing long afterwards, that Tiberius, nearly eighty years old, after a decent and strenuous life, plunged into debauchery?' Similar stories of the Regent Orleans and his daughter had circulated in his own time, but he never believed them. In relating such improbabilities the historian should have said there were rumours, there were suspicions. How could we believe that Agrippina frequently offered herself to her son at midday, and that Seneca saved the young Nero from incest by introducing Acte? Is there any need to believe that he sent his mother out in a leaky boat in the Bay of Naples? Was it not more probably an accident?' We should be equally prudent not to believe all the stories of Elagabalus. Over and over again Voltaire reminds us that probability is the first test to be applied.

That so many fables had become embedded in history was not solely the fault of the historian: credulous human nature itself was also to blame. 'If men were reasonable, they would only ask for

histories which would stress the rights of peoples, the laws by
which a father can dispose of his property, events of national
interest, treaties which connect neighbouring nations, the progress
of the useful arts, the abuses to which the majority are exposed by
the few. But this method is as difficult as it is dangerous. It would
involve effort for the reader, not relaxation. The public prefers
fables, so it gets them. *Audi alteram partem* is the obligation of
every reader of the story of rival princes who disputed for a crown
or of religious bodies which anathematised each other. Nothing
succeeds like success. If the *Ligue* had won, Henri IV would be
known as a little Béarn prince, debauched and excommunicated.
If Arius had won at the Council of Nicaea and Constantine had
taken his side, Athanasius would now be regarded only as an
innovator, a heretic, a fanatic who attributed to Jesus what did not
belong to him. The Romans decried Carthaginian sincerity, and
the Carthaginians suspected the *bona fides* of Rome. To judge fairly
we should have the archives of the Hannibal family. I should also
like the Memoirs of Caiaphas and Pilate, and those of the Court of
Pharaoh; then we should learn how it defended itself for having
ordered Egyptian midwives to drown all the Hebrew males, and
what was the use of this order for the Jews who only employed
Jewish midwives. It affords us pleasure to read the writings of the
Whigs and Tories. According to the Whigs, the Tories betrayed
England; according to the Tories, every Whig sacrificed the state
to his interests. Thus, if we are to believe these advocates, there
is not a single honest man in the nation.' The recriminations in
the Wars of the Roses were even worse. Voltaire was interested
but not wholly convinced by Horace Walpole's *Historic Doubts
concerning Richard III*, and wrote to the author in 1768. 'You seem
to have a liking for this hunchback. I can well believe he was not
so bad as he was painted, but I should not have liked to have
dealings with him.' That Pope Alexander VI was poisoned and
that Caesar Borgia prepared poison for several of the Cardinals
strikes Voltaire as improbable. There were many fakes in very
recent times such as the Testaments of Colbert and Louvois. This
should make us careful about the tales of antiquity.

Falsification was the deadliest sin. 'Of all writers so many men
of letters have been the worst calumniators, if one can give these
fanatics that title. For they fear nothing when they lie. The

Jesuits above all carried impudence to the furthest limit in the days of their power. When they were not writing *lettres de cachet*, they wrote libels. It is these men of detestable character who brought on their *confrères* the blows which have destroyed them and have ruined for ever an Order which contained some men worthy of respect. This multitude of calumnies piously vomited over Europe from infected mouths who call themselves sacred is beyond comprehension. After assassination and poison that is the gravest and that has been the commonest crime.' It was characteristic of Voltaire, a born fighter and a good hater, that his treatise should close with a kick at the Order whose suppression by Clement XIII provided one of the keenest satisfactions of his later life. *Pyrrhonisme de l'Histoire* was a plea, not for wholesale scepticism, but for caution in dealing with statements outside the limits of our experience. He was right to stress the fact that a mass of primitive ideology had floated down the ages. His mistake—and that of the Century of Reason—was to draw the frontiers of experience too narrowly. To the *Philosophes* it was unthinkable that what seemed inconceivable to them could appear credible to any other thoughtful mind. He saw only what was visible to the naked eye and was convinced that there was nothing else, ignoring the truth enshrined in the most illuminating of Pascal's *Pensées*: 'Le coeur a ses raisons que la raison ne connait pas'. The sub-rational and super-rational intuitions, ecstasies and torments of the soul were beyond his range.

In addition to the dissertations on *Histoire* and *Pyrrhonisme*, hundreds of articles in the *Dictionnaire Philosophique* are directly concerned with the events and problems of history, while hundreds more employ historical illustrations to explain a point. There is a closer resemblance both to the *Dictionnaire Critique* of 'the immortal Bayle, the glory of the human race', than to the *Encyclopédie*, but it is more personal and therefore more interesting than either. Though ranging over an immense variety of subjects, the author's ideology is simplicity itself. The philosopher, he declares, never claims to be inspired by the gods. The earliest and wisest of sages was Confucius, who proclaimed rules of conduct which have never been bettered and who never attempted to deceive. Belief in a Supreme Being was the foundation of all the world religions, for how else could the world be explained? That

was all we knew and all we could ever know. Everything else
was guesswork and most of the guesses were bad. The article on
Fanaticism concludes with a tilt against the limitless credulity of
mankind. 'Someone declares that there is a giant seventy feet high.
Then the doctors discuss the colour of his hair, the size of his
thumb, the length of his nails. They shout, intrigue, fight. Those
who maintain that his little finger is only fifteen inches in diameter
burn those who argue that it is only a foot across. But, gentlemen,
remarks a passer-by modestly, does your giant exist? What a
horrible doubt! cry all the disputants. What blasphemy! What
absurdity! Then they arrange a short truce to stone the passer-by,
assassinating him with the most edifying ceremonial, and then
resuming their conflict about his little finger and nails.'

Voltaire was academically interested in religious practices and
beliefs, like Sir James Frazer and other anthropologists a century
later, viewing them as a naturalist examines curious specimens in
a glass case. Seen in broad perspective the story of mankind might
be described as a duel between the philosophers and the priests.
'Poor creatures that we are! How many centuries were needed to
acquire a little reason?' The article on the Jesuits, written shortly
after the suppression of the Order by the Pope, decides that they
deserved their fate. There had been, and still were, men of rare
merit in their ranks. What then had caused their downfall?
'Pride. Their contempt was incredible for all the Universities in
which they had no part, for all the books they had not written,
for all ecclesiastics who were not *hommes de qualité*—of which I
have been witness a hundred times. Nearly all their polemical
writings breathe an indecent arrogance which estranged the whole
of Europe. Everything could be forgiven except pride. Hence all
the Parlements, whose members have usually been their pupils,
seized the first opportunity of destroying them, and the whole
world rejoiced in their fall. Under Louis XIV it was not considered good form to die without passing through the hands of a
Jesuit.' They had had their day and now it was over.

Voltaire's attitude towards marvels was conditioned by his
philosophic and scientific beliefs. No eighteenth-century thinker
was less of a sceptic, for there was no place in his brain for the
penumbra of doubt which is the essence of scepticism. 'I believe
in God—not the God of the mystics and the theologians, but the

God of Nature, the architect of the universe'. He fully accepted and continually proclaimed the argument from design: 'tout ouvrage démontre un ouvrier'. As Paley was to argue in his *Evidences of Christianity*, if we found a watch we should conclude that there was a watchmaker. *Si Dieu n'existait pas il faudrait l'inventer.* Voltaire's Deism, however, was as coldly intellectual as Rousseau's Savoyard Vicar in *Émile* was instinctive and emotional. When the *Être Sûpreme* had created the world and furnished it with the laws of nature, man had to look after himself: there was no need for intervention by a subsequent revelation or recurrent miracles. Christ, who never claimed to be the son of a virgin, was a moral teacher, *un enthousiaste de bonne foi*, like Socrates and George Fox. All experience, confirmed by recent scientific discoveries, pointed to the rigid uniformity of nature. Yet man was not a machine. The Divine Architect had provided him, not only with the material surroundings which rendered life possible, but with reason, the most precious of His gifts, to enable him to transcend the limitations of his physical needs.

The fullest exposition of his theology is provided in the article *Dieu* in the *Dictionnaire Philosophique*. 'Dans cet univers, composé de ressorts dont chacun a sa fin, on découvre un ouvrier très puissant, très intelligent.' Is this supreme artisan everywhere or in a particular place? How can we answer with our limited understanding? 'My reason indicates a Being who has arranged the matter of this world, but it cannot prove that He made the matter and created it from nothing. All the sages of antiquity believed matter to be eternal. So I believe the God of this world is also eternal. We shall never know more than Cicero. We feel we are in the hands of an invisible being; that is all, and we cannot advance a step further. It is insolence to wish to guess what this being is and how it operates.' Is the soul immortal? Here again we can only guess. The lengthy article on *Âme* reviews various hypotheses and concludes that no one can be sure.

Voltaire's theology is further explained in the elaborate dissertations on Miracles and Prayers. The Supreme Being is as distant and unapproachable as the stars. 'A miracle is a contradiction in terms; a law cannot be both immutable and violated. Why should God disfigure His own work? And why for particular individuals? Is it not the most absurd of follies to imagine that the Infinite Being intervenes in favour of three or four hundred ants on this little heap of mud? God's favours are vouchsafed in His laws. It would be a confession of His weakness, not His power. To attribute miracles to Him is to insult Him.' Since miracles are impossible, prayers are futile and indeed irreverent: that they are as old as mankind is no proof to the contrary. 'We know of no religion without prayers. All men have invoked the help of a divinity. The *Philosophes*, more respectful towards the Supreme Being, only pray for resignation: that is all that seems suitable between the creature and the creator. But philosophy is not made to rule the world, since it speaks a language which the crowd cannot understand.' The Eternal has His designs from all eternity. If the prayer is in accord with His immutable will it is useless to ask what He has already resolved to do. If one prays for the contrary of His intention, it begs Him to be weak, frivolous, arbitrary, inconstant. If you request something just, He owes it to you and will do it; if unjust, it is an insult. 'We pray to God only because we have made Him in our image, treating Him like a pasha, a sultan whom one can irritate or appease. All the nations pray to God; wise men resign themselves and obey.' For Voltaire Newton was the greatest man who had ever lived, for he had discovered that the reign of law prevailed throughout the universe.

A further reason for believing that the task of the Supreme Being began and ended with the act of creation was the human record, a sorry tale of cruelty and injustice, tyranny and superstition. If a benevolent God had been continually intervening, would not the picture have been very different, the sum of human agony vastly less, the tempo of progress far quicker? History reveals, not the guidance and goodness of God, but the struggles and the follies of man. Horror had succeeded horror, wars and massacres never ceased, and nature was as merciless as man. The Lisbon earthquake was the latest illustration of the blind forces at work. Was Lisbon, with its 30,000 victims, more wicked than Paris? The longer Voltaire reflected on the lamentable course of history, the stronger grew his conviction that the Supreme Being, if indeed all-powerful and benevolent, could not be pulling the strings, for it did not make sense. His philosophy of history is as clearly outlined in *Candide* as in the dissertations on History and Pyrrhonism.

Why the Creator had made so imperfect and suffering a world

we could not guess; but man had been furnished with two precious compasses to help him on his tempestuous voyage—reason and conscience. The latter was indeed the voice of God. Voltaire accepted the conception of *Jus Naturale* formulated by the Roman jurists, adopted by the Christian church, and retained by almost all modern publicists. The moral law, like the laws of nature, was immutable, since it was inscribed on the human heart. Though it was the least observed of laws, it revenged itself on those who infringed it. Man was free to choose, and he was punished if he chose wrong. 'It seems as if God has implanted it in man as a bulwark against the law of the stronger and the destruction of mankind by war, intrigue and scholastic theology.' 'Morality comes from God and is everywhere the same: theology comes from man and is everywhere different and foolish.' Since a future state of rewards and punishments after death could neither be proved or disproved, it was wise to act on the assumption of its reality. Voltaire's advocacy of religious toleration halted at the preaching of atheism, since without belief in God it might be impossible to govern the masses. He would have chuckled over Gibbon's celebrated aphorism that to the people all religions were equally true, to the philosopher all equally false, to the magistrate all equally useful. Since man was born neither good nor bad, education, example, the government, circumstances determined his course towards virtue or crime. 'In morals', we read in the article *Athée*, 'it is much better to recognise a God than not. It is certainly in the interest of all men that there should be a Divinity who punishes what human justice cannot repress. But equally clearly it would be better not to recognise a God than to adore a barbarian to whom human beings are sacrificed as in many nations. Atheism and fanaticism are twin monsters capable of devouring society. But the atheist retains his reason, while the fanatic is the victim of chronic madness.' Theism, the middle way between atheism and fanaticism, was the best and the most widely spread of religions; for even polytheism did not exclude belief in a Supreme Being. Confucius was a theist, and Mohammed, charlatan though he was, proclaimed the unity of God and rescued almost the whole of Asia from idolatry. It never occurred to Voltaire that his hypothesis—that the world was created by a Supreme Being and then left to sink or swim—was just as vulnerable as the rival ideologies which he despised. Philosophically speaking, Divine non-intervention is no more convincing than the doctrine of continuous creation.

Voltaire was neither a determinist, an optimist nor a pessimist, but, to use an expression of George Eliot, a meliorist: things could —but not necessarily would—be made better. His mind was far too critical to believe in a golden age in the past, like Rousseau, or in the future, like the utopians from Saint-Pierre to Condorcet. *Homo sapiens* was a teachable but unruly animal. 'Every day the question is asked if a republican government is preferable to a monarchy. The dispute always ends with the admission that it is very difficult to govern mankind.' The masses, he believed, were unlikely to change. Progress had always been and would doubtless remain an uphill fight waged by a minority of fearless crusaders. History was above all the record of the swaying conflict between reason and unreason. 'Reason survives despite all the passions which war against it, despite all the tyrants who would drown it in blood, despite all the impostors who would destroy it by super-stition.' Reason was not the only instrument of progress, for the urge towards greater material comfort and refinement of manners was strong. 'Men have always asserted that the good old times were much better than our own,' he wrote in the article *Anciens et Modernes*. 'Happy is the man who, free from all prejudices, is sensible of the merits both of ancients and moderns, appreciates their beauties and recognises their faults.' He might have said with Molière, *Je prends mon bien ou je le trouve*—in China, in Greece, in Rome, above all in Western Europe since the Renaissance. *Le Mondain*, written in 1756, saluted the amenities of civilisation and satirised the illusion of a simpler and purer age. 'Oh! le bon temps que ce siècle de fer!' he exclaims ironically. Life in Paris, London, Rome, was infinitely preferable to the Garden of Eden. 'Good wine never tickled Eve's joyless throat. Our ancestors knew neither silk nor gold. Is that a reason for admiring them? They lacked industry and comfort. Was that virtue? It was pure ignorance.' Free from financial anxieties Voltaire was something of an Epicurean, enjoying the goods things which life in a cultivated society could offer, but without excess. He would have agreed with the verdict of Talleyrand in old age that no one who had not lived in France before the Revolution had known *la douceur de la vie*. No one appreciated more fully the privileges of civilisation, and no one was more conscious how precarious were its foundations.

Voltaire's chief disciples in the sphere of historical interpretation were Turgot and Condorcet. When the former lectured at the Sorbonne in 1750 on the successive advances of the human mind, he had probably read the portions of the *Essai sur les Moeurs* which had appeared in *Le Mercure*. Though the work of a young man these astonishing discourses presented a more profound and illuminating analysis of the story of man than Voltaire was ever to achieve. He was more capable of understanding beliefs which he did not share, and he was more conscious of organic continuity. Between Voltaire and the historicism of the nineteenth century there is a gulf. Between Turgot and the genetic approach of Herder and Savigny there is no sharp dividing line. For the facile teleology of Bossuet he substituted the operation of innate energies and general causes. Historical study must begin not with events but with societies, which were shaped firstly by the nature, passions and reasoning faculties of man, secondly by environment, geography and climate. Every era was connected with all that had gone before, slowly moving forwards towards perfection, through alternations of repose and confusion: the units did not move at the same pace owing to differing circumstances. While Voltaire attributed progress exclusively to reason consciously warring against ignorance and passion, Turgot argued that man had moved instinctively in the right direction without visualising the goal. History was a record of crimes, follies and misfortunes, yet man had learned from his experiences. Even in dark times such as the Middle Ages there had been some advance. Christianity had been the agent, not the enemy, of civilisation. Turgot anticipated Comte's law of the three stages of intellectual development—theological, metaphysical, positive—the whole race moving steadily forward all the time. The Discourses at the Sorbonne steered a middle course between Voltaire's conception of haphazard advance and Condorcet's naïve belief in perfectibility. Compared with the wide vision of Turgot Condorcet was a doctrinaire. So strong was his faith that he composed his *Esquisse du Progrès de l'esprit humain* in prison while awaiting his summons to the guillotine. He was the last voice of the *Aufklärung*, of the Age of Reason, of the Century of Voltaire.

Before the Grand Old Man of eighteenth-century France closed his eyes in a blaze of glory at Paris in 1778, the Romantic Movement had begun with Rousseau, Richardson, and the young lions of the *Sturm und Drang*. The supremacy of reason was challenged, not from the angle of faith, but from the testimony of the human heart. The individual thinkers and lawgivers whom Voltaire had saluted as the principal agents of progress were dethroned in favour of the *Volk*, creating its laws and institutions, language and beliefs as it went along. A new standard of values was worked out and applied. The technique of the Rationalists had been to produce their yardstick and to censure what failed to pass the test. The deepest urge of the Romanticists was to admire and give thanks. While the *Aufklärung* had looked back with disdain and forward with confidence, the Romantic school revelled in tradition and glorified the Ages of Faith. The *lumen siccum* recommended by Bacon—the cold, clear light of day—was replaced by stained glass windows, resplendent with colour and symbolism. The Romantic Movement, in Watts-Dunton's revealing formula, was above all the renascence of wonder. Our ancestors were not fools, declared Justus Moser, the champion of social continuity and the forerunner of the historical school. Just as the critical empiricism of Voltaire constituted an advance beyond Bossuet, so the Romantic Movement, the foster-mother of the Historical School, represented an equally significant advance towards the reconstruction and interpretation of the past. Only by approaching the story of mankind without doctrinnaire suppositions could historians do justice to every type and every stage of civilisation. In the nineteenth century the bed of Procrustes was removed to the lumber-room. If France had contributed the conception of progress, Germany inaugurated the evolutionary method, in which the historian exchanges the rôle of the advocate, the prosecuting counsel and the judge for that of interpreter. The scornful astonishment with which Voltaire would have greeted Ranke's celebrated aphorism that all the centuries are equal in the eyes of God is a measure of the deeper insight of the nineteenth. The Age of Understanding was to bury the Age of Reason as the Age of Reason had challenged the Ages of Faith.

*Bibliographical Note.* The most recent edition of Voltaire's writings and correspondence is that of 1878 in fifty-two volumes edited by Louis Molland. Desnoiresterres, *Voltaire et la Société au XVIIIᵉ Siècle*, in eight volumes, remains indispensable. Of subsequent major works that of Georg Brandes (German translation, two volumes) is the most important. Among the shorter studies those by John Morley, David Friedrich Strauss, H. N. Brailsford, Alfred Noyes, Gustave Lanson and Émile Faguet are of interest. J. Churton Collins, *Voltaire, Montesquieu and Rousseau in England*, and Raymond Naves, *Voltaire et l'Encylopédie*, contain new material. Reusch, *Der Index der verbotenen Bücher*, summarises the reactions of the Vatican. The best discussions of his philosophy of history are by Meinecke, *Die Entstehung des Historismus*, Vol. I; Sir J. F. Stephen, *Horae Sabbaticae*, Vol. II; J. B. Black, *The Art of History*; Paul Sakmann, 'Die Probleme der historischen Methodik und der Geschichtsphilosophie bei Voltaire', *Historische Zeitschrift*, Vol. 97, and Alfred von Martin, 'Motive und Tendenzen in Voltaires Geschichtschreibung', *Historische Zeitschrift*, Vol. 118. The best and most recent survey of philosophies of history throughout the ages is in Fritz Wagner, *Geschichtswissenschaft*. A new edition of Voltaire's correspondence, containing thousands of hitherto unpublished letters, is appearing under the editorship of Theodore Besterman.

# 4

---

## BISMARCK'S LEGACY

### I

MAKERS of history from Julius Caesar to Adolf Hitler and
Winston Churchill have felt an urge to write about themselves, to explain to posterity what they have done and tried to do,
to justify the use they have made of their power, to cast the blame
on others for what went wrong. Bismarck's apologia stands at the
top of the list of political autobiographies, not merely because he
is the greatest man who ever wrote a full-length narrative of his
public career, and not merely owing to the earth-shaking events it
describes, but because its utility as a manual of statesmanship is un-
surpassed. It produces an almost overwhelming sense of power.
So long as rulers desire guidance on the discharge of their perilous
duties, and so long as students seek to unravel the tangled skein
of European diplomacy, his volumes are likely to be read. Compared with their dynamic force and their majestic sweep, the
lengthy narratives of Guizot and Bülow seem commonplace. Is it
an exaggeration to describe the Iron Chancellor's political testament as the most authoritative treatise on the art of government
since the 'Prince' of Machiavelli? As a factual record and interpretation of events it is as open to criticism as any other work of
its class. Its unique significance lies not only in the visualisation
of the greatest figure of the nineteenth century except Napoleon,
but in the maxims it enunciates and the warnings it suggests.

Some of the most celebrated books owe their origin to the accident of their authors' fall from power. Clarendon's two masterpieces were the fruits of his earlier and later exile. Napoleon
needed the boredom of St Helena to dictate his fragmentary
reminiscences. Émile Ollivier compiled the sixteen volumes of

*L'Empire Libéral* when the *débâcle* of 1870 terminated his brief political career. Differing widely in their importance, these and other writings of the same class have a family resemblance in their pose of superiority and injured innocence.

When the most famous and powerful performer on the world stage found himself at the age of seventy-five in the ranks of the unemployed, he determined to fight his battles over again. 'I cannot lie down like a hibernating bear,' he exclaimed in the bitterness of his heart. It was no sudden resolve, for when he was contemplating retirement in 1877 he planned to write his memoirs and determined that Lothar Bucher should lend his aid. When the blow fell in the spring of 1890 no time was lost. Accepting a tempting offer from Cotta of 100,000 marks per volume, he summoned his veteran associate of the Foreign Office, who, unlike the crafty Holstein, had remained loyal when the shadows began to fall. Busch and Poschinger coveted the job, but Bucher was clearly the better man. Encouraged not only by his indefatigable collaborator, who resided for long periods at Friedrichsruh and Varzin and sorted out the available materials, but also by his son Herbert, the old warrior dictated reminiscences and musings when he felt in the mood, which 'the pearl', as his employer called him, arranged in chapters. It was uphill work, for he kept irregular hours and—in his secretary's view—wasted a great deal of time over the newspapers. Since he trusted to memory and possessed few works of reference, the first draft swarmed with errors which it was Bucher's task to rectify in the libraries of Berlin. When *Buchlein*, as the faithful old scribe was named by Princess Bismarck, passed away in October, 1892, the foundations of the massive edifice had been laid. In the following year the first section was set up in type and served as a basis for the revisions which continued till the end.

The circumstances of its composition are reflected in the character of the work. It bears little resemblance to the comprehensive apologias whose authors possessed ample documentary materials and told their tale in orderly sequence from beginning to end. The original title *Erinnerungen und Gedanken* was restored in the critical edition published in 1937 as Volume XV of the 'Gesammelte Werke', edited by Gerhard Ritter. The first two volumes, which appeared immediately after his death in 1898 under the auspices of Horst Kohl, the editor of his collected speeches, close with the brief reign of the Emperor Frederick, and are immeasurably superior to the scolding supplement which could not emerge till the Hohenzollern Empire was swept away in 1918. The narrative of his fall, which forms its exclusive theme, was dictated in 1891, when the smart of the wound was fresh, and, like the later performance of Bülow, damages the author at least as much as the ruler whom both of them had served and despised.

William II is far from being Bismarck's only *bête noire*. Though the picture of his modest old master William I is painted with affectionate gratitude and is essentially true to life, and that of the Crown Prince Frederick is friendlier than was expected, his comments on rivals and enemies, among them the Empress Augusta, Count Harry Arnim and Gortchakoff, are vitiated by the exasperation of Prometheus chained to his rock. His vendettas had always been too violent to be hidden, and the self-portrait would have been unconvincing had the tiger's claws been kept out of sight. The faults of temperament which impair the authority of the book as a contribution to history and compel us to check every verdict by independent evidence enhance its value as a revelation of personality. Here is the whole authentic superman of blood and iron, fighting with the gloves off as he had fought all his life, hating and thundering to the last. In Meinecke's phrase the work is a wood of natural growth, not a well-laid-out park. No effort is made to cover the whole of the ground, for the main theme is foreign affairs. Domestic issues play a subordinate rôle, and economic problems are almost entirely ignored. Though on the whole he has been fortunate in his biographers, from Lenz and Marcks to Arnold Oskar Meyer and Erich Eyck, none of them— not even Busch—brings the reader so close to his innermost heart as his own dictated record, and none of them leaves such an impression of elemental greatness of brain and will. 'Not a work of art,' is the verdict of Marcks, 'but it is Bismarck.'

## II

Political apologias are not history but contributions to history. The least arresting portion of the narrative is the analysis of home

T

affairs, which is largely a running fight with his foes. Such major controversies and achievements of his later years as the nationalisation of railways, the tariff of 1879, the duel with the Socialists and the foundation of the Welfare State are described with tantalising brevity, and their lowly place indicates that foreign affairs dominated his thoughts till the end. The only domestic issue which receives fairly extensive treatment is the *Kulturkampf*, which is partially explained by the fact that his campaign against the Vatican was primarily a drive against the Poles. The first half of his public life was spent in founding the Reich, the second in combating disruptive elements—and their friends beyond the frontier —which seemed to threaten its cohesion. His methods in the later period were as ruthless as in the former. Political foes became personal foes. Throughout the book there are more broadsides than bouquets. When the failure of the *Kulturkampf* became obvious he made his peace with Leo XIII and drove his Kultus-Minister Falk like a scapegoat into the wilderness. Few would include magnanimity among the virtues of the founder of the German Empire.

The author skims lightly over his early years, and the narrative becomes dramatic only with his election to the United Landtag of 1847, when he emerged as the spokesman of the extreme Right. It was the era of Frederick William IV, the Hohenzollern Hamlet —more nerves than muscle, it was said—who is always mentioned with political disapproval and personal respect. During the first four years of his public life Bismarck's aim was to preserve the royal authority against the encroachments of the March revolution and the timidity of the ruler himself, not because he believed, like his master, in Divine Right, but because he regarded the dynasty as the core of the national strength. 'The unlimited authority of the old Prussian Monarchy was not, and is not, the final word of my convictions,' he wrote at the close of his life. 'Absolutism primarily demands impartiality, honesty, devotion to duty, energy, and inward humility in the ruler. These may be present, and yet male and female favourites (in the best case the wife), the monarch's own vanity and accessibility to flattery will nevertheless diminish the fruits of his good intentions, since he is not omniscient and cannot have an equal understanding of all branches of his office. My ideal has always been a monarchy so

far controlled by an independent national representation, prefer-
ably of classes or professions, so that neither Monarch nor Parliament could separately alter the position.' Though a Junker by
birth and tradition, his political ideology was much more modern
than that of his old friend Roon and his neighbours in the Mark.

In the second or Frankfurt period Bismarck's task as Prussian
envoy to the Diet was to establish the equality of Prussia with
Austria in the Deutscher Bund. A meeting between the aged
Metternich, returning to Austria from exile in 1851, and the newly
appointed Prussian envoy to the Diet symbolises the coming shift
of power in the second half of the century from Vienna to Berlin.
In the emotional reaction against Germany engendered by two
world wars there has been a tendency to discover virtues in the
Bund which were scarcely perceptible in the exhilarating era of
unification. It would have been wiser, it is argued, to continue
the Austro-Prussian partnership established after the fall of
Napoleon than to unleash a series of wars and to Prussianise Germany. This partial revival of the *Grossdeutsch* doctrine of Con-
stantin Frantz ignores the hunger for a nation-state which was felt
with equal intensity during the same era in Italy and the Balkans.
Bismarck's dispatches from Frankfurt, published by himself with
some omissions in the later years of his Chancellorship, record his
slow conversion to the belief that the Bund was an empty shell
which barred the way to nationhood. 'I had come to Frankfurt
well disposed towards Austria. The insight into Schwarzenberg's
policy of *avilir puis démolir*, which I there obtained by documentary
evidence, dispelled my youthful illusions. The Gordian knot was
not to be untied by the gentle methods of dual policy, and could
only be cut by the sword.' In Germany, he declared, there was no
room for both. It was equally clear that far-reaching changes were
impracticable so long as Frederick William IV sat on the throne,
since in his eyes the predominance of the Hapsburgs in the Bund
was as axiomatic as the Christian creeds. Part of Bismarck's intellectual equipment for the tasks of diplomacy was his sense of
timing. In his own expressive phrase, it is no good putting forward the hands of the clock for it will not go faster at your
bidding.

The most notable lesson he learned during his third phase—in
the Embassy at St Petersburg—was the necessity of covering the

Prussian flank in the event of a conflict in central or western Europe. 'It was not, and it is not, in our interest to stand in the way of Russia turning her surplus forces towards the East. In our position we ought to rejoice whenever we find Powers in whom we encounter no sort of competition of political interests, as in this case, so far, with us and Russia. With France we shall never have peace, with Russia never the necessity for war, unless Liberal stupidities or dynastic blunders spoil the situation.'

When Bismarck was called to the helm by King William in 1862 at the age of forty-seven his programme was ready: to challenge the *status quo* in central Europe, if necessary at the price of war with the Hapsburg Empire and its friends in the Bund; to create a nation-state under the Hohenzollerns as Cavour had just accomplished for the House of Savoy; to prepare for all eventualities by strengthening the Army; to avoid trouble with Russia by tolerating her plans in the Balkans. England hardly came into the picture, for her ambitions were oversea. The pregnant chapter entitled 'Retrospect of Prussian Policy' is a dirge on lost opportunities. Frederick the Great left behind him a rich inheritance and a belief in Prussian policy and power. 'Since his death our policy had either lacked definite aims or chosen or pursued them unskilfully.' In the words of Queen Luise, Prussia had gone to sleep on the laurels of her greatest king. At last, just a century after the close of the Seven Years War, a man was found to stretch the bow of Ulysses. 'Real responsibility in high politics can only be undertaken by a single directing Minister, not by numerous boards with majority voting.' The King's assent to a spirited programme was secured during a conversation in the train between Jüterbog and Berlin after the 'blood and iron' speech in the Budget Commission had echoed round the globe. Bismarck's hour was about to strike with the synchronisation of a resolute monarch on the throne, his old friend Roon at the War Office, and Moltke, the 'battle-thinker', waiting in the wings.

The narrative of the wars of unification forms the kernel of the book. Before 1866, we are assured, Prussia could claim the title of a Great Power only *cum grano salis*. Why should such humiliation continue when the balance of forces had changed? 'To reach my goal, North Germany under Prussian leadership,' he informed a French journalist on the eve of the struggle, 'I would face anything, exile, even the scaffold.' The stricken field of Königgrätz shattered the Bund, created a North German Confederation under Prussian leadership, and pointed towards a united Reich. He had staked his physical as well as his political survival on a throw of the iron dice, for defeat would have involved his suicide. A crucial factor was Francis Joseph's decision for dynastic reasons to entrust the command in Bohemia, where victory was problematical, to Benedek, who was ignorant of the terrain, while the command in Italy, where victory was reasonably certain, was given to the Archduke Charles.

If luck aided the Prussian cause on the battlefield, it was due to Bismarck alone that the fruits of victory could be gathered in. The chapter entitled 'Nikolsburg' describes his desperate struggle for a generous peace. Difficult though he had found it to persuade his master to fight Austria for the leadership of Germany, it proved still harder to hold him back when the fumes of victory mounted to his head. For three days he wrestled with the old monarch, and so painful was the scene that the man of iron nerve left the room and burst into a paroxysm of tears. The ruler's opposition was overcome only with the aid of the Crown Prince, and he grudgingly consented to what he denounced as a disgraceful peace. Bismarck's finest hour was not the proclamation of the Empire in the Galérie des Glaces but his decision not to turn a defeated rival into an irreconcilable foe. No annexations, no triumphal parade through the streets of Vienna, no crushing indemnity! Austria had been expelled from the Bund. The paralysing dualism was over. 'All we wanted was a free hand in Germany.' Why should he encourage the Hapsburgs to look towards Paris or St Petersburg by imposing needless humiliations? Austria's feelings were further spared by his refusal to punish her South German allies by merging them in Prussia as urged by the fiery young Treitschke, 'the Bismarck of the Chair'. Thirteen years later his foresight was vindicated by the conclusion of the Dual Alliance.

In a striking little book, *Bismarcks Friedensschlüsse*, Johannes Haller, best known as the biographer of Eulenburg, pronounces the Treaty of Prague not only the wisest of his settlements but as the perfect model for statesmen. Magnanimity played no part in it, for the Chancellor was the least sentimental of men; his moderation was the result of the coolest calculation. 'It was already quite clear to me that we should have to defend the conquest of the campaign in future wars. I did not doubt that a Franco-German war must take place before a United Germany could be achieved.' His next task was to postpone the conflict till Germany became strong enough to meet the challenge. Among other steps was the inclusion of adult male suffrage in the constitution for the new North German Confederation. 'Put the German people in the saddle and they will show they can ride,' he exclaimed. The autobiography confesses that it was a war measure designed to deter foreign monarchs from sticking their fingers into the German pie.

If the 'Nikolsburg' chapter exhibits the master of statecraft, the story of the Ems telegram reveals the cunning of the fox. France, he declares with truth, had no title to interfere with Spain's choice of a Hohenzollern for the vacant throne. 'Politically I was tolerably indifferent to the whole question.' That she would object to a Francophil Hohenzollern he could not anticipate. As a matter of fact she did not really object, for Spain in her irrevocable decline could never again be a danger, and the French Emperor, jealous of the growing might of Prussia since 1866, seized the pretext to unleash a war. This version sounded plausible till the diaries of King Carol of Rumania and other publications revealed that Bismarck had dispatched a secret agent to Madrid to encourage the project, the probable consequences of which he foresaw and designed. 'A trap for Napoleon', commented Lothar Bucher, who knew the truth. Whether the author was deliberately lying or his usually tenacious memory had failed is anybody's guess.

After securing the withdrawal of the Hohenzollern candidature Napoleon III demanded a promise that it would never be renewed, thereby presenting his antagonist with the winning card. Abeken's report of the interview between Benedetti, the French Ambassador, and the King at Ems reached the Chancellor when Roon and Moltke were his guests at dinner, and the narrative of the 'editing' of the telegram forms the most thrilling episode in the book. 'Now it has a different ring,' commented Moltke; 'it sounded like a parley; now it is like a flourish in answer to a challenge.' No alteration of the text had been made, but skilful abbreviation had changed its tone. Bismarck's action is defended by Marcks as a legitimate reply to a challenge which ought never to have been made, but foreign opinion has almost unanimously condemned it as a discreditable trick. He was proud of his handiwork, which was promptly published and produced the desired result of a French declaration of war. In a celebrated passage he describes the change of mood from gloom to gaiety produced on his guests. They knew that the Prussian army was ready and that the South German states would help; and the Chancellor had arranged that France should find no allies. Austria's defeat was too recent for her to burn her fingers again, and Russia had been squared by encouraging her to denounce the Black Sea clauses of the Treaty of Paris. England, connected with Germany by close dynastic ties, had no reason to keep Napoleon III on his throne. Italy had received Venetia from her Prussian ally in 1866, and a Franco-German war would ensure the desired evacuation of Rome by the French garrison and the end of the Temporal Power of the Pope. Diplomatically the road was clear, and the military conflict proceeded according to plan. The chapter on Versailles is disappointing, with growls at the Generals for conspiring to exclude the Chancellor from military decisions, at his master for reluctance to accept the Imperial title, and at 'the royal ladies' for striving to influence their husbands to be lenient to France.

When the nation-state was founded it had to be maintained. *Wir sind satt*, declared the master-builder; but other Powers were not, and he had to reckon with the resentments of the states which had felt his heavy hand. His system of insurance was as consummate an achievement as the creation of the Reich. His task would have been easier had not his desire to content himself with Alsace been overruled by his master and the Generals on the ground that a portion of Lorraine was essential to national defence. Here was his one major error as a diplomatist. 'I do not want too many Frenchmen in my house,' he remarked, and French-speaking Lorraine was to prove as indigestible as Polish Prussia. It is arguable that French sentiment might gradually have been reconciled to the loss of Alsace, all the more since she was allowed to retain Belfort; but the Chancellor realised that the annexation of Lorraine inflicted a wound too deep to heal. His excuse is that he had stood up to his master and the Generals in 1866 and could not face an even sterner ordeal. Moreover, the danger of France finding an ally, he believed, would be less under a Republic than under a

Catholic Monarchy which might perhaps attract the support of the Austrian Emperor and count on the sympathy of the Vatican, the incurable hostility of which to the new Protestant Empire is repeatedly proclaimed. Accordingly he endeavoured to distract the gaze of Frenchmen from 'the gap in the Vosges' by encouraging them to seek compensation in a colonial empire.

Since France could never launch another attack without an ally she had to be kept in quarantine, which was possible only if no other Great Power needed her help. The rumour that Bismarck was ready to fall on her in 1875, when she was beginning to recover her breath, is angrily dismissed as a lie invented by Gortchakoff, who resented German hegemony in Europe. The soldiers, it is true, favoured a preventive war, and the Chancellor himself was momentarily alarmed by certain military measures beyond the Rhine; but neither he nor his master had the slightest intention to draw the German sword. With England there would be no difficulty, for she did not make alliances and Bismarck craved neither colonies nor a fleet. The new Kingdom of Italy, weak as it was, had no reason to quarrel with Berlin. Austria, smarting under the humiliation of 1866, required watching, but her rivalry with Russia in the Near East placed a brake on her ambitions in Central Europe. For the remainder of his official life the Chancellor's chief anxiety was to prevent Russia and Austria flying at each other's throats. When Alexander II inquired what Germany would do in the event of an Austro-Russian conflict, he was informed that it was Germany's interest that neither combatant should be so weakened as to endanger its status as a Great Power: in other words, he refused a promise of neutrality. This was not enough for the Tsar, and Bismarck's detached attitude as 'honest broker' at and after the Congress of Berlin increased his resentment. So menacing indeed was his language that in 1879 the Chancellor found Austria willing to make the defensive alliance of which he had dreamed. At last the feud between Hohenzollerns and Hapsburgs which began with the seizure of Silesia in 1740 was closed. Andrassy's refusal to extend the promise of mutual assistance to cover an attack by France was a disappointment though hardly a surprise. The Dual Alliance was transformed into the Triple Alliance in 1882 by the adhesion of Italy who dreaded a clash with France over African colonies.

Confronted with an Austro-German bastion stretching from the
Baltic to the Adriatic, the Tsar changed his tune, and in 1881
Bismarck's loftiest aim was realised in the Three Emperors
League which was renewed in 1884 for a further three years.
When it broke down in 1887 over Austro-Russian friction about
Bulgaria the old chess-player concluded a secret treaty of neutrality with Russia for three years. Nothing scared him except 'the
nightmare of coalitions', and it was an axiom of his diplomacy to
have only one potential enemy at a time. In these delicate
manoeuvres, on which the security first of Prussia and then of the
Reich depended, he was a virtuoso. 'In Egypt I am English,' he
declared; 'in Bulgaria I am Russian.' The Balkans were 'not
worth the bones of a Pomeranian grenadier'. So anxious was he
to avert a collision with Russia that he would not grudge her Constantinople, which had been her dream ever since Catherine the
Great. That the first symptoms of a Franco-Russian *rapprochement*
were already visible on the eve of his fall is true enough, but they
materialised only when his Reinsurance Treaty of 1887 was
scrapped. When the Franco-Russian alliance was announced in
1895 he fired a broadside at the Emperor and his advisers by revealing the pact of 1887 and its lapse on the morrow of his fall.
His death in 1898, the year of the first Navy Law, spared him the
grief of witnessing the estrangement of England which paved the
way to the Triple Entente.

## III

The lessons of Bismarck's political testament and unique career
fall into two classes: those which concern statesmen of all times,
and those specifically addressed to his own countrymen. The
most important in the first category is enshrined in his celebrated
aphorism: 'Politics are the art of the possible', by which he meant
the meticulous adjustment of ends to means. *Qui trop embrasse mal
étreint.* Though nothing appears so obvious as the need for horse
sense on the stony paths of *haute politique*, no maxim has proved
more difficult to apply by those who scale the giddy summits of
power. The difference between practicable aims and *Caesaren-
wahnsinn* was sharply illustrated by the careers of Frederick the

Great and Napoleon. The former staked his fortunes on the seizure of Silesia, which events were to prove within his capacity to
accomplish and retain. Though he cherished and fulfilled other
territorial ambitions, he never dreamed of fighting for them.
Napoleon, on the other hand, intoxicated by his early victories in
Italy, followed his delusive star and ended at St Helena. The contrasted experiences of Bismarck and Hitler tell a similar tale. The
former set out with a bold but limited resolve, and when he
reached his goal he sheathed the sword. It was not a case of the
Prussian eagle borrowing the silky plumes of a dove, but a clear-
eyed perception that there were limits to the strength of the Reich.
Preventive wars he repudiated on the ground that no mortal could
read the cards of Providence. The outstanding figure of the era of
nationalism was neither an imperialist, for he never desired to
impose German rule on alien races, nor a Pan-German, since he
never aspired to bring all Germans into one fold. So long as he
remained at the helm it could not be seriously argued that the new
Reich had misused its strength. Hitler, on the other hand,
neurotic, inexperienced and trusting to his intuitions, was spurred
forward by ambition as insatiable as that of Napoleon, and even
before his appointment as Chancellor he confided to Rauschning
his fantastic dreams. Like Napoleon he never—in Byron's words
—learned 'that tempted fate will leave the loftiest star'.

From this general principle of limiting risks stemmed a salutary
exhortation to his countrymen, whose recurring temptation, located at the centre of the European chessboard without natural
frontiers, has been to hit out in all directions. During the medieval
*Kaiserzeit* it was an urge to the south, in the twentieth century the
call of East and West. A weak and divided Germany has always
been a tempting bait to greedy neighbours, a united and powerful
Germany a potential threat. Though Bismarck solemnly adjured
her rulers to avoid the simultaneous estrangement of East and
West, the warning was in vain. In that well-organised state, it has
been remarked, there was anarchy at the top. While Tirpitz, bent
on challenging Britain's naval predominance, urged the covering
of the German flank through an understanding with Russia,
Bethmann advocated friendly relations with England as a condition of forward moves in the Middle East. Both policies had their
advantages and their risks, and a choice should have been made

between them, but there was no Bismarck to make it. Had he revisited the scenes of his triumphs in the opening decade of the
twentieth century, he would have been appalled by the transforma-
tion of a friendly England and a neutral Russia into potential foes.
Had he returned for a second time at the close of the second decade, he would have pointed in grief and anger to the result of a
policy of uninsurable risks. Like the Emperor Augustus after the
defeat of Varus in the battle of the Teutoburger Wald, he might
have murmured: 'Give me back my legions.'

Statesmen can learn much of their trade in Bismarck's school
but not the whole. *Raison d'état* is a polite name for an ugly thing
—the divorce of politics from morals. This gospel of anarchy,
formulated though not invented by Machiavelli, has been practised, if not always professed, by men of all races and creeds, by
good and bad alike. 'If I see my opportunity,' exclaimed Frederick
the Great when the sudden death of the Emperor Charles VI
opened the road to Breslau, 'shall I not take it?' Napoleon dismissed as *idéologues* men who, as he believed, refused to look facts
in the face. In the latter half of the nineteenth century Cavour and
Bismarck played the familiar game with complete lack of moral
scruple and with consummate skill. 'If we did for ourselves what
we do for our country,' remarked the maker of United Italy,
'what rascals we should be.' Among the most ingenious of his
stratagems was the dispatch of a beautiful countess to win the
support of Napoleon III in expelling the Austrians from Lom-
bardy. Though Bismarck stressed the importance of *imponder-
abilia*, when the right hour struck he acted without hesitation and
let the world say what it liked. It is an error to regard Prussia as
more of an aggressor than Piedmont and Bismarck as morally inferior to Cavour. It was not till the shattering experience of the
First World War revealed the insufficiency of the sovereign state
in an increasingly interdependent world that Woodrow Wilson,
General Smuts, Lord Cecil and other practical idealists launched
a crusade for a system which seemed to promise less tragic results.

A second weakness in Bismarckian statesmanship was his neglect to train his countrymen for self-government. His grant of
adult male suffrage suggested confidence in their wisdom and
patriotism; but the Reichstag proved—and was intended to prove
—little more than a fig-leaf, to use Liebknecht's drastic expression,

to cover the nakedness of autocracy. That the power of the purse might have been put to better use is true enough, but the core of the Bismarckian constitution was the rentention of final decisions in non-elective hands. A further bar to the democratisation of Germany was the maintenance of the Three Class voting system invented by Frederick William IV for Prussia, which contained two-thirds of the population of the Reich and in which the rapidly growing army of urban workers did not count. So obsessed was Bismarck by the principle of undivided responsibility that, though he was prepared to admit to office Bennigsen, the trusty leader of the National Liberals, he declined the request to bring two of his Parliamentary colleagues with him, and the project of broadening the basis of government was dropped. When the Hohenzollern Empire fell with a crash in 1918 the problems of Weimar Germany had to be faced by amateurs.

It was not solely the fault of the Chancellor, for there was little demand for parliamentary government except among the Social-ists and the Radicals. Collaboration worked well enough in South Germany, but the Emperor and the army chiefs, the Jun-kers and the great industrialists of the Rhineland, objected to entrusting the proletariat with a substantial share of power. Con-servative historians such as Hans Delbrück and Adalbert Wahl regarded the Bismarckian Constitution as a model blending of popular representation with an irremovable executive, thus en-suring continuity in foreign policy and national defence. Liberal scholars, on the other hand, such as Ziekursch and Erich Eyck, censure him for ignoring the world-wide demand for parlia-mentary government. He could not live for ever, and no other superman was in sight. Officials nominated or dominated by the ruler are as liable to make mistakes as Ministers responsible to Parliament.

Bismarck bequeathed to his grateful countrymen a superb in-heritance: a nation-state, a Triple Alliance to ensure its safety, a federal constitution which satisfied the *amour propre* of the rulers of the component states, the beginnings of social security, colonial territory, and a prestige unknown since the Emperor Barbarossa. Almost all these assets were thrown away by the shortsighted successors who forgot that politics are the art of the possible. It is one of the ironies of history that his most enduring monument should be a book which would never have been written but for the accident of his dismissal. The action of a young ruler, so hotly resented by his victim, unwittingly set the seal on his immeasurable renown.

Bismarck spoke disdainfully of 'Professor Gladstone', but are the practitioners of Realpolitik as much wiser as they believe? Their weakness is to think too much of immediate returns and too little of the long-range results of their hammer strokes. Vast and splendid as was his intellect, he could see nothing and imagine nothing beyond the sovereign state pursuing exclusively its own supposed interests. For him Europe was only a geographical expression. The vision of an organised world, an international order resting on a willing partnership of self-governing national units, was beyond his ken. The presupposition of all profitable political and economic planning is a firm grasp of the unity of civilisation, but to the shaping of the human spirit for that supreme adventure he contributed nothing. He laboured exclusively for his countrymen—first for Prussia and later for a Prussianised Reich—and was satisfied with their applause. In a word, he dates, for we have learned by bitter experience that nationalism is not enough. Yet the twentieth century will have little right to throw stones at the nineteenth until all the Great Powers begin to operate a system more conducive to human welfare than that which the Iron Chancellor practised and preached.

# INDEX